THE
NEW
SCIENCE

Self-Esteem
Psychology

Robert N. Campbell, Ph.D.

UNIVERSITY
PRESS OF
AMERICA

LANHAM • NEW YORK • LONDON

Copyright © 1984 by

University Press of America,™ Inc.

4720 Boston Way
Lanham, MD 20706

3 Henrietta Street
London WC2E 8LU England

Library of Congress Cataloging in Publication Data

Campbell, Robert N.
  The new science.

  Bibliography: p.
  Includes index.
  1. Self-respect. 2. Motivation (Psychology) I. Title.
BF697.C26   1984   155.2   84-5085
ISBN 0-8191-3892-4 (alk. paper)
ISBN 0-8191-3893-2 (pbk. : alk. paper)

DEDICATED

to the

TRUTH

ABOUT OURSELVES

iv

ACKNOWLEDGMENTS

Special acknowledgment is made to the following for permission to quote from their copyrighted material:

Basic Books, Publishers, Ind. The Collected Papers of Sigmund Freud, edited by Ernest Jones, M.D. © 1959 by Basic Books, Publishers, Inc., by arrangement with The Hogarth Press Ltd. and the Institute of Psycho-Analysis, London.

Encyclopedia Brittanica, Inc. The Critique of Practical Reason, by Immanuel Kant, in vol. 42 of The Great Books of the Western World, copyright 1952 by Encyclopedia Brittanica, Inc.

The Free Press. The Structure of Evil, by Ernest Becker, reprinted by arrangement with George Braziller, Inc. Copyright © 1968 by Ernest Becker.

Sanford J. Greenburger Associates, Inc. The Individual Psychology of Alfred Adler. Copyright © 1956 by Basic Books, Inc. Reprinted by permission.

Harper & Row Publishers, Inc. Individual Behavior: A Perceptual Approach to Behavior, Revised Edition. Copyright, 1949, by Harper & Row, Publishers, Inc. Copyright © 1959 by Arthur W. Combs and Donald Snygg. Reprinted by permission of Harper & Row, Publishers, Inc.

Hutchinson Publishing Group Limited. The Moral Law, by Immanuel Kant. Trans. by H.J. Paton. Copyright 1950, Barnes and Noble.

The Johns Hopkins University Press. Reflections on Human Nature, by Arthur O. Lovejoy. Copyright © 1961 by The Johns Hopkins Press.

Journal of Experimental Social Psychology, 9 (Nov. 1973): 502-516. "Transgression and Altruism: A Case for Hedonism," by Robert B. Cialdini, Betty Lee Darby and Joyce E. Vincent. Copyright © 1973 by Academic Press, Inc.

THE NEW SCIENCE:

SELF-ESTEEM PSYCHOLOGY

CONTENTS

The message of this book will eventually become a basic given for the salesman, the advertiser and the politician, as well as for the educator, the psychologist and the theologian. The principles proposed in this book will be widely adopted as the starting point for the analysis and solution of problems of human behavior. The present book, despite its deficiencies in style and presentation, may make some modest contribution in bringing about that result. More influential, however, will be the current upsurge of books and articles proclaiming the same message—the centrality of the self-esteem motive in determining human behavior.

We propose the following Laws of Human Behavior:

First Law of Human Behavior: Each human organism seeks to maintain or increase its sense of its own excellence.

Second Law of Human Behavior: Each human organism seeks to maintain or increase its level of sensual gratification.

Third Law of Human Behavior: Virtually all human thoughts, words and actions spring from the two above motivations, operating singly or in combination.

Fourth Law of Human Behavior: In cases of conflict between the first and second motivation, the desire for a sense of excellence usually prevails.

Put in simplest terms: Virtually all of our human behavior springs from two motives: our desire for self-esteem and/or our desire for sense pleasure.

Acting as a brake on these desires is the Reality Principle. Serving to occasionally elevate them to a relatively altruistic level is the Principle of Identification.

We are not always conscious of our true motivation in a particular action. Often, our desire for a good self-image subconsciously influences us to attribute a nobler motive to our actions than the coolly objective observer would allow.

These Laws of Human Behavior are not proposed in the sense of either moral obligation or justification. It is far from our intention to lay any basis for an ethics of human behavior. These laws pertain to how human beings _do_ behave, quite abstracting from how they _should_ behave.

If other writers have realized much the same truths presented in this book, why another book? This book is justified, I believe, because it presents in a fuller and more precise way the laws undergirding a Science of Human Behavior.

INTRODUCTION

Self-esteem psychology is an idea whose time has come. An increasing tide of books and articles proclaim that self-esteem is what human beings desire above all. A variety of thinkers, starting from different ideologies and backgrounds, have come to the conclusion that the self-esteem motive can explain virtually every facet of human behavior. Proposed by psychoanalysts, psychologists and lay thinkers are self-esteem theories of aggression, of laughter, of anxiety, of suicide, depression, altruism, crime, etc.

What makes people do what they do? "Self-esteem!" chorus the authorities presented in these pages. We all want a good self-image. Each of us works incessantly and with ingenuity to brighten his or her self-image. To this conclusion point the observations of the astute observers of the human scene whose wisdom is harvested here. The assembled discoveries of these thinkers forms a collage of insights whose total impact proclaims that the self-esteem motive is the key to understanding—and controlling—human behavior. The correct analysis of any human problem must take the self-esteem motive into account; effective solutions to the problems lie in the proper channelling of the self-esteem motive.

Full appreciation of the scope of the self-esteem motive offers the basis for a more comprehensive and fruitful psychology. This is not an original discovery made by the present author; rather it is a swelling tide of awareness becoming ever more evident in the writings of experts on human behavior. Let Pulitzer prize winner Ernest Becker state the case in a chapter entitled "The New Science of Man:"

> The principle which explains the law of human character development in The Principle of Self-Esteem Maintenance . . . Thus, in the most brief and direct manner, we have a law of human development and its explanatory principle.
>
> I do not think it would be possible to overestimate the magnitude of this achievement for the science of man. It is a universal principle for human action akin to

gravitation in the physical sciences . . . .

Furthermore, like the principle of gravity—or any viable principle—our principle must explain apprent contradictory phenomena—which is exactly what it does: it explains the most disparate life-styles as variations around the single theme of self-esteem maintenance. Just as gravity explains both the northward course of the Rhine and the southward course of the Rhone, so the principle of self-esteem maintenance "explains" both schizophrenia and depression, sadism and masochism, hypersexuality and homosexuality, passivity and aggressivity, and so on. Not, of course, "all by itself," but with a properly elaborated theoretical structure. Given the achievement of this very structure in modern times, we have a perfect synthetic and deductive principle for our science.

Finally, and not least, it is—like gravity—an irreducible primary property. Just as innate attraction and repulsion are the irreducible primary properties of matter, self-esteem is the irreducible primary property of behaving organisms. There is no need at this time to seek further for a valid, nonreducible unifying principle. (18, p. 328-9).

Becker then asks why such a "simple and fertile" principle had not been discovered previously. He answers that it had been, and goes on to mention a dozen well-known thinkers of the past few centuries whose writings have implicitly embodied this discovery. Several of those authors will be cited in this book. Becker has the avant garde realization that proper application of the self-esteem principle gives entree into a New Science of Man.

Now a few words about the content of this book.

Chapter One considers the nature and sources of self-esteem and personality characteristics associated with high (and low) self-esteem. Our desire for self-esteem is insatiable, but is curbed by the moderating influence of the important "reality principle"—i.e.,

xiv

we must trim our self-esteem to conform to reality, otherwise we run the risk of ego-shattering confrontations with reality in the form of ridicule and social ostracism.

Chapter Two presents a second basic motivation in human nature, the desire for sensual pleasure, and its negative side, the desire to avoid pain and discomfort. This most obvious aspect of our desires is not as pervasive and powerful as the desire for self-esteem. Even activities such as eating, drinking and sex, seemingly motivated entirely by the desire for sensual gratification, are actually dominated by self-esteem considerations. History and philosophy show a broad dichotomy of personality types into Epicurean and Stoic, a division still important on the modern scene. The Epicurean or sensualist allies the sensual and self-esteem motives, deriving added self-esteem from the gratification of sensual desires. The stoic type, more commonly described as puritan or ascetic, has a life-style that places sensual and self-esteem motives in conflict with one another, and he derives part of his self-esteem from strict curbing of his sensual desires.

"I am persuaded that all men do all things for fame," says Plato in his Symposium. Chapter Three presents testimony from a variety of thinkers in agreement with Plato: underlying almost all of our behavior is the desire to win public acclaim or peer approval— acceptance, friendship, love, respect, admiration. And why are we so eager for this social approval? In order to be reassured that we are indeed lovable and worthwhile persons. This dominance of the deeper self-esteem motive, under its variety of names, is stressed by numerous observers of the human scene: Alfred Adler ("all our functions follow its direction"), William McDougall ("self-regard is the master sentiment"), Nathaniel Branden ("single most significant key to human behavior"), Robert Schuller ("ultimate will of man"), Mark Twain ("compels a man's every act"), psychologists Arthur Combs and Donald Snygg ("most crucial, if not the only task of existence"), psychologists George McCall and J.L. Simmons ("man's main concern"), and Pulitzer prize winner Ernest Becker ("the basic law of human life").

Even in the writings of the great Sigmund Freud, champion of the supremacy of the sex urge, we find abundant recognition of the importance of the drive for self-esteem. Certain key concepts in Freud's thought are expressions of the self-esteem motive. The relations between the ego and the super-ego, in which the ego strives to please the super-ego, or in other words, to fulfill the ego-ideal, is a quest for self-regard, self-respect, to use Freud's words. He frequently uses "narcissism" in the sense of the psyche's original state of deeming itself possessor of all perfection (having self-esteem to the nth degree) and states that the course of development of the ego is an attempt to regain that original state of high self-esteem. This is the "happiness that men seek." The important ego-defense mechanisms are strategems to protect the ego from unwelcome knowledge about itself, knowledge which would lower self-esteem. Chapter Four enlarges on these ideas. Additionally, a case is made from clues in Freud's writings that the self-esteem motive actually dominates the sex urge.

In Chapter Five, trend-setting philosophers Kant and Nietzsche are seen as glorifiers of the self-esteem motive. Kant presents his system aimed at enabling the common man to attain to the highest sense of personal worth and dignity. Nietzsche sees the drive for a sense of power as the single motivating force behind all our behavior. He urges the superior person to fully develop his intellect and sensuality, thus attaining the superman's supreme sense of power and excellence.

Chapter Six offers the testimony of perceptive observers from diverse backgrounds and ideologies who have come to the conclusion that self-esteem is the key factor in a number of human phenomena of crucial consequence. So central is self-esteem to these human concerns that each of them can be defined in terms of self-esteem. Depression, the emotional illness that afflicts all of us at times, lightly and passingly as "the blues," or cripplingly as chronic melancholia, is, in essence, a condition of low self-esteem. Anxiety, the curse of our modern age, casting a pall over the lives of countless millions, is apprehension of impending loss of self-esteem. Neurotic symptoms, the hairshirt that spoils our enjoyment of modern luxuries, "have as their object the task of safeguarding the patient's self-esteem." (Alfred Adler). Suicide, rising in incidence to become a leading cause of death, is most frequently caused by painfully low self-esteem with no perceived hope of recovery. Anger, the current American mood, according to some social critics, is a desire to restore self-esteem which has been wounded by another person or group. Violence and aggression, on the upsurge throughout the world, have roots in the desire to increase self-esteem at the expense of other human beings. Laughter and the appreciation of humor are expressions of pleasure resulting from a sudden increase of self-esteem. Even sex is a self-esteem game par excellence, with a rich variety of ego payoffs.

The frequent human tendencies to self-disparagement and even self-hatred seem to run counter to a self-esteem motive. Actually, however, self-depreciation, whether devious or sincere, is a tortuous manifestation of the drive for self-esteem, and has several ego payoffs. And self-hatred is, ironically, an expression of self-love; it is hatred not of the total self but of some aspect of self that is causing loss of esteem for the total self. Chapter Seven expands upon these themes.

We have portrayed human behavior as motivated entirely by self-oriented desires—self-esteem and sense pleasure. Does this mean that human beings are completely selfish in their motivation? Is self-concern and self-love necessarily selfish? How can such a theory explain the many acts of concern for the welfare of others that we see every day? Heroic acts of self-sacrifice, even to the point of death, surely cannot be explained by man's desire for self-esteem? Is such a noble sentiment as "greater love than this no man has, that a man lay down his life for his friend" to be comprehended under the rubric of self-esteem? These relationships between self-love and altruism and self-esteem are considered in Chapter Eight.

A word regarding quotation references: the first number following a quotation refers to the corresponding title in the bibliography; the second number is the page on which the quote is found.

CHAPTER I

SELF-ESTEEM—WHAT IS IT?

Definitions of Self-Esteem

In much of the rapidly expanding literature on self-esteem the authors offer no definition of the term, no doubt assuming that such a familiar concept scarcely requires definition. Such was my own assumption until someone remarked "your idea that the desire for self-esteem is the strongest motivating force is disapproved by the case of Nixon and his cronies. They were willing to give up their self-esteem in order to stay in power." This person was thinking of self-esteem as connoting self-respect dependent upon measuring up to a moral code, whereas for most writers on the topic the term self-esteem is much broader, embracing that type of self-respect and much more. The person who compromises his moral code to obtain more power is willing to dim one part of his self-image in order to brighten other parts which he considers more salient. Added power strengthens his sense of being an important person; it brings reassuring praise and admiration from others, it opens the door to further accomplishments. All this heightens his self-esteem.

To minimize misunderstandings, this chapter will spell out in considerable detail what we mean by "self-esteem." First, let us consider some definitions of self-esteem given by others.

William James, reknowned as a philosopher at the turn of the century, and also "generally considered to be America's greatest psychologist," has left us a much-quoted formula:

$$\text{Self-esteem} = \frac{\text{success}}{\text{pretensions}} \quad (99, \text{ p. } 310).$$

Thus, the greater a person's success in achieving whatever it is that he desires, the higher his self-esteem. Unless, of course, his "pretensions" increase accordingly, in which case the value of the fraction success/pretensions would be unchanged, and his self-esteem would not increase. By "pretensions" James means "what we back ourselves to be and do," "our supposed potentialities." This seems to correspond with what many current writers refer to as our "ideal self-image," or "ideal self-concept." Illustrative of his self-esteem formula, James says:

> I, who for the time have staked my all on being a psychologist, am mortified if others know much more psychology than I. But I am contented to wallow in the grossest ignorance of Greek. My deficiencies there give me no sense of humiliation at all. Had I 'pretensions' to be a linguist, it would have been just the reverse. So we have the paradox of a man shamed to death because he is only the second pugilist or the second oarsman in the world. That he is able to beat the whole population of the globe minus one is nothing; he has 'pitted' himself to beat that one; and as long as he doesn't do that nothing else counts. He is to his own regard as if he were not, indeed he _is_ not. (99, p. 310).

James makes an intriguing point that we sometimes lose sight of: self-esteem can be increased not only by further "successes" but also by diminishing our pretensions, i.e., cutting down on our aspirations and ambitions, or lowering our standards in some way. In a passage delightful for its elegance of expression and touch of humor, he suggests that this reduction of pretensions is in some cases the sensible thing to do:

> To give up pretensions is as blessed a relief as to get them gratified; and where disappointment is incessant and the struggle unending, this is what men will always do. The history of evangelical theology, with its conviction of sin, its self-despair, and its abandonment of salvation by works, is the deepest of possible examples, but we meet others in every walk of life. There is the strangest lightness about the heart when one's nothingness in a particular line is once accepted in good faith. _All_ is not bitterness in the lot of the lover sent away by the final inexorable 'No'. Many Bostonians, _crede experto_ (and inhabitants of other cities, too, I fear), would be happier women and men today, if they could once for all abandon the notion of keeping up a Musical Self, and without shame let people hear

2

them call a symphony a nuisance. How pleasant is the day when we give up striving to be young, —or slender! Thank God! we say, those illusions are gone. Everything added to the Self is a burden as well as a pride. A certain man who lost every penny during our civil war went and actually rolled in the dust, saying he had not felt so free and happy since he was born. (99, p. 311).

In this passage James several times equated happiness with high self-esteem, a valuable insight. His comment that self-esteem—and thus happiness—can be raised either by increasing successes or by diminishing pretensions points up the two basic ways that human beings have traditionally sought happiness, or if you prefer, tried to solve the problem of unhappiness. The way of the West, from Graeco-Roman times to the present, has been an attempt to increase "success": the way of pleasure, power, conquest, riches, fame, achievement, winning friends and influencing people. The way of the East, at least as embodied in the wisdom of Hinduism and Buddhism, is to decrease "pretensions": cut back on desires and ambitions, embrace asceticism and renunciation. Of course, that the way of renunciation may itself become an additional "pretension" is widely recognized.

Strictly speaking, James' formula is indicative of level of self-esteem, but it also gives us an insight into the nature of self-esteem. Similar is the definition proposed by psychologist Arthur Cohen:

> Self-esteem, then, may be defined as the degree of correspondence between an individual's ideal and actual concepts of himself. (33, 383).

Thus my self-esteem as a golfer today depends on how my score compares with what I hoped to shoot. I shot a 94 and was elated, felt like one helluva guy. My usual scores are with uncanny and unnerving consistancy between 104 and 108. My companion, who usually shoots in the 70's or low 80's, skyed to a 92. He ground his teeth in rage, muttering that he had played like an old woman, and one more round like this and he would break his sticks and henceforth devote himself to shuffleboard. Almost identical golf scores had brought joy to me and frustration to him because his self-concept as a golfer was so much higher than mine.

Cohen's "actual concept of himself" corresponds to James' "successes," and the "ideal concept of himself" corresponds to "pretensions." Cohen's formula, like James', is for <u>level</u> of self-esteem. His definition also indicates that self-esteem can be raised either by elevating one's actual self-concept or by scaling down one's ideal self-concept.

In any psychological discussion Freud's views must be taken into account. The variety and richness of his insights sheds light on any topic. Certainly Freud is not noted as a self-esteem theorist; nevertheless his genius has given us some valuable glimpses into the nature and operation of self-esteem. In a later chapter we will investigate more fully the place of self-esteem in Freud's thinking; for the moment let us see what he offers in the way of a definition of self-esteem. In a terse passage he offers us some clues. (Self-regard is Freud's favorite term in this context; occasionally he interchanges it with self-esteem).

> Part of the self-regard is primary—the residue of childish narcissim; another part arises out of such omnipotence as experience corroborates (the fulfillment of the ego-ideal), while a third part proceeds from gratification of object-libido. (56, p. 121).

By "childish narcissism" he refers in this case not to any autoeroticism, but to the infant's feeling of omnipotence. This feeling of omnipotence arises, says Freud, from the fact that the infant finds that all his desires are quickly satisfied. If his desires are not immediately satisfied, he can, through the magic of crying, soon obtain satisfaction. He thus seems to be totally in control of his world. Freud adds that regaining this oceanic feeling of omnipotence is the happiness that human beings seek ever afterward. The hard reality of life soon forces the child to relinquish his original feeling of omnipotence, except for "such omnipotence as experience corroborates," which is the individual's success in living up to his ego-ideal. Freud in this case is equating ego-ideal with super-ego, i.e., the indivi-

4

dual's personal moral and ethical code. The "gratification of object-libido" is the self-regard that arises when the person's love object returns his love.

> Love in itself, in the form of longing and deprivation, lowers the self-regard, whereas to be loved, to have love returned, and to possess the beloved object, exalts it again. (56, p. 121).

Putting together the three parts we have the components of self-esteem according to Freud: first, the enduring remnants of the infant's "I am the greatest" sentiments; second, faithfulness to one's own moral and ethical code; and third, love requited. No doubt, if pressed Freud would admit that this is not the entire self-esteem picture, but merely its major components.

Freud's follower Otto Fenichel, author of The Psychoanalytic Theory of Neurosis, a classic exposition of psychoanalytic thinking, condenses Freud's elements of self-esteem into one: the feeling of omnipotence.

> The individual's experiences connected with omnipotence lead to a most significant need of the human mind. The longing for the oceanic feeling of primary narcissism can be called the "narcissistic need." "Self-esteem" is the awareness of how close the individual is to the original omnipotence. (49, p. 40).

Fenichel makes it clear that he is referring not to any neurotic aberration, but to the normal condition of the human being. His condensation seems justified, in that omnipotence embraces the fulfillment of all desires, including those of requited love and moral rectitude. The definition by Fenichel can be paraphrased as: "self-esteem is the degree to which an individual feels that he is fulfilling all his desires." This amounts to the same thing as does the James' formula for self-esteem.

Psychoanalyst Edith Jacobson expands upon another strand of Freud's theory for her definition of self-esteem:

> . . . self-esteem is expressive of the
> harmony or discrepancy between the self
> representations and the wishful concept of
> the self . . . (98, p. 131).

Jacobson's "self representations" correspond to
what has come to be popularly known as "actual self-
image," and her "wishful concept of the self" corre-
sponds similarly to "ideal self-image." Thus her
definition of self-esteem is equivalent to a currently
popular one: self-esteem is the degree to which ac-
tual self-image matches ideal self-image. It is also
equivalent to the Freud-Fenichel definition in terms
of omnipotence, inasmuch as we are able to live up to
our "wishful concept of self" to the degree that we
are omnipotent.

Stanley Coopersmith, author of the comprehensive
Antecedents of Self-Esteem, sees self-esteem as a
"personal judgment of worthiness that is expressed in
the attitudes the individual holds toward himself."
This harmonizes with previous definitions we have
considered, in that a person judges his worthiness by
the degree that he measures up to his ideal self-
image. The latter is his personal standard of worthi-
ness.

Howard Kaplan, psychology professor at Baylor
College of Medicine, and author of Self-Attitudes and
Deviant Behavior, contributes:

> The self-esteem motive is defined as the
> need of the person to maximize the experi-
> ence of positive self-attitudes or self-
> feelings and to minimize the experience of
> negative self-attitudes or self-feelings.
> (103, p. 10).

This definition has the same basic note of "I'm
OK" as do the previous definitions we have con-
sidered.

Pulitzer prize winner and astute commentator on
the human scene, Ernest Becker presents several equi-
valent meanings of self-esteem in a passage emphasiz-
ing the importance of that motivation:

> We noted in Chapter I that answering the

four common human problems gave the actor the one thing he needed most: the sentiment that he was an object of primary value in a world of meaning. Data from anthropology support this fundamental place of self-esteem in human action. It seems that nowhere on this once-vast globe has man been able to act unless he had a basic sentiment of self-value. Unless the individual feels worthwhile, and unless his action is considered worthwhile, life grinds to a halt. Whole cultures have begun to expire in this way: Melanesians, Marquesans, reservation Indians, and, for a time after 1929, the world of Wall Street. (17, 113).

"Sentiment of being an object of primary value in a world of meaning;" "basic sentiment of self-value;" "individual feels worthwhile." These descriptions of self-esteem harmonize with and reinforce the definitions we have already presented.

Perhaps the tersest description of self-esteem is the "I'm OK feeling" used by Transactional Analysis followers (I'm OK—You're OK, by Thomas Harris) of Eric Berne to describe the goal of human relations; each participant is seeking to establish for himself an "I'm OK" feeling (and ideally should be seeking to confirm his partner in the human transaction in that same good feeling).

This sampling of descriptions of self-esteem is enough to reveal the common element—a sense of personal worth. This is precisely—so it seems to me— the most common meaning assigned to self-esteem in ordinary conversation. "A good opinion of oneself," says Funk and Wagnalls. And adds a second meaning: "overestimation of oneself." This latter perjorative connotation is a species and limitation of the general "good opinion of oneself" to the case where that good opinion is unjustified. In this book we do not intend to so limit the word.

The definition we have found most serviceable and will use throughout this book is: "self-esteem is an awareness of possession of desirable qualities or objects by oneself." This definition has the advantage that it not only points up the "good opinion of self" aspect but also shows its cause, perceived possession of desirable qualities or objects. By "desirable qualities or objects" we mean anything that the particular individual may consider desirable— material possessions, good personality, success, good physique, illustrious ancestors, many friends, love, intelligence, high aspirations, virtue, great potential, even such outre qualities as viciousness, competancy as a killer[1], or proficiency as a rapist. As a short-hand phrase we will use the words "good," "goods," or equivalently, "excellence." These seem to be the most apt words, but each has a disadvantage: the word "good" might be misunderstood as necessarily involving some notion of morality; "goods" may convey to mind merely material possessions; and the word "excellence" may be misunderstood as necessarily connoting superiority to others. To repeat, when we define self-esteem as "awareness of good (goods, excellence) possessed by self," the word "good" (or goods or excellence) merely means something considered as desirable by the particular individual, even though that something may be considered by society in general to be irrelevant or even abhorrent.

The good possessed may be actual or potential. The youth of "great potential" derives considerable self-esteem not only from his present capabilities, but also from envisioning the great things he hopes to accomplish in the future. Hope is of such vital importance in our estimation of our lot; sometimes one is tempted to think that our vision of our future possibilities means more to us than do the present realities of our situation. The convinced Christian patiently bears with poverty and adversity, looking forward to the glory of eternal life; the ardent communist bears the privations of his present life, be-

---

[1]Historically, one of our most cherished sources of self-esteem has been proficiency in killing one's fellow man. Most cultures exalt their "great warriors"; the distinction of being the "fastest gun in the West" finds its counterpart in many cultures and times. When the women of Israel sang "Saul slew his thousands; David his ten thousands" they were proclaiming a criterion of excellence which well may be No. 1 on the human hit parade.

lieving that this is setting the stage for the workers' paradise; the gambler stuffs more cardboard into his shoe, munches his peanut butter sandwich in his bleak room and consoles himself with thoughts of the "big hit" or "hot hand" which is just around the corner. Each of us has a cherished hope that carries us through lean times.

The possession of excellence may be <u>direct</u> or <u>vicarious</u>. Mrs. Jones has a solid self-esteem about her own social skills, and she radiates pride in recounting the accomplishments of "my son the doctor." The excellence of any person, group, movement, ideology, etc., with which you identify becomes your excellence, vicariously. When your football team wins the Superbowl, you stand just a little taller. When your candidate wins the presidential election you feel a glow of personal achievement.

The <u>awareness</u> of good possessed by self may be explicitly conscious, as when an individual prides himself on being highly successful in his profession, or it may be inchoate and implicit, in the case of a person who experiences a warm glow on being treated with consideration, without explicitly adverting to the source of his increased sense of well-being. The awareness of good possessed may be factual or illusory. One may consider himself the best bowler in his league and have the scores to prove it, or he may consider himself the wittiest person in his group even when others consider him a crashing bore.

If anyone demands the meaning of the word "self" in our definition, the only thing we can offer is "the entire you; you in all your aspects and prospects, you in all your identities and identifications."

<u>Self-esteem is awareness of good (excellence, goods) possessed by self.</u>

Once more we should add the <u>caveat</u> that "good" does not necessarily have any moral implication, nor does "excellence" necessarily mean superiority to others, nor does "goods" necessarily imply material possessions. Rather, each means "anything the person considers desirable for himself."

9

Other Terms Equivalent to Self-Esteem

A few years ago the term "self-esteem" carried in popular usage a negative connotation, almost synonymous with conceit. However, current use of the term usually connotes something totally good, the equivalent of psychological well-being. Some present self-esteem literature does take a third and broader view, using the term to embrace a self-regard that may be valid or illusory, justified or overweening. In this book we use self-esteem in this fuller sense, embracing both "good" and "bad" self-esteem.

Common usage offers quite a variety of terms that are more or less interchangable with self-esteem. All have the core meaning of "awareness of good possessed by self." In the richly informative book Self-Esteem authors Wells and Marwell list several of these terms:

> A sample of related names might include terms such as self-love, self-confidence, self-respect, self-acceptance (or rejection), self-satisfaction, self-evaluation, self-appraisal, self-worth, sense of adequacy or personal efficacy, sense of competance, self-ideal congruency, ego or ego-strength . . . . However, self-esteem is currently the most popular term for self-evaluative behaviors, and the body of information bearing on the conceptualization and measurement of self-regard is generally known as "the self-esteem literature." (185, p.7)

In addition to the above, we find the following terms used in much the same sense: pride, self-image, self-concept, honor, self-feeling, self-complacency, amour propre, sense of human dignity, and the "I'm OK feeling."

As they are commonly used, some of the terms carry only a positive nuance. Such would be self-respect, self-regard, sense of adequacy (or competance or human dignity), honor. Others customarily carry a vaguely negative nuance—such as self-satisfaction, ego, amour propre, self-complacency. Still others are neutral in content: self-image, self-concept, self-evaluation.

The term "pride" sometimes carries the same positive connotation as self-respect ("we are poor but we have our pride"), and sometimes carries a negative implication ("pride goes before a fall"). The term "honor", strictly speaking, refers to esteem rendered to an individual by others, but it is often loosely used as an equivalent for self-esteem.

The term "self-love" can mean either self-complacency, which is <u>awareness</u> of good possessed by self, or it can mean self-seeking, which a <u>desire</u> for good to be possessed by self. The French <u>amour propre</u>, often used in English as well, customarily carries an implication a bit less harsh than its English equivalent.

The variety of these terms and the frequency of their use is testimony to the basic importance of the underlying concept—awareness of good possessed by self.

Complexity and Variability of Self-Esteem

Research literature that compares "high self-esteem people" with "low self-esteem people" might leave the reader with the impression that self-esteem is a single, fixed entity, much like a person's height. Actually, each person may have a high self-esteem in some aspects of his life and low self-esteem in other aspects. There is a multiplicity of facets in your life, in each of which you can have a different level of self-esteem: physical appearance, intelligence, wit, suavity, your country club, your new car, your children, your identity as a Democrat, as a liberal, as a Presbyterian, as the best bowler in your company league, etc.

Perhaps you are very pleased with your ability to relate to people on a one-to-one or small group basis, but terrified to speak before a large audience. You may have a pleasant assurance about your competance to make a comfortable living, but feel that you fall far short of the social ease and polish you would like to have. Einstein justifiably had a great self-esteem as a mathematician but was painfully shy. Johnny Carson, whose easy self-confidence before a national TV audience is legend, is said to be frequently ill-at-ease in dinner party situations. J. Paul Getty had a su-

preme self-esteem as a financial wizard, but was un-
happy about his social presence. "I wish I had a
better personality. Sometimes I feel that I am a
boring person," he said. (Elsa Maxwell was unkind
enough to snap in reply "you are entirely right.")

Not only do we have many self-esteems of differ-
ent levels, but some of them can vary in level from
day to day, even from moment to moment. Getting off a
clever bon mot gives a boost to your self-esteem as a
wit; committing a social gaffe depresses your sense of
social competence. You beat handily one of your usual
tennis cronies and revel in a feeling of invulnerabil-
ity. Next you play a young hot-shot, can barely get
your racquet on his stinging returns, and are dis-
gusted with your ineptitude. Receiving signs of self-
esteem and affection from that certain someone gives a
lift to your spirits, expands your horizons, and makes
the world a brighter place. Which is to say, pro-
saically, it has increased your sense of self-worth.

Psychoanalyst Karen Horney remarked that "all
neurotic persons are markedly unstable in their self-
evaluation, wavering between an inflated and a de-
flated image of themselves." The same is true of
young persons who have not yet "found themselves" or
established a "solid identity." But it is also true
of all of us, to varying degrees. Researchers in
self-esteem have found it easy to put some of their
subjects into moods of temporarily elevated self-
esteem and others into temporarily depressed self-
esteem by the simple expedient of telling them they
had done well, or poorly, in a previously administered
aptitude test. Psychologists Kenneth Gergen, Mary
Gergen, and Kenneth Meter report:

> In the case of self-esteem, a trait dispo-
> sition par excellence, research has shown
> that self-esteem scores are highly suscep-
> tible to situational shifts. Simple expo-
> sure to a boaster, another's good opinion,
> or the mere presence of a person of shabby
> appearance all prove sufficient to alter
> self-esteem scores radically . . . . Self-
> esteem itself may be a moment-to-moment
> affair. (73,123)

The close correlation that researchers have found

between high self-esteem and happy moods, and between
low self-esteem and depressed moods, suggests that
your self-esteem is every bit as variable—or stable,
in the case of some persons—as your moods.

"Chronic" Self-Esteem

Although a person's self-esteem is subject to
fluctuations, it seems realistic to speak of a general
level of self-esteem that is characteristic of each
individual. We all know people we would describe as
self-assured and confident, and others who are timid
and unsure of themselves. Granted, there are unusual
occasions when this confident person might show less
self-esteem that does the timid person, but the over-
all tone of his life is one of stronger self-esteem.
This customary level of self-esteem characteristic of
an individual is referred to by researchers as his
"chronic" or "global" self-esteem.

Limitation on Self-Esteem: The Reality Principle

Our appetite for sense pleasure is, in its more
obvious aspects, quite satiable. Sometimes we satisfy
our desire for the pleasure of eating or drinking to
the degree that additional food or drink presented to
us brings a feeling of revulsion. Sexual satiety is a
fact of common experience. Judging from the frequency
with which they treat the subject, Ann Landers and
Dear Abby are snowstormed with letters from wives
complaining that their husband's sex drive is perma-
nently satiated. One is reminded of Joan Rivers' joke
about telling her husband that she had heard sex is
good for the complexion and that she intended to have
sex three hundred times during the coming year.
"Great," he responded, "sign me up for two." Legend,
possibly apocryphal, has Sigmund Freud going into
sexual dormancy at about the age of 40, or 45, accord-
ing to other stories. At least, his wife wrote Dear
Abby letters to a friend bewailing her fate.

But of self-esteem we never get enough. Our
appetite is insatiable. We all have the desire to be
number 1, the greatest, the best. We may proclaim
modest ambitions, but satisfy those ambitions and we
are going on for higher things, excelsior, ever up-
ward. Each of us has the urge to achieve his own
concept of perfection, a perfection that expands and

13

yet recedes as we progress. John Adams commented on the ubiquity and insatiability of our passion for public esteem and thus for self-esteem:

> If we attempt to analyze our ideas still further upon this subject, we shall find, that the expressions we have hitherto used, <u>attention</u>, <u>consideration</u>, and <u>congratulation</u>, comprehend with sufficient accuracy the general object of the passion for distinction, in the greater part of mankind. There are not a few—from him who burned a temple, to the multitudes who plunge into low debauchery—who deliberately seek it by crimes and vices. The greater number, however, search for it, neither by vices nor virtues; but by the means which common sense and every day's experience show, are most sure to obtain it; by riches, by family records, by play, and other frivolous personal accomplishments . . . . But for our humiliation, we must still remember, that even in these esteemed, beloved, and adored characters, the passion, although refined by the purest moral sentiments, and intended to be governed by the best principles, is a passion still; and therefore, like all other human desires, unlimited and insatiable. No man was ever contented with any given share of this human adoration. When Caesar declared that he had lived enough to glory, Caesar might deceive himself, but he did not deceive the world, who saw his declaration contradicted by every action of his subsequent life. Man constantly craves for more, even when he has no rival. (1, Vol 6, p. 248).

Weight is lent to the above testimony by the fact that it comes from a man who received the highest honor the Unites States can confer, election to the presidency. Sartre puts the same thought more tersely: "man is the desire to be God."

When Freud speaks of the infant's desire for omnipotence, he is describing the basic condition of all of us. When he describes the child's all-consuming narcissism, this is you and me he is describing,

14

the basic you and me, underlying the adjustments we have been forced to make as a result of the impact of reality on our lives. The ego of the infant, Freud observes, "deems itself the possessor of all perfections." To this feeling we all strive to return, insofar as reality permits. In Freud's thought, the infant feels a sense of omnipotence, generated by the fact that his every wish is granted. Throughout life we seek to recover this sense of omnipotence, of being the possessor of all perfections.

> To this ideal ego is now directed the self-love which the real ego enjoyed in childhood. The narcissism seems to be now displaced on to this new ideal toy, which, like the infantile ego, deems itself the possessor of all perfections. As always where the libido is concerned, here again man has shown himself incapable of giving up a gratification he has once enjoyed. He is not willing to forego his narcissistic perfection in his childhood; and if, as he develops, he is disturbed by the admonitions of others and his own critical judgment is awakened, he seeks to recover the early perfection, thus wrested from him, in the form of an ego-ideal. (56, p. 116).

> One more important function remains to be mentioned which we attribute to this super-ego. It is also the vehicle of the ego ideal by which the ego measures itself, which it emulates, and whose demand for ever greater perfection it strives to fulfill. (59, p. 64).

The same ever-upward[1] urge is noted by Adler, citing Goethe in support:

> Among others, Goethe also points out that while perception is connected with the practical satisfaction of needs, man leads

---

[1]This ever-upward urge does not necessarily mean toward moral or spiritual perfection. Rather it is the urge to be Number One, supreme, all-powerful, adored.

a life beyond this, a life of feelings and
imagination. Thereby the coercion toward
enhancement of the self-esteem has been
excellently comprehended. This also be-
comes clear from one of Goethe's letters to
Lavater where he remarks: "This passionate
desire to drive the pyramid of my ex-
istence, the base of which is given to me,
as high as possible outweighs everything
else and barely admits momentary forget-
ting. (5, p. 123).

We all have the basic desire to drive the pyramid
of our existence as high as possible, to fulfill the
demands of our ego for ever greater perfection, to
obtain a greater share of glory and adoration. But
inevitably, that basic desire is modified, humbled,
cut down to size, by the impact of reality. Repeated
confrontations with failure, or let us say, the in-
ability to achieve my desires in the fullest, forces
me to the realization that my talents and abilities
and luck are limited, and I will never be the great-
est, never Number One in anything. That realization
comes hard. It has to be beaten into us by sharp
collisions with reality, or at least such is the case
with slow learners as myself.

Ambition to be the greatest in areas where suc-
cess has some very objective standard of measurement
is the first casualty in the battle with reality. I
can develop a very glowing image of my ability as a
tennis player, and of my potential for future great-
ness, as long as I am playing with inferior players.
However, as soon as I move into more advanced company
and suffer humiliating defeats, and this continues for
some months, I am at last forced ruefully to admit
that I will probably always be a very mediocre player.
Whereas my desire for self-esteem was the motivator of
my visions of being a tennis great, that same desire
for self-esteem now dictates that I bow to reality and
accept my limited abilities. Otherwise, with con-
tinuing exalted ambitions, the gap between expectation
and performance would be too painful for my self-
esteem. Acceptance of reality is hard on the self-
esteem initially, but we soon learn that it is ac-
tually easier on the self-esteem in the long run.
Acceptance of our limitations can spare us many a
later disgruntlement. The person who attempts to

maintain an exalted self-image in defiance of reality is courting suffering—he becomes known as conceited, vain, arrogant, out of touch with reality (all of which he is), and friends begin to shun him, and make biting remarks in an attempt to get him to face reality. So most of us early learn that bucking reality, at least in its more obvious aspects, is counterproductive, self-esteem-wise.

At What Age Does Self-Esteem Begin?

Self-esteem involves having a concept of oneself; equivalently, it means having a sense of identity. Originally, my impression was that these are somewhat involved thought processes and thus probably do not appear in human development until, say, the age of three or four, or possibly even at the so-called "age of reason," about the seventh year. However, observation of children just old enough to speak shows that they operate on the same self-esteem patterns as adults, but with less subterfuge. "Me good boy," the two year old will proudly assert. In those "terrible two's" children are given to self-assertive stamping of feet and shouting "No. I will not!" in response to mother's directives. And could it be that these feelings of self-esteem antedate even the ability to speak? Numerous psychologists and psychoanalysts believe that it does.

Some psychoanalysts, taking their cue from Freud, assert that even the suckling infant has feelings of self-esteem. Freud states that the infantile ego "deems itself the possessor of all perfections." (56, p. 116). This is the sense of "oceanic omnipotence" which the infant has, arising from the fact that all his desires are soon satisfied. "Self-esteem, as the psychoanalysts aptly note, begins to grow with the intake of the maternal milk," says cultural anthropologist Ernest Becker. Psychoanalyst Otto Fenichel states "The first supply of satisfaction from the external world, the supply of nourishment, is simultaneously the first regulator of self-esteem." (49, p. 40).

This development of self-esteem in the infant is summarized by psychoanalyst William Silverberg:

Thus the infant's doing or aggression

17

is felt by him as effective to the extent
to which the mother fulfills his needs.
The more alert the mother, the briefer and
less frequent will be the periods of dis-
turbed homeostasis, and in accord with his
subjective bias, the more effective and
powerful the infant will feel himself to
be. It would seem that such a sense of
adequacy and competence, despite its ob-
jective inaccuracy, must be basic to self-
esteem and must form the foundation of the
healthy ego. (166, p. 65).

In successive months of the infant's life an
increasing sense of reality diminishes his earlier
feeling of omnipotence, and thus decreases his self-
esteem. But at the same time there is a partially
compensatory increase of self-esteem due to the
child's heightened realization of parental approval:

The self-esteem of the one year old is not
so absolute or indestructible as it was in
infancy; it is more relative and more pre-
carious, but it exists on the more realis-
tic basis of the actual capacities of the
child and has the additional support of
parental approval. (166, p. 67).

Concurring with Silverberg that self-esteem be-
gins in the child's earliest years is Alfred Adler:

The first realization we obtained was
that the strongest impulses toward building
the mental life have their origin in earli-
est childhood . . . . the secret goal of
the child's attitude is identical with the
individual's attitude of later years. (5,
p. 189).

And what is this "strongest impulse" and secret
goal"? It is, in Adler's psychology, the "striving
for superiority" which motivates everything that we
do. In our later consideration of Adler's psychology
we will see that this striving for superiority is a
striving for self-esteem. For the present, the fol-
lowing quote from Adler will suffice:

The origin of humanity and the ever-

repeated beginning of infant life impresses
with every psychological act: "Achieve!
Arise! Conquer!" This feeling, this long-
ing for the abrogation of every imperfec-
tion, is never absent. (5, p. 103).

The infant's self-esteem is not an involved pro-
cess of self-reflection. He need not even be able to
distinguish between himself and the external world; it
is sufficient that he has the simple "I'm OK" feeling
which is the core of self-esteem.

Characteristics of the High Self-Esteem Person
And of the Low Self-Esteem Person

Having a high self-esteem is what life is all
about. High self-esteem is the basis for a good per-
sonality and effective social functioning. You cannot
love others unless you first love yourself. Love
yourself and others will love you. A high self-esteem
enables you to win friends and influence people. High
self-esteem is mental health. Self-esteem is hap-
piness. These and similar axioms are the message of
numerous popular books today. As Dorothy Briggs says
in Your Child's Self-Esteem: "if your child has self-
esteem, he has it made . . . in fact, self-esteem is
the mainspring that slates every child for success or
failure as a human being." (24, p. 3).

There is considerable research which supports
such a glowing appraisal of high self-esteem. Stanley
Coopersmith, behavioral scientist at the University of
California, Davis, with a team of colleagues made an
eight-year study of the self-esteem and other per-
sonality characteristics of a group of normal, middle
class urban boys, beginning at the age of ten to
twelve years and continuing until the subjects were in
early adulthood. The boys' level of self-esteem was
determined by self-report, by teachers' testimony, and
by psychological tests designed to reveal unconscious
self-evaluation. (The three methods yielded closely
agreeing results.) The boys' behavior and careers
were closely followed for eight years. Coopersmith's
description contrasting the high self-esteem boys with
the low self-esteem boys is most detailed and force-
ful:

We found, not very surprisingly, that

youngsters with a high degree of self-esteem are active, expressive individuals who tend to be successful both academically and socially. They lead rather than merely listen in discussions, are eager to express opinions, do not sidestep disagreement, are not particularly sensitive to criticism, are highly interested in public affairs, showed little destructiveness in early childhood and are little troubled by feelings of anxiety. They appear to trust their own perceptions and reactions and have confidence that they will be well received. Their general optimism stems not from fantasies but rather from a well-founded assessment of their abilities, social skills and personal qualities. They are not self-conscious or pre-occupied with personal difficulties. They are much less frequently afflicted with psychosomatic troubles—such as insomnia, fatigue, headaches, intestinal upset—than are persons of low self-esteem.

In contrast, boys with low self-esteem presented a picture of discouragement and depression. They felt isolated, unlovable, incapable of expressing or defending themselves and too weak to confront or overcome their deficiencies. They were fearful of angering others and shrank from exposing themselves to notice in any way. In the presence of a social group, at school or elsewhere, they remained in the shadows, listening rather than participating, sensitive to criticism, self-conscious, pre-occupied with inner problems. (36, p. 98).

Surprisingly, the boys with medium self-esteem were not "medium" in the qualities described above. They were similar to the high self-esteem boys in most qualities of behavior and attitude—optimistic, expressive and able to take criticism. They were more likely than either high or low self-esteem boys to accept and comply with middle-class values and norms, and were more eager in their search for social approval. For these reasons Coopersmith insists on a clear distinction between uncertainty about one's

worth (medium self-esteem) and conviction of infer-
iority (low self-esteem).

A similar contrast between high and low self-
esteem persons was revealed in a study by Jup-chung
Leung of two hundred college students at San Diego
State University. The high self-esteem subjects were
found to be significantly happier, more emotionally
mature, and more self-controlled. (114, p. 62). The
low self-esteem individuals were more likely to be
unhappy, discouraged, discontented, quick-tempered,
procrastinators, prone to over-indulge in eating,
drinking and smoking, and socially alienated. "The
alienation of the low self-esteem individuals appeared
to be due to their reported feelings of insecurity,
rejection, and self-consciousness, their lack of emo-
tional poise, their suspicious attitude toward people,
and their quick tempers." (114, p. 76).

Mercifully, these findings by Coopersmith and
Leung are general trends rather than absolutes. Ex-
ceptions to their findings do exist. Thus, a par-
ticular low self-esteem person may be emotionally
mature, socially effective, have several close
friends, and be highly successful and regarded. A
possible example is John Quincy Adams, who after a
distinguished career as senator, U.S. ambassador to
major European nations, and president of the United
States, could say "my whole life has been a succession
of disappointments. I can scarcely recollect a single
instance of success in anything that I ever under-
took." (194, p. 1).

Further comparison of high versus low self-esteem
characteristics was made by O'Brien and Epstein at the
University of Massachusetts. The subjects (19 females
and 10 males) were asked to describe each week over a
period of six weeks the experience that had most
raised their self-esteem that week, and also to fill
out a psychological questionnaire to show how they
felt after that experience. They did the same for the
experience of the week that had most deflated their
self-esteem.

> When self-esteem was raised, there was an
> elevation in happiness, security, affec-
> tion, energy availability, alertness, clear-
> mindedness, singleness-of-purpose, lack of

restraint and spontaneity. When self-
esteem was lowered, there was an elevation
in unhappiness, anger, threat, sluggish-
ness, withdrawal, disorganization, con-
flict, feelings of restraint and self-
consciousness. (141, p. 385).

Interestingly, the self-esteem deflating experi-
ences had stronger impact than did the self-esteem
boosting experiences. The reason for this, the re-
searchers suggest, was that the subjects' happiness in
the boosting experiences was tempered by the fear that
they might be building themselves up for a let-down.

A summary of several studies concludes that "in-
dividuals with high self-esteem are assertive, trust-
ing, competent, autonomous, achieving, respected by
peers, and generally efficacious in meeting personal
goals and aspirations." (195, p. 355).

Cloyed by all these "perfect Boy Scout" descrip-
tions of the high self-esteem individual, one is al-
most refreshed to discover a piece of research which
concluded that criminals have higher self-esteem than
does the average person. The study compared 46 white
male prisoners with 46 non-criminal males, equated as
far as possible with the prisoners as to age, educa-
tion and economic status. Researchers Worchel and
Hillson conclude: "The mean self-concept of the crimi-
nal is relatively favorable and significantly superior
to that of the normal person." (196, p. 180). Among
the items contributing to the higher self-esteem of
the criminal were significantly less dissatisfaction
and guilt about their sexual activities, and less
awkwardness in their dealings with the opposite sex.
The researchers see these apparently good qualities as
due to "callousness to problems of sex."

Confirming the high self-esteem of the criminal
is a British study of "40 normals, 120 neurotics, and
31 psychopaths." Researcher Foulds, comparing his
results with two similar studies, says:

Although agreement between these three
studies is not perfect and although a nor-
mal group was lacking in one study, there
is certainly broad agreement as to trends.
It would seem likely that psychopaths and

criminals tend to have a more favorable, and neurotics a less favorable concept of themselves in relation to others, than do normal people. These attitudes would appear to be in line with the views of Adler, as Worchel and Hillson pointed out. (197, p. 83).

It is confusing to find a criminal element among the high self-esteem people, the latter being described in such radiantly glowing terms by other researchers. But isn't it possible for a criminal to be emotionally mature, socially effective, popular, active, assertive, a natural leader, purposeful and happy? Some popular folk heroes among criminals seem to fit this description nicely.

But trumpeting to the rescue of conventional morality comes a piece of research that suggests that the high self-esteem scores of convicted criminals may be largely due to what is referred to as "social desirability" (the subject's desire to make a good impression) and "machiavellianism" (the subject's tendency to manipulate others to his own ends). The person in a correctional institution is likely to have a hunch that the way he answers the self-esteem questionnaire will have some impact on his future in the institution. When faced with a question such as "do most people who know you like you?" he will be strongly motivated to answer the question in the way that will make a good impression on the "authorities." To test this hypothesis, J. Rounds, former supervisor of the Central Planning Unit, Massachusetts Department of Correction, gave fifty inmates tests to measure self-esteem, machiavellianism, and urge toward social desirability. The subjects ranking high in self-esteem also were high in machiavellianism and social desirability. The researcher concludes that "test-taking defensiveness" (machiavellianism and social desirability) may have been at least partially responsible for the high self-esteem scores obtained by the criminals. (157, p. 87).

Of course this raises the broader question: even when administered to the average person, to what extent do self-report tests of self-esteem actually measure self-esteem, and to what extent do they measure the subject's inclination to make a good impression on some vague public—or more likely, the subject's desire to appear well in his own eyes. Self-deception being so endemic to the human psyche, to what extent are self-esteem tests really a measure of the subject's skill at concealing from himself his shortcomings? Such artificially inflated self-esteem is referred to by some researchers as "defensive" self-esteem. No fully satisfactory method of distinguishing between genuine self-esteem and defensive self-esteem has been generally accepted.

The above problem is only one of the many issues yet to be resolved in self-esteem psychology. Although the last dozen years have produced a great deal of self-esteem literature, the field is still in its infancy. However, there is virtually unanimous agreement that genuine self-esteem goes hand-in-hand with mental health, happiness and social effectiveness. The fulsome descriptions given by Coopersmith, Leung and others of the high self-esteem person seem to be justified.

Self-Esteem Not Proposed as Criterion
of Personal Excellence

In view of the fact that self-esteem is what we desire most of all, and in view of the outstanding personal characteristics of the high self-esteem individual, is it reasonable to conclude that an individual's level of self-esteem is the best measure of his worth as a person? In other words, is level of self-esteem the best criterion of personal excellence? Is the person with higher self-esteem, self-respect, self-confidence, ipso facto the better person? Maxwell Maltz, in his book The Search for Self-Respect, says:

> For if there is anything that I have learned in my sixty-five plus years in this world, if there is anything that has survived the ups and downs of my life, it is this knowledge: That there is no more accurate measure of an individual's value than his own degree of self-respect. (189, p. 2)

Actually, such a value judgment poses several problems. First, self-esteem may be based upon false standards of excellence. A Billy the Kid may have a high self-respect based upon being the fastest and coolest gun in the West; a tycoon may have a high self-respect because of his shrewdness and success in business; an actress may have a high self-esteem because of the adulation she receives from her fans; no doubt many a storm trooper had a high self-esteem because of his ruthless efficiency in combatting the enemies of the Third Reich. None of these is a reliable gauge of personal excellence.

Second, since self-esteem is higher to the extent that the individual's actual self-esteem approximates to his ideal self-image, the self-esteem can be raised by scaling down his ideal self-image, that is, by lowering his standards. In terms of William James' oft-cited formula, "self-esteem = successes divided by pretensions," this means that self-esteem can be increased by cutting down on "pretensions," i.e., goals, ambitions, desires, standards. The thus-augmented self-esteem can scarcely be equated with an augmented excellence.

Also, self-deceit often plays a part in maintaining self-esteem. Two persons may have the same level of successes and failures, but person A maintains a higher self-esteem by rationalizing away his failings, whereas the esteem of person B suffers because he honestly faces up to his failings.

Even though self-esteem is highly correlated—in general—with many qualities of personal excellence there are too many ambiguities in the picture to be confident that a person's self-esteem is a reliable guide to his personal worth, everything considered.

Sources of Self-Esteem

Self-esteem is awareness of goods possessed by self. Therefore, any goods possessed by self are factors contributing to self-esteem. Also, any goods which one _thinks_ he possesses, but does not, equally contribute. Thus, helping to increase or maintain self-esteem is any good, actual or potential, that one can consider as his own: his ancestry, nationality, affiliation with other groups, physical attributes and competencies, intelligence, achievements, material possessions, virtues, aspirations, talents, friends and loved ones (and any good that they possess, inasmuch as his identification with them can lead him to take pride in their excellences), social status, attention and acceptance and love from others, one's standard of values, his beliefs, profession, chances for achievement—the list is endless.

The factors contributing to self-esteem are the topic of the excellent book <u>The Antecedents of Self-Esteem</u> by Stanley Coopersmith. He groups the "several major conditions and experiences that seem to be associated with the development of positive and negative self-attitudes" into three categories—success, values and aspirations, and defenses. (35, p. 38). Success has four elements: power—the ability to influence and control others; significance—the attention, acceptance and affection from others; virtue—adherence to moral and ethical standards; and competence—successful achievement. Whatever success the individual thinks he has in any of these areas enhances his self-esteem. Coopersmith's conclusion about values and aspirations is somewhat ambiguous. He suggests that an individual may enhance his self-esteem by stressing the value of areas where he is more competent and minimizing the value of his less effective areas. However, "evidence on this point is scant." Also, he assumes that the gap between aspirations and performance contributes to low self-esteem, but this assumption has only "mixed and uncertain empirical support." By defenses Coopersmith means the individual's strategy and ingenuity in interpreting his experiences in such a way as to maintain or enhance his self-esteem. These strategies include but are still broader than the standard defense mechanisms. Summing up, Coopersmith says that we enhance our awareness of good possessed not only by acquiring more good, but also by juggling our subjective attitudes, i.e., by value shifts and by defenses.

Coopersmith refers us to William James' treatment of the same problem. James' analysis "provides us with three possible influences on self-esteem." James is more categorical than Coopersmith regarding the role that values and aspirations play in influencing our self-esteem. As we have seen previously, James uses the word "pretensions" for our aspirations, ambitions, standards, goals, etc., and his famous formula "Self-esteem = successes/pretensions" shows that self-esteem can be increased by cutting down on our aspirations, etc. As he says, "such a fraction can be increased as well by diminishing the denominator as by increasing the numerator. To give up pretensions is as blessed a relief as to get them gratified . . ." (99, Vol. I, p. 310). However, despite the general validity of James' formula, it does not allow for the power of self-deception. By the magic alchemy of self-deception we can rationalize away our failures to live up to our goals and standards, and continue to revel in the fact that we have such high standards. Even though I have grossly failed to measure up to my high standards and to achieve my high ambitions, I still pride myself on having such high standards and ambitions, which I feel sets me apart from the "common herd." The reality of the situation, that I am no closer to measuring up to these high standards than is the "common herd," I can easily evade by a thousand rationalizations, subterfuges, and repressions. In this manner the smallness of the "success" numerator in the fraction "Self-esteem = successes/pretensions" is easily explained away or ignored, and the large "pretensions" denominator inflates rather than deflates my self-esteem.

The other two influences on self-esteem that Coopersmith finds in James' theory are success and "the value placed upon extensions of self." By success he means how well a man measures up to society's standards for material status.

> The normal provocative of self-feeling is
> one's actual success or failure, and the
> good or bad actual position one holds in
> the world. A man . . . with powers that
> have uniformly brought him success with
> place and wealth and friends and fame, is
> not likely to be visited by the morbid
> diffidences and doubts about himself which
> he had when he was a boy, whereas he who
> has made one blunder after another and
> still lies in middle life among the fail-
> ures at the foot of the hill is liable to
> grow all sicklied over with self-distrust,
> and to shrink from trials with which his
> powers can really cope.

James' third source of self-esteem, extensions of self, includes:

> The sum total of all that he can call his,
> not only his body and his psychic process,
> but his clothes and his house, his wife and
> his children, his ancestors and his
> friends, his reputation and works, his
> lands and horses, and yacht and bank ac-
> count. All these things give him the same
> emotions. If they wax and prosper, he
> feels 'triumphant'; if they dwindle and die
> away, he feels cast down—not necessarily
> in the same degree for each thing but in
> much the same way for all.

Also included in extension of self is a man's social self:

> . . . social self which is the recognition
> he gets from his peers . . . . A man has
> as many social selves as there are people
> who recognize him and carry an image of him
> in their mind. To wound any of these, his
> images, is to wound him. (99, Vol. I, p.
> 219).

The sources of self-esteem mentioned by James and by Coopersmith are much the same, with the exception that the latter gives more place to ego defense mechanisms.

Building upon the contributions of James and Coopersmith, the following is our own analysis of the means we use to maintain or enhance our self-esteem. Self-esteem is awareness (valid or illusory) of goods (anything desired) possessed (actually or potentially) by self (directly or vicariously). This reveals a number of possible avenues for enhancement of self-esteem.

First, with regard to good, we can divide this into the testimony of others (social approval) and good which we possess in a manner not immediately dependent upon the opinion of others. The former is the attention, acceptance, admiration, friendship, love, etc., which we receive from others and which conveys to us the implicit message that there exists in us some good that has merited this recognition. The second type of good is that which we have and take comfort in regardless of the opinions of others—our own qualities, achievements, and possessions. Thus a man may derive self-esteem from being able to exert power over others, despite possible unpopularity. "They may hate me, but I can make or break any of them," a certain type exults. The mountain man, trapper or hermit of old had a quiet pride, or perhaps a fierce pride, in his survival skills, even though no one else might know of them, much less praise him for them. A J. Paul Getty may lament that Elsa Maxwell and others consider him a bore, but he consoles himself with the thought of his success in amassing billions. A Thomas More may be denounced or pitied by friends and foe alike for his intransigence, but he has the consolation that he is being true to his principles.

The nature of good as "anything desired" opens another possibility for enhancing or preserving self-esteem. This is the method, mentioned by James and Coopersmith, of adapting our aspirations, ambitions and "pretensions" to what is most feasible, considering our circumstances. In effect, this is adjusting our definition of the desirable to suit our situation. Each person can increase his awareness of good possessed by adapting his concept of good to what he already has or is very likely to get. The pro football player can be expected to rate "physical coordination" higher in the hierarchy of values than does the college professor. Rather than call this process self-deception it seems more accurate to refer to it as a "placing of emphasis" or "personal value system" or as some researchers term it, "selective saliency."

Considering the qualifications on the word "awareness" means we can increase self-esteem either by acquiring more good, or increasing our illusory awareness of good possessed, that is, by self-deception. This we do either by a variety of ego defense mechanisms which aim at protecting us from loss of self-esteem, or by what we will choose to call ego-enhancement mechanisms. A later section of this book provides a fuller description of our ingenious means of self-deception.

Another source of self-esteem is our estimation of what the future holds in store for us. Good possessed only potentially is a great comfort to us, as we have pointed out previously. As long as we have an ego-ace-in-the-hole in the form of a dream, a hope, an ambition, we can laugh at the present slings and arrows of fate. But this can prove to be a two-edged sword: having high ambitions can give us a lift while we still entertain hopes of fulfilling them, but as Coopersmith and James pointed out, when we fail to achieve our goals, the gap between aspirations and success, between actuality and ideal self-image, lowers our self-esteem.

The fact that we derive self-esteem from the success of persons and groups with which we identify opens another avenue of increasing self-esteem. We can be selective in our process of identification. We join the best fraternity or country club (if possible), choose our friends for their qualities that we consider to be excellences, identify with athletic teams that have a good chance of winning, etc. We will consider this process of identification in more detail in a later section.

We protect our self-esteem from loss by using this process in reverse. We try to dissociate ourselves from persons or groups that would reflect unfavorably on us. Only hardcore fans care to identify with a team with a 0-11 record. The number of those who were willing to admit having voted for Nixon diminished sharply after Watergate. Most people assiduously avoid "life's losers" lest the stigma rub off on themselves.

In addition, to avoid awareness of lack of good possessed we employ another technique, which we have not previously mentioned. This is to diminish our level of awareness. This comes under the heading of "blowing your mind," a curious phenomenon which owes its popularity at least in part to the temporary surcease it offers from a hurting ego. After a couple of drinks we can forget our troubles and inhibitions. Narcotics and other devices for temporarily paralyzing our critical faculties accomplish the same end.[1] Sleep, by temporarily eliminating awareness itself, also helps us to escape from a painful awareness of lack of good possessed. Suicide is the ultimate gam-

---

[1]We are not presenting this as the only appeal that alcohol and narcotics offer.

bit in this genre.

At this point we are not clear just where in this schema to locate another device we all use to avoid awareness of lack of good possessed, that is, withdrawal from situations which are likely to cause us a vivid awareness of that lack. Most prominent is social withdrawal, autism being the extreme.

The following outline sums up the ways in which we seek to increase or preserve our awareness of good possessed, i.e., self-esteem. Where the term "positive" (P) appears it signifies ways to increase self-esteem; "negative" (N) means ways of avoiding loss of self-esteem. The various categories are not always mutually exclusive. We do not claim the list is exhaustive; undoubtedly there are general ways of increasing self-esteem which have escaped our attention.

WAYS OF PRESERVING OR INCREASING SELF-ESTEEM

(Awareness of Goods Possessed by Self)

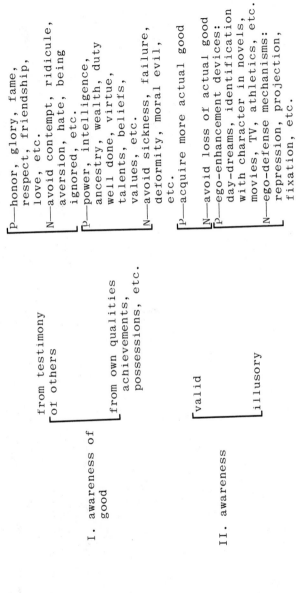

I. awareness of good

- from testimony of others
  - P—honor, glory, fame, respect, friendship, love, etc.
  - N—avoid contempt, ridicule, aversion, hate, being ignored, etc.
- from own qualities achievements possessions, etc.
  - P—power, intelligence, ancestry, wealth, duty well done, virtue, talents, beliefs, values, etc.
  - N—avoid sickness, failure, deformity, moral evil, etc.

II. awareness

- valid
  - P—acquire more actual good
  - N—avoid loss of actual good
- illusory
  - P—ego-enhancement devices: day-dreams, identification with character in novels, movies, TV, athletics, etc.
  - N—ego-defense mechanisms: repression, projection, fixation, etc.

III. good possessed

- presently—as in I and II
- potentially—in hopes, aspirations, ambitions

IV. self

- identical
  - P—as in I, II, and III
  - N—as in I, II and III
- expanded self
  - P—by identification with higher prestige persons or groups
  - N—by dissociation from lower prestige persons or groups (includes discrimination)

V. level of awareness

- heightened—drugs taken to increase level of sensory awareness
- decreased—diminish awareness of personal deficiencies and problems by use of drugs, alcohol, sleep, and suicide

33

The Two Most Significant Sources of Self-Esteem

Most significant in the consideration of self-esteem sources is the dichotomy between <u>other-dependent</u> sources and <u>self-dependent</u> sources. This is the division in Part I of the preceding schema. Other-dependent sources of self-esteem are the manifestations of esteem that others give us—acceptance, praise, friendship, respect, love, etc. Self-dependent sources are those which are relatively independent of what others think of us. Among these are intelligence, strength, talents, ancestry, wealth, living up to one's own ethical code, etc.

This dichotomy has been emphasized by several writers on self-esteem. William V. Silverberg, psychoanalyst and author of <u>Childhood Experience and Personal Destiny</u>, terms these two "inner" and "outer" sources. A stable self-esteem depends upon development of "inner" sources.

> Throughout life, self-esteem has two sources: an <u>inner</u> source, the degree of effectiveness of one's own aggression; and an (<u>outer</u>) external source, the opinions of others about oneself. Both are important, but the former is the steadier and more dependable on; the latter is always more uncertain. Unhappy and insecure is the man who, lacking an adequate inner source for self-esteem, must depend for this almost wholly upon external sources. It is this condition seen by the psychotherapist almost universally among his patients. (165, p. 29). (emphasis added)

The same note is sounded by Franks and Marolla, writing in the journal <u>Sociometry</u>. They use the term "social approval" to correspond to outer, other-dependent sources, and "efficacious action" to correspond to inner, self-dependent sources.

> Self-esteem is conceptualized here as a function of two processes: (1) the reflected appraisals of significant others in one's social environment in the form of social approval, and, (2) the individual's feelings of efficacy and competence derived

from his own perceptions of the effects he has on his environment. The former give rise to feelings of self-worth, the latter is more closely associated with feelings of power and competence. (51, p. 325).

Sandor Rado, one of the first Freudians to expand upon Freud's hints about the relation between narcissism and self-esteem, and the importance of self-esteem in the psychic economy, notes the same two basic sources of self-esteem. He further comments that people disposed to moods of depression are too reliant upon outer, social approval for their self-esteem. Rado's article in the International Journal of Psychoanalysis appeared while the great gray eminence Freud was still flourishing (1928). Rado says:

> Those pre-disposed to depression are, moreover, wholly reliant and dependent on other people for maintaining their self-esteem; they have not attained to the level of independence where self-esteem has its foundation in the subject's own achievements and critical judgment. They have a sense of security and comfort only when they feel themselves loved, esteemed and supported and encouraged. Even when they display an approximately normal activity in the gratification of their instincts and succeed in realizing their aims and ideals, their self-esteem largely depends on whether they do or do not meet with approbation and recognition. They are like those children who, when their early narcissism is shattered, recover their self-respect only in complete dependence upon their love objects.

> Thus the favorite method employed by persons of this type for increasing their self-respect is that of attracting to themselves narcissistic gratification from without. (147, p. 422).

Fellow Freudian Otto Fenichel, discussing the psychology of jealousy, distinguishes between "internal regulation of self-regard" (as for example, living up to one's ego-ideal) and "external narcissistic supplies," by which he means not only social approval but also "oral supplies," such as food, drink and drugs. Insufficient development of internal self-regard, with corresponding over-reliance upon external narcissistic supplies, is conducive to a variety of psychological problems:

> . . . in certain orally fixated people, the regulation of whose self-regard remains continuously and more or less exclusively dependent upon the external world. Just as the infant needs external material supplies in order to survive, so do they need "external narcissistic supplies" in order to maintain their self-regard. An "internal regulation of self-regard" (as carried on, say, by the relationship between ego and superego) has not, or has not sufficiently, developed, or has been regressively lost in favor of an "external" regulation. This is the same disposition as that which underlies the "oral" or "self-regarding" neuroses, that is, in the first place, manic-depressive phenomena, addictions and other impulsional neuroses, and the "masochistic character." (50, p. 350).

Some Freudians following Freud's frequent description of the superego as a merciless tyrant, critizing and hounding the poor defenseless ego, have assigned the superego the role of villian in the psychic drama. More recently, other Freudians have taken their clue from Freud's statements that the ego feels a sense of triumph whenever it pleases the superego, and that "for the ego, living means being loved by the superego." In the latter vision the superego is the knight in shining armor, hastening to rescue fair maiden ego from the loathsome ogre id, and his henchmen, external vicissitudes. Recognition of the importance of inner self-esteem and its major component, approval of the ego by the super-ego, lends itself to the knight-in-shining-armor picture of the superego. Living in harmony with the superego has the effect of stabilizing the self-esteem and providing a bulwark against neuroses. The above quote by Fenichel supports this view.

More explicit is psychoanalyst Edith Jacobson. She points out that the superego aims at harmony between its moral codes and the ego behavior, and thus establishes a relatively stable self-esteem, able to resist "dangerous external and internal instinctual influences." She says:

> This cathetic stability normally finds expression in the maintenance of a sufficiently high average level of self-esteem, with a limited margin for its vacillations, apt to withstand to some extent psychic or even physical injuries to the self. Thus the superego accomplishes, in general, a central regulation of the narcissistic and object cathexes and promotes the stability of both.
>
> In summary, the superego introduces a safety device of the highest order, which protects the self from dangerous internal instinctual stimuli, from dangerous external stimuli, and hence from narcissistic harm. (98, p. 132).

Thus, this distinction between inner and outer sources of self-esteem has significant practical consequences. Developing inner sources of self-esteem adds stability to one's emotional life and is the key to increased psychological freedom and security.

CHAPTER II

IS SELF-ESTEEM THE ONLY HUMAN MOTIVE?

Sensuality as a Basic Motivation

Some observers of the human scene maintain that only one motive is necessary to explain all behavior. Alfred Adler offers the drive for superiority (a self-esteem motive) as the single motivating force. Mark Twain says "we ignore and never mention the Sole Impulse which dictates and compels a man's every act: the imperious necessity of securing his own approval, in every emergency and at all costs."

Freud, by contrast, gave the place of primacy to sensual gratification. Is the desire for sensual pleasure a motive in its own right, a sort of co-partner (or at times, rival) with the self-esteem motive? Or is the sensual pleasure motive merely another expression of self-esteem, a case of Little Jack Horner glowing "what a good boy am I!" as he smacks his lips over the delicious plum?

Certainly our desire for sense pleasure (by this we intend to include not only gratification of the five senses, but also comfort, and the negative aspects, i.e., the desire to avoid pain, discomfort and whatever is displeasing to the five senses) is so intimately tied up with self-esteem considerations that it is difficult to separate the two in particular cases. Do the physical pleasures of sex ever exist apart from psychological pleasure in the real or imagined possession of a desirable partner? Do the pleasures of eating or drinking ever exist in what might be called a "pure" state, unalloyed with self-congratulation on one's competence at having provided so well for himself, or at least self-congratulation on one's good fortune?

It might seem that a case can be made for the independent existence of sense pleasure motivation, considering the behavior of an infant. The infant's world seems to be one of only sense gratifications— eating, drinking, being comfortable. But as we have seen already, some psychologists maintain that the self-esteem motivation is present in infancy. Even the infant needs the self-esteem gratification of being loved. Some justification for this view is offered by the repeated observations that infants tend to wither away if they do not receive enough fondling and affection. Therefore we hesitate to say that even in the infant does sense pleasure exist apart from the self-esteem drive.

The case of the dieting person may seem to offer proof that we have a sense pleasure drive which can be independent of self-esteem motivation. The dieter sometimes lets his desire for sense gratification impel him into gobbling goodies, all the while hating himself for this affront to his self-esteem. But research into the matter of compulsive eating has revealed that it can be a complex combination of motives, most of them having self-esteem roots. Therefore we cannot rely on this argument in favor of sense pleasure motivation as an entity in its own right.

However, consider the times when you have turned on the hot water to wash, put your hands in the stream, and jerked them away from scalding hot water. Is this not strictly a sense pleasure reaction—in its negative aspect, the desire to avoid pain? It does not seem necessary or plausible to bring self-esteem into the picture here. This type of example can be multiplied in our daily life—scratching an itch, shifting to a more comfortable position, turning up the thermostat, answering a painfully urgent call to go to the bathroom even in a social situation where going to the bathroom may be somewhat embarrassing, etc.

For these reasons we conclude that sense pleasure is a motivation having an independent existence of its own, that is, it cannot be reduced to merely another expression of the drive for self-esteem. However, ordinarily the two motivations have a constant and mutual interaction as we shall consider more fully later.

Which Desire Predominates?

Which of these two desires predominates in motivating our behavior? Sense pleasure motivations are more readily apparent, leading sometimes to the conclusion that they must be dominant. Sex is obviously a sense pleasure activity, less obviously a self-esteem source. Sense pleasure in eating, drinking, and being comfortable forces itself upon our attention, whereas sel-esteem motivations are often difficult to ferret out. We have a curious penchant for hiding our self-esteem motivations from ourselves, and bristle defensively when someone points them out. It is as though a self-esteem motivation revealed is a self-esteem motivation defeated.

Actually, the predominance of self-esteem motivation over sense pleasure motivation, both in frequency and power, is, upon reflection, so evident that one is slightly embarrassed to belabor the obvious by offering evidence. Is getting up in the morning primarily motivated by sense pleasure or self-esteem considerations? Is going to school or to work primarily motivated by sense pleasure or self-esteem considerations? Are one's conversations with others primarily motivated by sense pleasure or self-esteem considerations? We must opt overwhelmingly for self-esteem in all these cases. We cannot discount the independent influence of sense pleasure, but it is easy to see why Alfred Adler and others could come to the conclusion that our desire for a feeling of superiority, an exalted self-concept, was the total explanation for our behavior.

Relation Between Sense Pleasure and Self-Esteem

Two Types of Pleasure

What is pleasure? Is it not merely satisfied desire? Is it not true that every time we experience pleasure it is due to the satisfaction of some desire? To test this, let us consider some examples of pleasure that seem most remote from satisfaction of desire. You see a total stranger do a kindly deed for another total stranger, and feel a warm glow of pleasure. What desire of yours is being satisfied here? There are several possibilities. First, we find a pleasure in seeing or hearing something that agrees with our own moral code, or standard of values, because this offers additional confirmation that we are right, that our judgment in this important matter is good. Secondly, just as we often feel uneasy in the presence of a harsh interchange between two strangers, an uneasiness due at least in part to the awareness that a harsh world bodes ill for our own welfare, so

41

also when we see kindness between two strangers it gives us the comfortable feeling that this is not such a bad world after all, which augers well for our own welfare. And thirdly, even though the others are total strangers, we can identify with them as fellow human beings, with the result that the good experienced by them is good experienced by ourselves, in these extended selves. Naturally, such considerations are seldom explicitly in our consciousness, nor need they be in order to effectively give us a warm feeling of pleasure.

Or suppose you feel pleasure at seeing the first yellow crocus of spring. What desire of yours is being satisfied in this case? The sight of the brave little flower is a promise of better weather to come. Also, this refreshing glimpse satisfies to a small degree our ever-present desire for beautiful sights.

Accepting for the moment the idea that all pleasure comes from satisfied desire, is it also true that all satisfied desire yields pleasure? We have all desired something, obtained it, and been disappointed rather than pleased. Is this a case of satisfied desire not bringing pleasure? Instead, was it not a case of our desire not being satisfied by the thing we thought would do so. For instance, we order a filet mignon, wait with anticipation, and receive something that is tough, stringy and overdone. Disappointment rather than pleasure. But also, not satisfied desire. Our desire was not just to receive a steak, but to sink our teeth into a tender, juicy steak.

Sometimes desire is satisfied but is followed by regret. The prospect of gain or pleasure may lure us into an action that is contrary to our moral code. However, in this case we actually do experience some pleasure when the desire is satisfied, but remorse follows when we begin to realize what we have done to our self-respect. This then is a case of satisfied desire with pleasure, followed by frustration of a more basic desire, with attendant displeasure.

But is it more accurate to say that pleasure is satisfied desire, or rather that it is a state of mind, or state of being, resulting from satisfied desire? As always, we should opt for the simpler version, unless it proves to be inadequate. In this case we see no need to bring "state of mind" or "state of being" into the equation, so we will settle for the position that pleasure is satisfied desire. This we are prepared to modify if subsequent considerations indicate that it is inadequate.

Pleasure being satisfied desire, we can expect types of pleasure to correspond to types of desire. Here we suggest that human beings have two basic types of desire: those which we have in common with other animals, and those which are uniquely human. In common with animals we have desires for gratification of the senses. The type of pleasure corresponding to these "animal" desires is sense pleasure.

And, as we noted earlier, desires unique to human beings are those which involve some psychological awareness for their gratification. They involve an appreciation of ourselves as possessors of some good. We want money not only for the creature comfort it makes possible, but also for the accompanying sense of security, for a sense of keeping up with the Joneses, for the feeling of personal worth it can give us, for the accompanying vision of expanded horizons. The desires unique to human beings we suggest can all be embraced under the rubric of "psychological awareness of good possessed by self." And here self includes those extended selves, the other human beings with whom we may identify. This principle of identification we will develop more fully in a later chapter.

The two basic desires then in the human economy are for a sensory awareness of good possessed, and for a psychological awareness of good possessed. The two basic corresponding pleasures are sense pleasure and self-esteem. Here we find ourselves in agreement with the English philosopher Thomas Hobbes:

> Now whatever seems good, is pleasant, and relates either to the sense, or the mind. But all the mind's pleasure is either glory, (or to have a good opinion of one's self), or refers to glory in the end; the rest are sensual, or conducing to sensuality, which may be all comprehended under the word conveniences. (91, p. 260)

Although Hobbes had a detestation of the Scholastics, and misses no opportunity to express his aversion, on this point he is in unwitting agreement with the foremost of the Scholastics, Aquinas himself, who says:

> Now pleasure is twofold, as we shall state later on: one is in the intelligible good, which is the good of reason; the other is in good which is perceptible to the senses. (11, I-II, Q. 30, a. 1, corp.)

Personality Types Resulting From The Relation Between Sense Pleasure and Self-Esteem

The individual may develop a life-style in which sense pleasure and self-esteem are allies one with the other, or a life-style in which they are in conflict. He can derive self-esteem from satisfaction of sense desires, or he can derive self-esteem from curbing his sense pleasures. The "great lover" builds his self-image largely upon his sexual prowess, the gourmet preens himself upon his discriminating taste, and the average person to a lesser degree finds ground for self-congratulation in his sensual activities. "Grab all the gusto you can get!" But there is another type—variously called Spartan, Stoic, Puritan, ascetic, etc.—who builds his self-image largely upon his self-discipline, self-denial, and control of his sense desires. The "allies," sensual, type of relationship between sense pleasure and self-esteem comes to us more easily and naturally, and in most cultures is the predominant adjustment. Of course, as in all typologies, "pure types" are rare.

For centuries, Epicurean and Stoic philosophies competed for men's loyalties, and indeed continue to do so today, although today as implicit Weltanschauugen rather than as formal philosophies. For the Epicureans, all pleasures were good, good both in the sense of desirable and morally praiseworthy. This does not mean that Epicurus and his disciples passed their days in orgies or debauchery. Actually, they favored a simple, retiring life as most conducive in the long run to fullest pleasure of mind and body and avoidance of cares and pains. Epicurus himself was a man of moderate, temperate life, teaching his disciples that over-indulgence resulted in pain out of proportion to the pleasure obtained.[1] This pleasure/

pain calculus led the apostle of pleasure to the paradoxical observation "Sex never benefitted any man, and it's a marvel if it hasn't injured him!" (175, p. 206). His experience with sex had led him to the same conclusion that Epicurean Oscar Wilde voiced 2000 years later: "The pleasure is momentary, the posture ridiculous, and the price damnable!" However, despite this apparently ascetic attitude toward sex, Epicurus' basic doctrine was that all pleasures are, in themselves, good, and are the crtieria for personal excellence. The better man is he who is achieving in his life the greater balance of pleasure over pain. Thus the true Epicurean, prudently enjoying sense delights, was at the same time increasing his self-esteem.

Also seeking a solution to the problem of human happiness/unhappiness, the Stoic followed a different path. He considered that placing his happiness in pleasure, especially physical pleasure, made him too vulnerable to external conditions. "Sickness, poverty, the malice of other men and a multitude of other causes can deprive me of pleasure. I want to be master of my own destiny, to find happiness—and perhaps more important, to escape unhappiness—in a way that is not subject to the vagaries of fortune." The answer seemed to lie in self-control, in disciplining oneself to accept with equanimity of spirit whatever trials or blessings fate might send. The most obvious obstacle to achieving this constant tranquillity was the appeal of physical pleasure, whose siren song constantly lures the individual back to a vulnerable dependency on external circumstances. As a result, the Stoic came to regard physical pleasure as a fifth columnist within his own psychological camp.

> It seems that the true Stoic found something repulsive in any admission, however guarded, of the value of pleasure—of any qualifications, however cautious, of the stern, inescapable demands of duty. (184, p. 171).

---

[1]Some of Epicurus' later followers (Julius Caesar, "every woman's husband," "lock up your daughters, Caesar is in town") did not take such a long range view in their pleasure seeking, and have given Epicurus' philosophy its popular reputation for sensual abandonment.

Roman Emperor Marcus Aurelius, "one of the finest and greatest men who ever lived," (140, p. xxiii) (a judgment supported by the fact that during his nineteen years of almost absolute power over the civilized world, Marcus maintained his sterling character, an outstanding exception to the principle enunciated by Lord Acton, "power corrupts, and absolute power corrupts absolutely") writes in his notes to himself:

> Show those qualities that are absolutely within thy power, sincerity, gravity, endurance of labour, aversion to pleasure, contentment with thy portion and with few things, benevolence, frankness, no love of superiority, freedom from trifling magnanimity. (15, p. 47). (emphasis ours)

The dichotomy of attitudes toward sense pleasure—"sense pleasure is good and I pride myself on getting lots of it," versus "sense pleasure is demeaning and I pride myself on my self-denial"—serves as the basis for contrasting personality types who customarily view each other with dislike. Stoic Cicero in the Roman Senate denounced Epicurean Marc Anthony as a lecher, a drunkard and a waster of public funds. Anthony had Cicero beheaded and preserved his head and hand to gloat over. In our own day the personal animosity between steak-and-lobster John F. Kennedy and cottage-cheese-and-ketchup Richard M. Nixon did not issue in a beheading—although some of the more wild-eyed theory-concocters have hinted at the equivalent.

In summary, sense pleasure and self-esteem are separate entities; neither is merely a function of the other. Both are expressions of our desire to be aware of possession of good. Which is to say, both are expressions of our desire for happiness. In many cases of human behavior, both sense pleasure and self-esteem considerations are present, mutually interacting. A fundamental basis for a typology of personality is the habitual relationship between sense pleasure and self-esteem in the individual's life style. The Epicurean or "average Joe" type gets a self-esteem boost from enjoying sense pleasures—"grab all the gusto you can get"—while the Stoic, Puritan, ascetic type gets a self-esteem boost from curbing sense pleasures.

Evidence thus indicates that self-esteem does not play the sole role in determining human behavior. However, the entrance of the sense pleasure motivation into the psychic drama does not challenge the top billing that must be given to the self-esteem motive. The great bulk of our moment-to-moment activities are traceable to self-esteem rather than to sense pleasure; when the desires conflict, self-esteem customarily wins out—when has the urge to "go to the bathroom" been so imperious that you have relieved yourself in public view? The great decisions in our lives are more influenced by considerations of prestige and social approval than by desires for comfort and sensual pleasure. Even those most sensual activities, such as eating, drinking and sex, are increasingly seen by psychologists as controlled by consideratins of peer approval and ego compensation. The strong dominance of self-esteem in this working partnership justifies the billing "Self-Esteem Psychology."

Instinct for Self-Preservation?

In addition to the desires for self-esteem and for sense pleasure, is there a third distinct motivation in human nature, namely the instinct for self-preservation? At first we are inclined to say, yes, of course. After all, "self-preservation is the first law of nature." Also, human beings are usually willing to undergo considerable humiliation or pain if this is necessary to save their lives. How many times have we seen the Western movie character take a swig of whiskey, bite the bullet, and willingly submit to having his gangrenous leg hacked off with a bowie knife? This would seem to testify to a drive for self-preservation even more basic than the desire for sense pleasure.

At the opposite end of the bravery spectrum, we saw many Union soldiers in Red Badge of Courage fling down their rifles and flee from the charging Rebs. They were willing to risk living with a coward self-image in order to save their lives. Once again, self-preservation seems the more basic and powerful motive.

And yet we find some psychologists who say that there is no instinct for self-preservation per se, that is, human beings do not have a desire to preserve their existence as such, but only have the desire to preserve their existence as the necessary basis for the satisfaction of other desires. When people are convinced that there is no further hope for continued gratification of their desires for self-esteem and sense pleasure, they simply lose the will to live.

Alfred Adler concluded that the self-preservative urge is merely an expression of our drive for superiority:

> I began to see clearly in every psychological phenomenon the striving for superiority . . . . Whatever premises all our philosophers and psychologists dream of—self-preservation, pleasure principle, equalization—all these are but vague representations, attempts to express the great upward drive. (5, p. 103).

Presumably, by the above statement Adler means that we only desire continued existence as the necessary substratum for continued and increased superiority. It is well to remember that by superiority Adler does not in all cases mean superiority to others, but sometimes means superiority to obstacles that impede growth. Put quite simply, Adler does not concede the existence of an instinct for self-preservation, as such, but instead he posits a drive for superiority, which ordinarily dictates self-preservation as a necessary means to its fulfillment.

Among the psychologists who have come to the conclusion that the drive for self-preservation is not an entity in its own right, but is desired merely as a means to gratify other drives, are Anna Freud and the Snygg/Combs team, whose theory we consider in the next chapter. Anna Freud explains Cyrano de Bergerac's determination to save Christian's life as being due to Cyrano's implicit realization that only through the union of Christian and Roxanne can he, Cyrano, realize the vicarious fulfillment of his own desires. She then states the general principle:

> Analysis shows that both the anxiety and the absence of anxiety are due rather to the subject's feeling that his own life is worth living and preserving only in so far as there is opportunity in it for the gra-

tification of his instincts. (53, p. 145).

By "instincts" Anna Freud does not have precisely in mind the desires for self-esteem and sense pleasure, but the basic idea is there: self-preservation is not a drive in its own right, but is only directed toward the satisfaction of other desires.

Psychologists Snygg and Combs maintain that what seems to be an urge for self-preservation of physical life is actually an urge to preserve and enhance the "phenomenal self." By this term they mean the self-concept.

> If this struggle to maintain the integration of the organism is seen in a purely objective sense, the only conclusion possible is that the fundamental motive of human behavior is the preservation of the physical organism. But, this is inadequate because many things men do are not directed toward their physical survival. They risk their lives in war and sports, they drive too fast, use alcohol, drugs, and even commit suicide. How can such activities be motivated by a need for self-preservation? Seen simply in terms of this need such behaviors do indeed seem paradoxical. When we observe them, however, as attempts by the individual to maintain the organization of his phenomenal self, they become completely consistent. What the individual is seeking to preserve is not his physical self but the self of which he is aware, his phenomenal self. (170, p. 56).

In the same vein, Snygg and Combs state:

> The soldier in wartime is not torn between a desire for self-preservation and self-destruction as he faces the coming battle. On the contrary, he is concerned solely with the preservation or enhancement of his phenomenal self. Although the situation will vary from individual to individual, it might roughly be described as follows: He may risk death on the one hand to preserve his phenomenal self against be-

49

coming the kind of person who "lets his buddies down" and on the other hand to en-hance his phenomenal self by being the kind of person who is "one of the gang," or as brave as the rest. (170, p. 61).

"Death before dishonor" sounds quaint to modern ears but still has considerable validity. Each year hundreds of thousands of people choose to directly end their lives by suicide rather than to continue living with a lacerated self-esteem. How many millions more seek relief from the pain of a depressed ego by means of indirect suicide—self-destructive life-styles and psychosomatic illnesses—is impossible to estimate.

One becomes ready to question the existence of any instinct for self-preservation when he reads of suicide epidemics. Some instances:

> Herodatus, speaking of the Crestonaeans of Thrace, says that no sooner does a man die than "a sharp contest" follows among his wives as to which has the best right to share her husband's grave. Prescott, in his History of the Conquest of Peru, writing of events two thousand years later, goes out of his way to emphasize a similar eagerness among the Incas. When a great man died a number of his attendants and favorite concu-bines were immolated with him, and, says Prescott, "the women have been known, in more than one instance, to lay violent hands upon themselves when restrained from testi-fying their fidelity by this act of conjugal martyrdom."

> Caesar, when he tells how certain picked warriors, or soldurii, were unwilling to survive their chieftain, is merely in-stancing a form of institutional suicide found in the most divers countries . . . . (48, p. 20).

> Somewhere into this sacrificial cate-gory must also be fitted the Jaina sect of Southern India, who threw themselves under the wheels of the Juggernaut, and the devo-tion of the Japanese divinity Amida, who,

amidst applause, made hecatombs for their
divinity, throwing themselves into the sea
or burying themselves alive . . . . Among
the Northern peoples the fabled death of
Odin resulted in approved and almost insti-
tutional suicides. (48, p. 24).

More contemporary examples are given by Meerloo:

During World War II, several examples of
mass suicide were observed. When people
fail as a group and believe they have no
future, they surrender "en masse" to death.
An example of this attitude is given in
Robert Sherrel's report of the taking of
Saipan as quoted by Lindsay. He describes a
Japanese officer cutting off the heads of
his kneeling men with a Samurai sword;
crowds of civilians and soldiers walking off
cliffs or wading into the ocean, while
others blew themselves up with grenades.
"Three women sat on the rocks and deli-
berately combed their long black hair. Fi-
nally they joined hands and walked slowly
into the sea." A hundred soldiers on the
rocks at Marpi Point bowed to the Marines
from the clifftops, spread a large Japanese
flag on the rocks, and then pulled the pins
from grenades which the leader handed them.
(198, p. 83).

These and a multitude of similar episodes support
the contention of Anna Freud, Adler, and Snygg/Combs
that human beings do not have an urge to preserve
their physical existence as such, when devoid of any
possibility of future self-esteem and sense pleasure.
We do however strive to continue our existence when it
is seen as the necessary condition for continued gra-
tification of our desires for self-esteem and sense
pleasure.

The "Born Again" Motivation

"I went to a Bible study group with my
wife. It was just a Bible study, but it
angered me. I thought, "These people talk
like they have God in their hip pocket."
But I went eight Wednesdays in a row. The

51

last Wednesday evening, while everyone was praying, I got down on my knees and gave my life to the Lord and I have never been the same since. It was an emotional experience, but it hasn't passed. That was nine years ago."

Once such words would have been identified, and uncharitably patronized, as the essence of Southern redneck religion. But they were uttered last week at a thoroughly Episcopal church in Darien, Conn., an almost stereotypically proper and affluent Northeastern suburb. The speaker, Lee Buck, 54 is a senior vice president of the New York Life Insurance Co. "Before, I wanted to be successful in the world," says Buck. "Now I want to exalt the Lord."

These are the opening lines of the cover story "Back to the Oldtime Religion" in Time Magazine, Dec. 26, 1977. The story documents the "burgeoning new empire of Evangelicalism" that has burst upon the American scene in the past decade. The "born again" movement, variously called evangelicalism or fundamentalism (purists distinguish the two, occasionally with some acerbity, but the difference is almost imperceptible to the outsider), and typified by the theology and preaching of Billy Graham, has captured public attention by the number and celebrity of its converts. The last three Presidents of the United States—Gerald Ford, Jimmy Carter and Ronald Reagan—have been reputed (perhaps by overzealous image-makers) to be "born again" Christians. Ex-sinners Charles Colson and Eldridge Cleaver have appeared on the same platform to witness to their re-birth in Christ; every pro football team seems to have its cadre of zealous re-born "athletes for Christ." Says Time Magazine: "Gaudy and vital, U.S. Evangelicalism is booming . . . most active and vital aspect of American religion today . . . set off hopeful echoes in the national spirit."

Evangelical theology maintains that when a person is "born again" through faith in Jesus Christ, he receives a new nature. He is now a child of God in the fullest sense, sharing in God's nature. Dominating his life is a new motivation, the desire to serve

52

and glorify God. Capturing the essence of this motivation are the words of New York Life vice president Lee Buck, "Now I want to exalt the Lord." The desire for self-esteem is not dead, but it is dominated by the desire that the Lord be esteemed. Traditional Protestant and Catholic theologies concur in the essentials of this belief: the regenerate person shares in God's nature, and his dominant motivation is the desire to glorify God.

The regenerate person has been given a share in God's nature

It is intrinsic to the concept of "generation" that the living being generated has the same nature as its progenitors. We, born of human parents, have a human nature. The person who is born again is born of God, as the Scripture assures us. This carries the implication that the regenerate person now has a new nature in addition to his human nature, a nature which is a share in God's nature. Pointing to this new nature are various Scriptural references to the born-again person as being a "new creature," a "new man." "Therefore if any man be in Christ, he is a new creature." (2 Cor. 5:17). "Being born again, not of corruptible seed, but of incorruptible, by the word of God." (1 Peter 1:23). "Put on the new man, which after God is created in righteousness and true holiness." (Eph. 4:24). Most explicit is the apostle Peter: "Whereby are given unto us exceeding great and precious promises: that by these ye might be partakers of the divine nature, having escaped the corruption that is in the world through lust." (2 Peter 1:4).

This sharing in the divine nature is not to be confused with possession of the divine nature in all its fullness, as Jesus has. Jesus, truly a man with human nature, has also the divine nature in all its perfections—omniscience, omnipotence, eternity, etc. He is truly God, equal with the Father in all things. Our sharing in the divine nature of course does not give us all the perfections of the divine nature, but does raise us to a new level of kinship and fellowship with God. It consists principally in this, that we now have a new operating principle guiding our lives. Now, the dominant motivation in our lives is no longer the desire for self-esteem or sensual gratification, but is now the desire that God be obeyed, loved, and glorified. This new motivation is well expressed in the beginning of the Lord's prayer: "Hallowed be thy name, thy kingdom come, thy will be done on earth as it is in heaven." This new motivation, new operating principle, of the new man is the same as God's operating principle, which may be variously described as "love for the Supreme Good above all," or "dominant desire that God be glorified."*

Protestant evangelical tradition recognizes "sharing in God's nature"

One of the founding fathers of evangelical Protestantism, Martin Luther himself, has powerful words in commentary on Peter's "you become partakers of the divine nature":

> Through the power of faith, he says, we partake of and have association or communion with the divine nature. This is a verse without a parallel in the New and the Old Testament, even though unbelievers regard it as a trivial matter that we partake of the divine nature itself. But what is the divine nature? It is eternal truth, righteousness, wisdom, everlasting life, peace, joy, happiness, and whatever can be called good. Now he who becomes a partaker of the divine nature receives all this, so that he lives eternally and has everlasting peace, joy, and happiness, and is pure, clean, righteous, and almighty against the devil, sin, and death. (226, Vol. 30, p. 155).

In John Calvin's commentary on the same passage in Peter, he says: "he then shews the excellency of the promises, that they make us partakers of the divine nature, than which nothing can be conceived better." Calvin then warns against misinterpretations of

---

*Terms such as "desire" or "motivation" are only an analogy when used in connection with God's action. Such terms imply an aim at some good not yet possessed, whereas God already possesses all good.

The expression "sharing in God's nature" is not to be understood in a pantheistic sense, as though we were a part of a single existing reality which is God.

54

this passage, as by Manicheans who "dreamt that we are a part of God," and by "at this day fanatics who imagine that we thus pass over into the nature of God, so that his swallows up our nature."

A giant of the American evangelical tradition is Jonathan Edwards, eighteenth century theologian, whose voluminous writings are enjoying a revived vogue today, due to his rich insights into human psychology and its relation to the Christian life. Regarding our participation in the nature of God, Edwards says of the redeemed:

> They have spiritual excellency and joy by a kind of participation of God. They are made excellent by a communication of God's excellency. God puts his own beauty, i.e., his beautiful likeness, upon their souls. They are made partakers of the divine nature, or moral image of God.
> 2 Peter 1:4. (227, p. 115)

Probably no one is more representative of the current American evangelical scene than is Billy Graham. His staff of research assistants and his frequent contacts with evangelical leaders throughout the country keep him in touch with prevailing evangelical attitudes. (This is not to overlook the fact that the Protestant evangelical world is certainly no monolith; there exists a variety of views, even mutally contradictory views, on some important theological issues.) In his World Aflame, Graham says of those who have been born again: "They have been born from above. God's nature has been imparted to them." And, "The moment we receive Christ as Saviour, we receive the divine nature of the sons of God." (p. 140.) Graham adds the reminder, universal in Christian tradition, that our old nature is still with us, battling for dominance: "It is true that the Christian possesses a new nature, but the old nature is still there . . . we are to feed the new nature, and to starve the old nature." (p. 144-5)

Catholic tradition recognizes "sharing in God's nature"

According to 2 Peter 1,4, the Christian is elevated to participation in the

Divine nature: "By which (His own power and glory) He (God) hath given to us most great and precious promises, that by these you may be made partakers of the Divine nature." Again, the scriptural texts which represent justification as generation or birth from God (John 1,12 et seq.; 3,5; 1 John 3,19; Tit. 3,5; James 1,18; 1 Peter 1, 23), indirectly teach the participation of man in the Divine nature, as generation consists in the communication of the nature of the generator to the generated. (Fundamentals of Catholic Dogma, by Ludwig Ott, p. 256).

The author of the above quote notes that the participation in God's nature is not to be interpreted in a pantheistic sense of transformation of the human soul into Divinity, nor on the other hand is it a mere imitation of the moral perfections of God. Rebirth in Christ "assimilates the soul to God and unites it with Him in a manner transcending all created powers."

In the Dictionary of Dogmatic Theology (1945) this sharing in the Divine nature is "identified by the best exegetes with that supernatural life, kindled and sustained by the Holy Spirit in the Christian, which St. Paul calls 'grace' and 'spirit.'" In order that a human being be capable of knowing and loving God in a supernatural way, he must be really elevated to a divine level. This elevation to a divine level, this sharing in God's nature, is traditionally known in Catholic theology as "sanctifying grace."

The regenerated person acts with the operating principles of the Divine nature

Traditional Christian theology proposes that the operating principles of God's nature are his knowledge of himself and love of himself. God's knowledge of himself is the Word, the Second Person of the Trinity. God's love for himself is the mutual love between Father and Son, and is the Third Person of the Trinity, the Holy Spirit.*

---

*Augustine sees an image of the Holy Trinity in the human mind's knowledge of self and love of self. In this parallel the self corresponds to God the Fa-

56

The individual to whom God has given a share in the Divine nature can now act with the operating principles of that nature—he knows God in a supernatural way, and he loves God above all. "Neither knoweth any man the Father, save the Son, and he to whomsoever the Son will reveal him." (Matt. 11:27). "Thou shalt love the Lord thy God with all thy heart, and with all thy soul, and with all thy mind, and with all thy strength: this is the first commandment." (Mark 12:30). God only commands that which is possible for us, aided by his grace. The regenerated person loves God above all, but does not yet perfectly fulfill this great command. This is the ideal toward which he is striving, with God's help.

Acting in accord with the Divine nature in which he participates, the born-again person loves God with a God-oriented love rather than a self-oriented love. Quite apart from any advantage to self or reference to self, he rejoices that God is supreme good, supreme truth, supreme holiness, supreme in love, majesty and beauty; rejoices that God has infinite knowledge and power, that he always was and always will be; rejoices that God is three Persons, Father, Son and Holy Spirit. He praises God for these things, and desires that all beings praise and glorify God, love him and obey him and serve him. The doxology has well captured the essence of this God-oriented love: Glory be to the Father, and to the Son, and to the Holy Spirit, as it was in the beginning, is now, and ever shall be, world without end, Amen. An even more capsulated version is Alleluia! (All hail to him who is, praise God!) The same desire is expressed by the first petition of the Lord's prayer: hallowed be thy name. The next two petitions, "thy kingdom come, thy will be done," are God-oriented in that they ask that God be glorified, but an element of self-orientation begins to enter in. The petitioner will share in the blessings from God's kingdom and his will being done.

---

ther, its knowledge of its own excellence corresponds to God the Son, and its love for that excellence corresponds to God the Holy Spirit.

Can we thus say that self-esteem is an image of the Holy Trinity? The person's knowledge of his own excellence and love for that excellence is precisely the essence of self-esteem.

The New Testament is of course filled with further exhortations to the Christian to give expression to this God-oriented love by giving glory to God, praising him, obeying and serving him. Even our most mundane actions can and should be directed to the glory of God. As the apostle Paul says: "Whether therefore ye eat, or drink, or whatsoever ye do, do all to the glory of God." (I Cor. 10:31).

The Christian also has a self-oriented love for God

A self-oriented love for another is a desire to be united to the other because of the benefits that self derives from the other. Often joined to this is a love of benevolence toward the other, that is, a desire to promote the welfare and happiness of the other. Even this benevolent love is self-oriented in its origin, namely, a consideration of the benefits that the other has conferred upon self, and may confer in the future. Our desire for God's approval, for union with him here and hereafter, for eternal life and the joys of heaven, for the peace and joy that the Holy Spirit can give us now—all these are self-oriented desires. The apostles reported that they loved Jesus because he first loved them, and they were concerned about what reward they would have for following him. This desire for personal benefits is an inescapable part of human nature and is encouraged by Jesus. The petition, "give us this day our daily bread," and the petitions that follow, are requests for personal benefits. Jesus' numerous appeals to our desires for peace of soul (Matt. 11:29), rewards (Matt. 6:1-6), everlasting life (Matt. 19:29), honor from God (Jn. 5:44), joy (Jn. 15:11), etc., put his stamp of approval on these self-oriented desires. The type of love for God that flows from seeing him as the source of all that we hope for, is a self-oriented love. But it is pleasing to God because it is based on faith in truths revealed by him, faith in his promises.

These desires for the benefits God confers are traceable to the basic operating principle of our nature, the self-esteem motive.* What can give a

---

*Our self-esteem motive leads us to desire God's blessings, but only when so moved by God's grace.

person a more secure and exalted self-esteem than to
receive honor from the One who knows all and judges
justly. What can give a person a greater sense of his
own worth than to be united to the Supreme One—a
worth not independent of God but totally dependent
upon him, and even more desirable and triumphant for
that very reason. Such noble exaltation of self-
esteem, from sharing in God's nature and gifts, can go
hand in hand with a deep realization of one's own
viciousness, misery and nothingness, by one's own
nature apart from God. Testimony to this paradox of
deep self-contempt accompanied by an inner peace and
buoyant joy is frequent in the writings of Christian
believers.

Empirical evidence for the born-again motivation?

Can concrete empirical evidence be offered to
establish the existence in some human beings of this
motivation to promote the interests of God, indepen-
dent of any reference to self? What examples of human
behavior can be found which cannot be explained by the
desires for sense pleasure and self-esteem, but only
by the desire that God possess good—i.e., be glori-
fied, loved, obeyed and served? In casting about for
such examples, cases of willing martyrdom seem like
possibilities. But here we run into the difficulty
that even persons who do not believe in God are some-
times willing to die for a cause. Also, even St. Paul
admits the possibility of martyrdom for motives other
than love for God: "Though I bestow all my goods to
feed the poor, and though I give my body to be burned,
and have not charity, it profiteth me nothing." (I
Cor.3:13).

Can we accept as evidence for the existence of
this self-transcending love for God the attitudes and
behavior of some Christians who have made it their
concern to act contrary to the desires for sense plea-
sure and self-esteem? Hagiographies are replete with
examples of persons who, after conversion, spent the
rest of their lives denying themselves creature com-
forts and inflicting pain upon themselves. This cer-
tainly is contrary to our desire for sense pleasure,

Without the prior help of God's grace we can neither
think nor desire anything pleasing to him.

but might be explained by the desire for an exalted self-image as a dedicated, holy person. However, many of these people also seemed to act against the desire for a good self-image, desiring instead to be held in contempt by others, to be ridiculed, hated, ignored, despised, and further, to have a correspondingly low self-regard, considering themselves as vile, sinful, despicable. The discernable rationale offered for thus acting contrary to sense pleasure and self-esteem is that these are the desires competing with love for God in the psychic arena. To the extent that sense pleasure and self-esteem flourish, love for God will wither. And to the extent that sense pleasure and self-esteem are curbed, cut back, then love for God and truly altruistic love for others can flourish.*

But is such an expressed attitude to be accepted as empirical evidence for the existence of this third motivation, the love for God above all? Or is it possible that even in his humility and self-abasement the individuial is actually but unwittingly seeking to nourish his self-image as a person on fire with love for God, as a holy saint, as one of the elect? Concern on this very point is found in the writings of outstanding Christians, anxious lest all their heroic efforts, ostensibly directed to the glory of God, were actually directed to self-glorification. Thus it seems that any empirical evidence that might be cited for the existence of this love for God transcending all self-interest is ambiguous, subject to interpretation as merely another expression of the desire for a good self-image. Of course no empirical evidence is necessary for the person who is convinced by the Scripture and his own inner experience of the existence of a self-transcending desire to glorify God.

---

*A contrary theory has been widely promoted in popular religious literature (evangelical, liberal Protestant, and Catholic) in the last fifteen years. According to this view, the self-esteem desire is not a competitor with love for God, but rather, an ally. That is, a person can only love God and neighbor to the extent that he loves himself. By "loving self" the proponents of this theory mean having a solid self-esteem. To adequately evaluate this view, which at first glance seems so contrary to Christian tradition, would require another volume.

Relevance of the "born again" motivation

In a consideration of the basic motives which constitute the principles for a science of psychology, what place is there for a motive which can only be known from supernatural revelation? For persons who do not accept this revelation, the "greater glory of God" motive is credible only if it can be established empirically. This I am not able to do, though conceding that it may be possible for someone more discerning and knowledgeable than I. It is not the purpose of this book to investigate the role this motivation might play in the science of psychology as it is applied to "secular" concerns, that is, to analysis and treatment of behavioral problems, personal and social.

However, for the Christian who accepts on faith —corroborated by his own inner experience—that God has given to some human beings a new nature, with a new operating principle, any science of psychology is incomplete unless it takes this God-oriented motive into account. But even in this case it might be argued that for practical purposes the supernatural motivation can be safely ignored in assessing human behavioral situations. It is possible that the number of situations where the desire to glorify God is the dominant factor are so few as to have no practical impact? In the sum total of day to day human actions, what percent are determined by the desire to glorify God? Very few, it seems, taking a world-wide perspective. Even in the life of the devout believer, what percent of his actions are determined by this motive? An honest analysis might reveal very few. And even those actions which the believer stoutly avers are from the desire to glorify God, how many are actually from more self-interested motives, masquerading under the title of giving greater glory to God.

Nevertheless, for the Christian's psychology of his personal relationship with God, the supernatural motivation is of supreme importance. The essence of Christian spiritual growth is living ever more completely for God's glory.

Christian writers down through the centuries have shown an intense interest in psychology, in its core aspect, human motivation. Repeatedly they stress the importance of self-knowledge. By this they mean peeling away our usual layers of self-deception to arrive at an honest glimpse of what sort of persons we really are. This in turn means honestly facing up to our true motivations. This is the true humility—honest knowledge about self, about self in its most important aspect, its loves, values, and motives. And when we have said "motives," we have said loves and values.

True humility requires a ruthless ferreting out of our secret motives, no matter how depressing it may be to admit them to consciousness. This honest confronting the corruption and deceitfulness of our own motives is a necessary first step in Christian growth. "The heart is deceitful above all things, and desperately wicked: who can know it?" (Jer. 17:9). The Christian can know it, and yes, must know it, guided by the grace of God.

The importance of self-knowledge, humility, is well summed up in Augustine's famous sentiment, here roughly paraphrased. "What is the most important virtue for the Christian to develop? Humility. And the second most important is humility. Likewise the third. This is the foundation upon which the Christian life must be built, if it is to be genuine. As deep as the foundation of humility is laid, so high will reach the temple of charity that is built thereon."

When the Christian is faced with a decision of importance in his life, he asks himself what are his motives for the various alternatives that seem most logical. He wants to be doing the will of God at all times, and this too demands an honest examination of his motives. Am I seeking God's glory, or am I seeking my own glory? He realizes that the former way leads to true happiness, and the latter leads away from God. He realizes how easy it is for him to fall into the attitude of the Pharisee in the parable of the Pharisee and the publican. Human nature constantly pulls in that self-glorifying direction. How is one to avoid falling into that trap? Ultimately of course everything depends upon the grace of God, but his grace moves us to make every human effort to achieve the desired end, namely, purity of desire to love and serve God.

For the Christian then, the born-again motive, the God-oriented desire that God be loved, obeyed, served and glorified, is all-important in his daily psychology. His daily struggle is to assert the dominance of this motive over his desire for self-esteem and sense pleasure.

The relationship between this "divine nature motive" and the motives of human nature is a topic which can only be adequately treated in a separate book. The purpose of the present book is merely to make a case for the fact that human nature operates on two basic motives, the desire for self-esteem and the desire for sense pleasure.

CHAPTER III

EVIDENCE FOR THE PRIMACY OF THE SELF-ESTEEM MOTIVE

PART I: WE DESIRE SOCIAL APPROVAL TO INCREASE SELF-ESTEEM

The first part of this chapter presents testimony from a variety of thinkers, ancient and modern, stressing the all-pervasive importance of the human desire for esteem from others. Then we see additional testimony to the effect that we desire this esteem from others in order to increase the esteem from "number one," self. The desire for self-esteem is the more basic wellspring from which the desire for social esteem flows. Thus, whatever is said of the ubiquity and influence of desire for esteem from others is said a potiori of the self-esteem motive.

The second part of this chapter offers the witness of numerous observers of the human scene concluding that the self-esteem motive is the cause and explanation of human behavior. Thus the first part points to the primacy of the self-esteem motive because it is the cause of our powerful and pervasive desire for social approval, while the second part provides direct testimony to the primacy of the self-esteem motive.

In addition to the experts cited in this chapter, Freud also has passages hinting at the supremacy of the self-esteem motive, despite his avowed allegiance to the primacy of sexuality. Because of Freud's importance as a psychologist, and because of the richness and variety of his insights, we have devoted a full chapter to examination of his clues regarding self-esteem.

The Desire for Esteem from Others

Our lives seem to be ruled by our desire for approval from others. We want to be noticed, accepted, praised, loved, admired, respected, held in high esteem. Give a few moments consideration to your behavior and your plans and reveries and you will find the great bulk of them traceable to this desire for social approval from the "significant others" in your life. Writers down through the ages have commented on the sweeping importance of this motivation in our lives.

Over two thousand years ago Plato developed this theme in his Symposium. He uses as his literary vehicle a group of friends dining and discussing love. Plato presents as his main protagonist Socrates, who tells the group of his philosophy of love, which he learned from Diotima of Mantineia, "a woman wise in this and many other kinds of knowledge . . . she was my instructress in the art of love. . . ." (1445, p. 159). Diotima has taught Socrates that men are motivated by their desire for social approval, as widespread and as lasting as possible, which she refers to as the "love of the immortality of fame." She says:

> "Of that, Socrates, you may be assured—think only of the ambition of men, and you will wonder at the senselessness of their ways, unless you consider how they are stirred by the love of an immortality of fame. They are stirred to run all risks greater far than they would have run for their children, and to spend money and undergo any sort of toil, and even to die, for the sake of leaving behind them a name which shall be eternal. . . . I am persuaded that all men do all things, and the better they are the more they do them, in hope of the glorious fame of immortal virtue. . . ." (145, p. 167).

Socrates expresses his agreement with the views of his teacher:

> Such, Phaedrus—and I speak not only to you, but to all of you—were the words of Diotima; and I am persuaded of their truth. (145, p. 172).

Aristotle presents a similar motivation in his description of what he considers to be the most excellent type of man, the proud man, also referred to as "great-souled man" or "magnanimous man". This proud man "thinks himself worthy of great things" and is quite correct in his estimation.

Now the proud man, since he deserves
most, must be good in the highest degree;
for the better man always deserves more,
and the best man most. Therefore the truly
proud man must be good. . . . Therefore it
is hard to be truly proud; for it is impos-
sible without nobility and goodness of
character. (12, Bk. 4, sec. 3).

And what motivates this truly proud man? First
and foremost he seeks honor, that is, esteem from
others:

If, then, he deserves and claims great
things, and above all the great things, he
will be concerned with one thing in parti-
cular. Dessert is relative to external
goods; and the greatest of these, we should
say, is that which we render to the gods,
and which people of position most aim at,
and which is the prize appointed for the
noblest deeds; and this is honour: that is
surely the greatest of external goods. . .
And even apart from argument it is with
honour that proud men appear to be con-
cerned for it is honour that they chiefly
claim, but in accordance with their des-
serts. (ibid.)

Whereas Aristotle applauds this human desire for
honor, Augustine, 600 years later and from the point
of view of the Christian saint, condemns it as an
enemy to love for God. But both agree as to its pow-
erful motivating force:

. . . the love of praise which goes around
as it were canvassing and collecting votes
for the advancement of one's personal dis-
tinction. It still tempts me even when I
condemn it in myself; indeed it tempts me
even in the very act of condemning it;
often in our contempt of vainglory we are
merely being all the more vainglorious. . .
(14, p. 252).

Although love for honor is distinct from vain-
glory, they are both expressions of man's desire for
the approval of his peers.

In the same tradition as Augustine but 1200 years later, Blaise Pascal, who possessed the unusual combination of mathematical genius and psychological insight, had some trenchant things to say about man's penchant for social approval. Arthur Lovejoy, in his scholarly and perceptive Reflections on Human Nature, cites quotes from the Giraud edition of Pascal's Pensees:

> The quest of glory (la recherche de la gloire) is the quality that is most ineffaceable from the heart of man. . . . However much of health and of essential comforts he may have, he is not satisfied unless he have a place in men's esteem. . . The sweetness (douceur) of glory is so great that we love any object to which it is attached, even death. (117, p. 132).

And again:

> Vanity is so anchored in man's heart that a soldier, a camp-follower, a cook, a porter, boast and wish to have admirers; and the philosophers wish the same; and those who write against the desire for glory, glory in having written well; and those who read it, desire to have glory for having read it; and I who write this have perhaps the same desire; and also those who will read what I write.

Contemporary with Pascal but totally opposed in ideology is English philosopher John Locke, who agrees with Pascal on this point if no other:

> He who imagines commendation and disgrace not to be strong motives to men, to accommodate themselves to the opinions and rules of those with whom they converse, seems little skilled in the nature or history of mankind: the greatest part whereof he shall find to govern themselves chiefly, if not solely, by this law of fashion; and so they do that which keeps them in reputation with their company, little regarding the laws of God or the magistrate. . . . (199, Bk. II, Chap. 28, sec. 12).

A century later than Locke, shrewd observer of human behavior Dr. Samuel Johnson writes in his weekly journal The Rambler:

> Proportionate to the prevalence of the love of praise is the variety of means by which its attainment is attempted. Every man, however hopeless his pretensions may appear, to all but himself, has some project by which he hopes to rise to reputation; some art by which he imagines that the attention of the world will be attracted; some quality, good or bad, which discriminates him from the common herd of mortals, and by which others may be persuaded to love, or compelled to fear him. (100, No. 164).

John Adams of Boston adds his agreement in describing a passion that was to carry him to the presidency of the United States and into a determined glory-rivalry with Thomas Jefferson. Adams lamented on his deathbed "Thomas Jefferson still lives." In his Discourses on Davila he says:

> The same nature therefore has imposed another law, that of promoting the good, as well as respecting the rights of mankind, and has sanctioned it by other rewards and punishments. The rewards in this case, in this life, are esteem and admiration of others; the punishments are neglect and contempt; nor may anyone imagine that these are not as real as the others. The desire of the esteem of others is as real a want of nature as hunger; and the neglect and contempt of the world as severe a pain as the gout or stone. . . . Every personal quality, and every blessing of fortune, is cherished in proportion to its capacity of gratifying this universal affection for the esteem, the sympathy, admiration and congratulations of the public. (1, Vol. 1, p. 234).

I am persuaded that all men do all things for fame. (Plato.) Honor is the greatest of external goods. (Aristotle.) The quest of glory is the quality that is most ineffaceable from the heart of man.

(Pascal.) Every good thing is cherished in proportion to the public esteem it may bring us. (Adams.) All this testimony as to the basic and all-powerful nature of our desire for esteem from others seems opposed to the principal thesis of this study, namely, that our most basic and compelling motivation is our desire for self-esteem. Actually, this testimony is supportive of rather than contradictory to our thesis. Why are we so avid for social approval? Primarily, to reinforce our self-esteem. Esteem from others conveys to us the message "you possess good which merits our approval." This bolsters our self-image. This theme we will develop at length in the next section. Thus, testimony as to the basic and powerful nature of our desire for social approval is <u>a fortiori</u> testimony supporting the basic and powerful nature of our desire for self-esteem.

We Desire Esteem from Others in Order to Reinforce Self-Esteem

The fact that we seek the esteem of others in order to reinforce our self-esteem is of importance throughout this study and thus deserves further examination.

The central theme of Arthur Lovejoy's excellent book <u>Reflections on Human Nature</u> is the overwhelming importance in human behavior of the motivations which he refers to as approbativeness (desire for the esteem from others), self-approbativeness (self-esteem), and emulation (desire for superiority to others). Emulation, or emulativeness, he clearly sees as deriving from the desire for self-esteem. We desire to be superior to others as a proof to ourselves of our own excellence.

> Nor does Hume neglect the potency of the passion of emulativeness, which is of course a form of the desire for self-esteem. (117, p. 187).

However, on the relation between self-esteem and approbativeness Lovejoy is ambiguous. He cites some writers who can be interpreted as favoring the position that self-esteem is the more basic and approbativeness is the derivative, and other quotes lend themselves to the opposite interpretation.

Favoring the "approbativeness is more basic" position, Lovejoy cites Jacques Abbadie, a "French Protestant theologian famous in his day, and of considerable influence, especially in England, to which he emigrated."

> Nor will Abbadie admit that the craving for the esteem of others is a derivative of self-esteem, that the good opinion of our fellows is valued simply because "it confirms the good opinion we have of ourselves." For the two desires vary independently; and men in general, he thinks, "prefer to have faults that are esteemed than good qualities which society (le monde) does not esteem," and like "to gain consideration for qualities which they know very well they do not possess."
> (117, p. 161)

In response to Abbadie's comments we offer the following considerations. When we observe in another the desire to be praised for qualities which "he knows he does not possess," are we certain that he is truly convinced of his lack of those qualities? He may protest as much, but may not his desire for praise in reality be a willingness to be convinced that he is wrong in his self-deprecation? He wants to be reassured that he truly does possess those praised qualities. If a person is truly convinced that he does not have such and such good qualities, he is likely to be somewhat suspicious, rather than pleased, when he is praised for those qualities. "Does this flatterer take me for a fool? What is he trying to set me up for?" However, on those occasions when men do take pleasure in having a reputation which they know full well is not justified, we suggest that their pleasure in basking in public esteem derives from its self-esteem value. First, there may be a feeling of self-congratulation on one's cleverness at having thus gulled the public. Second, even though one knows that the immediate reason for the admiration is false, still in the glow of receiving the admiration one can easily shove into the back of his mind that falsity and "kid himself" into thinking that the praise is somehow well-deserved. Also, the mere fact of receiving attention, even were it adverse attention, can contribute to our self-esteem. "Better to be criticized than ignored," is a sentiment one sometimes hears. A fortiori, better to be falsely praised than ignored. Another consideration: recognized false praise can be pleasing if it provides entree to some other advantage, let us say business success, which in turn is desired as a testimony to our competence, i.e., is a self-esteem booster.

In response to Abbadie's other comment, that men prefer to have faults that are esteemed than good qualities which society does not esteem, perhaps such men agree with society's judgment, and consider those "faults" to actually be good qualities, and those "good qualities" to be of little value. Thus awareness of possession of the "faults" boosts one's self-esteem. In those cases where the individual recognizes society's standards as false, most of what we have said in the previous paragraph applies.

Supporting the "self-esteem is more basic" position, i.e., the contention that we desire social approval (attention, fame, admiration, love, etc.) in order to confirm our sense of self-worth, we find the following passages in Lovejoy. He quotes the English philosopher Hume:

> This constant habit of surveying ourselves, as it were, in reflection, keeps alive all the sentiments of right and wrong, and begets, in noble natures, a certain reverence for themselves as well as for others, which is the surest guardian of every virtue . . . . Our moral sentiment is itself a feeling chiefly of that nature, and our regard to a character with others seems to arise only from a care of preserving a character with ourselves; and in order to attain this end, we find it necessary to prop our tottering judgment on the correspondent approbation of mankind. (117, p. 183).

Here Hume, according to Lovejoy, is suggesting "that the desire for the approval of others is merely a derivative of self-esteem, as a means of corroborating or correcting our good opinions of our own favorable judgments of ourselves, or our qualities, or behavior; self-admiration is, here, apparently the more fundamental passion."

Also, Lovejoy presents Rousseau proposing that
the difference between savages and civilized man con-
sists in the former's tendency to "live within him-
self," that is, to derive his sense of his self-esteem
from his own testimony, whereas civilized man "lives
outside himself," deriving his sense of worth from the
testimony of others. The savage is not aware that:

> there exists a kind of man who comptent
> pour quelque chose les regards du rests de
> l'univers, who look upon the thoughts of
> the rest of the world about them as a thing
> of consequences—men who are able to be
> happy and content with themselves upon the
> testimony of others rather than their own.
> Such is, in fact, the true cause of all
> these differences [between the savage and
> civilized man]: the savage lives in him-
> self, l'homme sociable, the socialized man,
> always outside of himself. He is capable
> of living only in the opinion of others,
> and it is, so to say, solely from their
> judgment that he draws the feeling of his
> own existence. (117, p. 231).

In this passage Rousseau has presented the savage
as not concerned with the opinions of others. How-
ever, in another of his works, operating no doubt upon
the principle that a foolish consistency is the hob-
goblin of little minds, he assures us of the contrary,
as Lovejoy points out:

> For, he assures us, among savages, "public
> esteem is the only good to which each of
> them aspires, and which they all of them
> merit." In short, le bon savage lives
> "outside of himself" more than civilized
> man does. (117, p. 233).

In the final analysis then, Rousseau presents
both civilized and savage man as "living outside him-
self," deriving the "feeling of his own existence"
from the judgment of others.

We find more explicit support for our contention
that we desire esteem from others in order to increase

our self-esteem in other writers. In William James we find:

> A man's Social Self is the recognition
> which he gets from his mates. We are not
> only gregarious animals, liking to be in
> sight of our fellows, but we have an innate
> propensity to get ourselves noticed, and
> noticed favorably, by our kind. No more
> fiendish punishment could be devised, were
> such a thing physically possible, than that
> one should be turned loose in society and
> remain absolutely unnoticed by all the
> members thereof. If no one turned round
> when we entered, answered when we spoke, or
> minded what we did, but if every person we
> met 'cut us dead,' and acted as if we were
> non-existing things, a kind of rage and
> impotent despair would ere long well up in
> us, from which the cruellest bodily tor-
> tures would be a relief; for these would
> make us feel that, however bad might be our
> plight, we had not sunk to such a depth as
> to be unworthy of attention at all. (99,
> Vol. 1, p. 293).

The thing he has singled out as the supreme per-
sonal evil, worse than "the cruellest bodily tortures"
is the feeling of being unworthy of attention. A
feeling of being unworthy is precisely a lack of self-
esteem. Why is lack of attention, and thus lack of
esteem from our fellows, so terrible a thing? Because
it leads to our feeling unworthy, to our lack of self-
esteem.

Coopersmith also sees William James as holding
that social esteem is desired because of its effect on
self-esteem:

> "A man has as many social selves as there
> are people who recognize him and carry an
> image of him in their mind. To wound any
> one of these, his images, is to wound him."
> The enhancement of a man's extended self,
> be it his body, race, father, or reputa-
> tion, would thus be expected to raise self-
> esteem, and derogation would be expected to
> have the opposite effect. (35, p. 30).

Coopersmith finds sociologist G. H. Mead proposing the same idea:

> The end result of regarding and speaking to and of himself as others have spoken is that he assumes the properties of a social object. When this occurs he tends to conceive of himself as having the characteristics and value that others attribute to him. . . . From Mead's formula we would conclude that self-esteem is largely derived from the reflected appraisal of others. (35, p. 31).

In his work On Narcissism Sigmund Freud says:

> Everything we possess or achieve, every remnant of the primitive feeling of omnipotence that experience has corroborated, helps to exalt the self-regard . . . where the erotic life is concerned not being loved lowers the self-regarding feelings, while being loved raises them. . . . Love itself, in the form of longing and deprivation, lowers the self-regard; whereas to be loved, to have love returned, and to possess the beloved object exalts it again. (56, p. 120).

In this passage Freud offers us the insight that everything we possess or achieve, not only the social esteem we receive, serves to raise our self-esteem.

Aquinas proposes the question "Whether the actions of others are a cause of pleasure to us?" and in his response is the following that is pertinent to our present issue:

> . . . the action of another may cause us pleasure in three ways. . . . Secondly, from the fact that another's action makes us to know or appreciate our own good; and for this reason men take pleasure in being praised or honored by others, because, to wit, they thus become aware of some good existing in themselves. . . . And as love is for something great, so it is pleasant to be loved and admired by others, inasmuch as a

man thus becomes aware of his own goodness
and greatness, through their giving pleasure
to others.
(11, I-II, Q. 32, a.5, corp.)

Thus, to be praised, honored, loved and admired
is pleasant because it makes us aware of good existing
in ourselves, i.e., it raises our self-esteem.

Contemporary Testimony

Among modern psychologists there is a widespread
realization that people seek approval from others in
order to bolster self-esteem. A comment by Loring
Woodman, author of Perspectives in Self-Awareness,
sets the tone:

The important thing, however, is the gen-
erally acknowledged observation that we
find our self-esteem through the past (and
present) experiences of social acceptance.
(187, p. 5).

In the same vein, researchers David Franks and
Joseph Marolla see social approval as one of the fac-
tors administering to self-esteem:

Self-esteem is conceptualized here as a
function of two processes: (1) the re-
flected appraisals of significant others in
one's social environment in the form of
social approval, and (2) the individual's
feelings of efficacy and competence.
(51, p. 325).

Psychiatrist William Silverberg, in a quote we
have presented in a previous chapter, comes to the
same conclusion, and adds the cautionary note that
over-dependence upon social approval is associated
with neuroticism:

Throughout life self-esteem has these
two sources: an inner source, the degree of
effectiveness of one's own aggression; and
an external source, the opinions of others
about oneself. Both are important, but the
former is the steadier and more dependable
one; the latter is always more uncertain.

Unhappy and insecure is the man who, lacking an adequate inner source for his self-esteem, must depend for this almost wholly upon external sources. It is the condition seen by the psychotherapist almost universally among his patients. (166, p. 67).

Psychologist Harvey Mindess, in Laughter and Liberation, states the case vividly:

The data before us suggest that being treated as trivial or inconsequential is far more damaging to our self-esteem than any experience we can name. It appears, therefore, that above all else we need to matter: to be taken seriously for better or worse.

Our egos require it. Our pride, our conceit requires that other people look on us as important, that they treat us with respect. Otherwise, we are afraid that we amount to nothing. (134, p. 128).

Even those who seem most immune to any eagerness for social approval actually covet it—perhaps without being fully aware of their desire—as a gauge of their worth. Ernest Becker states:

Self-esteem depends upon our social role, and our inner-newsreel is always packed with faces—it is rarely a nature documentary. Even holy men who withdraw for years of spiritual development, come back into the fold of society to earn recognition for their powers. Nietzsche said of Schopenhauer that he was a model for all men because he could work in isolation and care nothing for the plaudits of the human market-place. The implication is that he had his sense of value securely embedded in himself and his own idea of what his work was worth. Yet this same Schopenhauer spent his lonely life scanning the footnotes of learned journals to see whether there was ever going to be recognition of his work. (19, p. 70).

Esteem from others is gratifying because its implicit message "we see some excellence in you that calls forth our esteem" reassures us that we are indeed worthwhile persons.

Thus, when astute observers of the human scene tell us that "we do all things for fame," and "every good thing is cherished in proportion to the public esteem it may bring us," they are offering indirect witness to the power of self-esteem, the motive that leads us to seek fame and public esteem.

WITNESSES TO THE DOMINANCE OF THE SELF-ESTEEM MOTIVE

Duality of Motives

In the previous section we have seen that our behavior is motivated by the desire to win approval from the "significant others" in our life; and that we desire their esteem principally to maintain and increase the esteem we get from the most significant other, namely one's self. We have also maintained that although this desire for self-esteem is by far the most powerful and pervasive influence on behavior, there is a second thread of motivation in human nature. This is a motivation we have in common with animals, a desire for sensual gratification. We enjoy and seek out activities that please our senses and seek to avoid physical pain or discomfort.

Of course this is not the first time this particular duality of motivations has been offered as the explanation of all human behavior. Three and a half centuries ago a French writer named Jean La Placette published his _Traite de l'Orgueil_, in which he

> . . . subsumes all man's numerous desires under two classes: _la volupte_, which is not peculiar to man, and the love of glory, praise, and the like, which is; and he somewhat hastily concludes that the motives of man's activities—or at least of his "sins"—are about equally divided between the two. (117, p. 146).

English philosopher and political theorist Thomas Hobbes, writing about the same time as La Placette, also maintains that all human behavior can be explained by sense pleasure and self-esteem:

> Now, whatsoever seems good, is pleasant, and relates either to the sense, or the mind. But all the mind's pleasure is either glory, (or to have a good opinion of one's self), or refers to glory in the end; the rest are sensual, or conducing to sensuality, which may be all comprehended under the word _conveniences_. (91, p. 260)

By the term "glory" Hobbes means self-esteem, as
he indicates in the parentheses. Substantiating this
we have his definition of "glorying":

> Joy, arising from imagination of a man's
> own power and ability, is that exultation
> of the mind which is called glorying: which
> if grounded upon the experience of his own
> former actions, is the same with confi-
> dence: but if grounded on the flattery of
> others; or only supposed by himself, for
> delight in the consequence of it, if called
> vain-glory. . . . (91, p. 197).

Strictly speaking, Hobbes' passage reduces all
pleasures to two, sense pleasure and self-esteem. But
inasmuch as pleasure results from satisfied desire, he
has equivalently reduced all man's desires to the same
two.

In modern times Harry Stack Sullivan has proposed
this same duality in human motivation, under the names
satisfaction and security. We seek satisfaction of
those needs which we have in common with lower ani-
mals. As thinking beings we seek security—a sense of
self-worth—and seek to avoid insecurity, anxiety,
that is, any feeling of threat to self-esteem. We
will consider Sullivan's theories more at length later
in this chapter.

Psychoanalyst Karen Horney too recognizes this
same dichotomy. She says "Man is ruled not by the
pleasure principle alone but by two guiding princi-
ples: safety and satisfaction." (94, p. 73). "Satis-
faction" she equates with the pleasure principle and
with "instinctual gratification," both of which seem
to be the equivalent of sensual gratification. By
"safety" Horney means freedom from "basic anxiety,"
which she defines as "a feeling of helplessness toward
a potentially hostile world." From this condition of
low self-esteem the individual seeks throughout his
life to be free.

Dominance of Self-Esteem Motive

Jean-Jacques Rousseau (1712-1788), still popular
and influential as the apostle of the view that man's
nature and impulses are good ("noble savage") and that

the evil in our world has come from corrupt institu-
tions, was an early proponent of the dominance of the
self-esteem motive. He sees self-esteem as the very
essence of the happiness that we all seek:

> In what is called honour, there is a
> material distinction between that which is
> founded on the opinion of the world, and
> that which is derived from self-esteem.
> The first is nothing but the loud voice of
> foolish prejudice, which has no more sta-
> bility than the wind; but the basis of the
> latter is fixed in the eternal truth of
> morality. The honour of the world may be
> of advantage with regard to fortune; but as
> it cannot reach the soul, it has no in-
> fluence on real happiness. True honour, on
> the contrary, is the very essence of feli-
> city; for it is that alone that inspires
> the permanent interior satisfaction which
> constitutes the happiness of a rational
> being. (158, p. 84).

As an aside, Rousseau's association of self-
esteem with "the eternal truth of morality" is very
much in accord with his most cherished principle that
"the first impulses of nature are always right; there
is no original sin in the human heart." However, such
an attribution of morality to self-esteem is going
beyond our present concerns, which are <u>not</u> with how
people should or should not behave.

Rousseau's apotheosis of the common man is dia-
metrically opposed to the Neitzsche-like glorification
of the superman found in the writings (<u>Breaking Free</u>,
and <u>The Psychology of Self-Esteem</u>) of California ther-
apist Nathaniel Branden. However, the two agree that
self-esteem is the essence of the happiness that we
all seek. Branden extols self-esteem as an indivi-
dual's most priceless possession and "the single most
significant key to his behavior," and adds:

> Man experiences his desire for self-
> esteem as an urgent imperative, as a basic
> need. Whether he identifies the issue
> explicitly or not, he cannot escape the
> feeling that his estimate of himself is of
> life-and-death importance. No one can be

indifferent to the question of how he judges himself; his nature does not allow man this option. (21, p. 110).

Poles apart in their ideological views are enthusiastic evangelical TV preacher Robert Schuller and bitter skeptic Mark Twain, but they agree that the desire for self-esteem is "what makes us tick." Mark Twain summarizes the results of his years of shrewd observance of the human scene in the words of the Old Man in his essay What Is Man?:

> Young Man. Well, let us adjourn. Where have we arrived?
> Old Man. At this. That we (mankind) have ticketed ourselves with a number of qualities to which we have given misleading names. Love, Hate, Charity, Compassion, Avarice, Benevolence, and so on. I mean we attach misleading meanings to the names. They are all forms of self-contentment, self-gratification, but the names so disguise them that they distract our attention from the fact. Also we have smuggled a word into the dictionary which ought not to be there at all—Self-Sacrifice. It describes a thing which does not exist. But worst of all, we ignore and never mention the Sole Impulse which dictates and compels a man's every act: the imperious necessity of securing his own approval, in every emergency and at all costs. To it we owe all that we are. It is our breath, our heart, our blood. It is our only spur, our whip, our goad, our only impelling power; we have no other. Without it we should be mere inert images, corpses; no one would do anything, there would be no progress, the world would stand still. We ought to stand reverently uncovered when the name of that stupendous power is uttered.
> Young Man. I am not convinced.
> Old Man. You will be when you think.
> (31, p. 352)

The name of that "stupendous power" is of course the desire for self-esteem, or in Mark Twain's words, "the imperious necessity of securing one's own approval."

Schuller, in his popular <u>Self-Love</u>, states the case equally emphatically:

> I strongly suggest that <u>self-love</u> is the ultimate will of man—that what you really want more than anything else in the world is the awareness that you are a worthy person. It is the deepest of all the currents which drive man onward, forward and upward. All other drives—pleasure, power, love, meaning, creativity—are symptoms, expressions or attempts to fulfill that primal need for personal dignity. . . Even the will to love is a clever mask hiding the deeper and undetected will to self-love. . . .So we go through life driven by the compulsion to love—unaware that what we really seek is not love as an end in itself, but as food to nourish our self-love. . . . Even the will to meaning, under critical analysis, will often prove to be an expression of the will to self-love . . . Meaning is empty unless it feeds and nourishes your self-esteem.
> (161, p. 21-25).

In this powerful and comprehensive statement Schuller equates self-love with a desire for an "awareness that you are a worthy person," with a "need for personal dignity," —both aspects of self-esteem—and with the desire to "nourish your self-esteem," and sees it as the wellspring of all of our behavior.

Now we will see in more detail the views of several psychologists—and one anthropologist—who have arrived at the conclusion that the desire for self-esteem is the prime mover in human behavior.

Alfred Adler

Adler (1870-1937) was an early disciple of Freud but came to disagree with Freud's central thesis that the sexual drive is the prime determinant of human behavior. Adler's ideas have come to considerable prominence under the name of Individual Psychology.

Starting from contradictory premises, Freud and Adler arrived at the same conclusion, although of course these two warring geniuses never admitted any substantial agreement. Freud envisions the infant as having a sense of "oceanic omnipotence" (total self-esteem) which is gradually lost, and asserts that human beings ever afterward seek to regain that un-limited self-regard. "This is the happiness that men seek." Adler begins with the contrasting premise that the child from its earliest years is oppressed with a feeling of inferiority. All of his or her subsequent behavior flows from the desire to escape this painful feeling of low self-esteem and attain to an unlimited feeling of superiority. Both thus conclude that human beings desire unlimited self-esteem. Freud offers this insight in a few brief snippets and never devel-ops it, whereas Adler builds his entire psychology on this self-esteem motive.

Although Adler is a thorough-going self-esteem psychologist, neither he nor his followers have given much explicit recognition to that fact. Looking through the Journal of Individual Psychology, the voice of Adlerian psychology, one finds no articles in the ten-year span 1968-1977 with "self-esteem" in the title, and only two articles dealing with any roughly synonymous topic (self-concept in both cases.) During this ten-year period some psychological jour-nals carried a score or more articles on self-esteem. Ansbacher and Ansbacher, editors of The Individual Psychology of Alfred Adler, list in their book the twelve basic propositions of Adlerian psychology with-out mentioning self-esteem. It is however implicit in proposition #1:

> 1. There is one basic dynamic force behind all human activity, a striving from a felt minus situation toward a plus situa-tion, from a feeling of inferiority towards superiority, perfection, totality. (5, p. 1).

This single human driving force was referred to by Adler in his earlier writings as the "aggression drive," "the masculine protest," and "striving for power," and later as "striving for superiority," "over-coming," "seeking for perfection." Underlying all of these expressions is the idea of striving to progress from a feeling of inferiority to one of superiority. Adler did realize that this goal, the feeling of superiority, is equivalent to self-esteem, but ordinarily he uses the term self-esteem in a limited sense as the goal of the neurotic. The reader of Adler can get the impression that he considers the self-esteem motive as a self-glorification that is either self-deceptive or "socially useless." This would readily explain why his followers have not seen Adler as a self-esteem psychologist.

In the following passages Adler describes the neurotic's goal as the enhancement of self-esteem:

> The neurotic purpose is the enhancement of the self-esteem. . . All neurotic phenomena originate from these preparatory means which strive toward the final purpose of superiority. They are psychological readinesses for initiating the struggle for self-esteem. . . His realm is not of this world and he cannot free himself from the deity which he has created for himself, the enhancement of the self-esteem.

> The pathological fear, which we find in patients, is always the fear of loss of the goal of superiority, the fear of loss of self-esteem. . . . Through the safeguarding tendency the individual aims at getting rid of the feeling of inferiority in order to raise himself to the full height of the self-esteem, toward complete manliness, toward the idea of being above. . . .

> So far we have considered the guiding force and final purpose of the neurosis to be a desire for enhancement of the self-esteem which always asserts itself with special strength. This is merely the expression of a striving which is deeply founded in human nature in general. . . .

> The constitutional inferiority and similarly effective childhood situations give rise to a feeling of inferiority which demands a compensation in the sense of an enhancement of the self-esteem. (5, pp. 108-111).

Peeping through these passages is the glimmering realization that this is a description not only of the neurotic, but of all of us, although the manifestations are more restrained, and less bizarre perhaps, in the "normal" person. As the editor remarks "when Adler speaks here of the normal, it is an extrapolation from the neurotic." The neurotic in the above passages is guided by the identical motivations that Adler in his later writings ascribes to human beings in toto: "strive toward the final purpose of superiority," "rid of the feeling of inferiority," "toward the idea of being above."

A few passages from Adler reveal more fully his awareness that the desire for self-esteem is the dominant life principle not only of the neurotic but of all people. Speaking now of basic human nature, Adler asserts that self-esteem dominates even such powerful desires as sensual gratification and self-preservation:

> In what manner do these two admittedly effective incentives [pleasure and self-preservation] subordinate themselves to the main guiding line which drives toward enhancement of the self-esteem [even where they seem to dominate]? (5, p. 122).

Adler goes on to answer that cases where pleasure or self-preservation seem to be dominant are actually cases in which the individual is seeking his self-esteem through pleasure or self-preservation, and therefore it is actually self-esteem which is the root motivation. In the following paragraph he once again spells out the dominance of the striving for perfection, and its equivalency with self-esteem.

> Human beings are in a permanent mood of inferiority feeling, which constantly spurs them on to attain greater security. The pleasure or displeasure which accompany this striving are only aids and rewards received on this path. . . . Thereby the coercion toward enhancement of the self-esteem has been excellently comprehended. This also becomes clear from one of Goethe's letters to Lavater where he remarks: "This passionate desire to drive the

pyramid of my existence, the base of which
is given to me, as high as possible out-
weighs everything else and barely admits
momentary forgetting." (5, p. 123).

What distinguishes the neurotic from the normal
individual is the degree to which the former seeks
superiority in ways that are socially useless or even
harmful, while the latter to a large extent channel-
izes his drive for superiority in ways that are soci-
ally useful. This latter tendency Adler refers to as
"social interest." Social interest is not a new
drive, not a second drive, but is the ultimately
desireable avenue for seeking superiority. Thus soc-
ial interest is not a drive independent of the stri-
ving for superiority, but is a manifestation of the
latter. Social interest seems to be an identification
with others and concern for their welfare—or at least
it is an enlightened self-interest which leads the
individual to ways of behavior that contribute to the
welfare of others.

Harry Stack Sullivan

Sullivan (1892-1949) is the founder of a new
"school" of psychology known as the "interpersonal
theory of psychiatry." His premise is that all dis-
tinctively human behavior involves interaction between
people. Therefore the unit of study should be the
interpersonal situation, rather than the individual.*
Psychoanalyst William Silverberg says of Sullivan:

Sullivan is the only psychiatrist known to
me who might conceivably have made Freud's
contributions if Freud had not existed, for
he was possessed of great genius and fear-
less originality and his powers of obser-
vation were uncanny. (165, p. 5).

Sullivan maintained that human beings operate on
two basic principles: the desire for satisfaction and
the desire for security. By "satisfaction" he means

---

*However, the interpersonal situation is composed
of individuals, and thus in considering the interac-
tion Sullivan is forced to analyze the behavior of its
elements, namely, individuals.

relief of "biological tensions," i.e., satisfaction of those desires which belong to what might be called our animal nature. In this category he mentions hunger, thirst, and lust. "Security" is the sense of being a worthwhile, esteemed person. Interchangeably with security Sullivan uses the expression "freedom from anxiety." Anxiety is the apprehension of <u>not</u> being a worthwhile, esteemed person.

> Each of you, when you think about it, will see that you have had experience in the past—and the effects of that experience are still manifest in the present—in which you were esteemed by somebody as good, important, worthy, or you were considered in an unfavorable, derogatory or depreciatory way. The most general term I have ever found for the states which are attendant upon being valued, respected, looked up to, and so on, is a feeling of personal security; and the term, insecurity, works out even more impressively when one looks for a general term to encompass all the states and all the processes that are called out by situations in which that is not the case.
>
> This differentiation between pursuits of satisfaction and the maintenance of security—that is, the avoidance of anxiety —I think, one of the most important classifying principles in all that we will have to say about living. (191, p. 11).

In the above passage from Sullivan we see that the feeling of security is equivalent to a feeling that others esteem us, which is one of the two major sources of self-esteem. (The other source is our own powers and achievements independent of what others think of us. This aspect of self-esteem is not emphasized by Sullivan. His is the <u>interpersonal</u> theory of psychiatry, and thus gives no prominence to self-feelings which are independent of other persons.)

Patrick Mullahey, editor of a symposium on Sullivan, sees the security motivation as meaning a desire for esteem from others and for self-esteem, more especially the latter:

Security here has a special meaning which I
hope gradually to clarify. It refers rough-
ly to what we mean by the maintenance of
self-esteem. The absence of this state of
security or, more precisely, its opposite
is called anxiety. The collision of the
needs for satisfactions, with the need for
security, for self-respect and self-esteem
often leads to what Sullivan called "con-
flictful integrations" which are so out-
standing in psychiatric work. In essence,
security means a feeling that one enjoys
the respect of the other person in a situa-
tion and that one respects oneself. (192,
p. 23).

Judging from the time he devoted to it in his
writings, and from the range of human phenomena ex-
plained by it, Sullivan considers the desire for se-
curity to be of much greater consequence than is the
desire for satisfaction.

The opposite of security, anxiety, is an impor-
tant concept in Sullivan's theory of human behavior:

Insofar as you grasp the concept of anxiety
as I shall be struggling to lay it before
you, I believe you will be able to follow,
with reasonable success, the rest of this
system of psychiatry. (190, p. 8).

The infant first feels anxiety through empathy
with anxiety his mother is feeling. Anxiety arouses
in the infant what Sullivan describes as a "bad-me"
feeling.

Bad-me, on the other hand, is the beginning
personification which organizes experience
in which increasing degrees of anxiety are
associated with behavior involving the
mothering one in its more-or-less clearly
prehended interpersonal setting. That is
to say, bad-me is based on this increasing
gradient of anxiety and that, in turn, is
dependent, at this stage of life, on the
observation, if misinterpretation, of the
infant's behavior by someone who can induce
anxiety. (190, p. 162).

On Sullivan's concept of anxiety psychiatrist Mullahey remarks:

> One gets anxious when a person anticipates, whether rightly or not, that the regard of another person will decrease, that his regard and respect for you will become less, or that one's own regard for oneself will decrease. Anxiety is related to the loss of esteem for one by oneself or by others. (293, p. 33).

Thus anxiety is apprehension of an imminent bad-me concept, i.e., apprehension of imminent loss of self-esteem.

Another important concept in Sullivan's psychology is the "self-system." This is a psychological process (sometimes conscious, sometimes subconscious, but always operating) aimed at increasing or maintaining security (the good-me feeling) and avoiding anxiety.

> From the essential desirability of being good-me, and from the increasing ability to be warned by slight increases of anxiety. . there comes into being the start of an exceedingly important, as it were, secondary dynamism[1]. . . This secondary dynamism I call the self-system. . . . . The self-system thus is an organization of educative experience called into being by the necessity to avoid or to minimize incidents of anxiety. (190, pp. 164-5).

To sum up, in Sullivan's system the dominant human motivation is the desire for security, that is, the desire to increase and maintain the good-me self-concept. This same motive he also refers to as the desire to avoid anxiety, the bad-me self-concept. In brief, the dominant motive is the desire to maintain and increase self-esteem.

---

[1]The primary dynamism is the drive for satisfaction of purely physical needs. It is primary in the time of origin in the infant, but secondary in importance in explaining human behavior.

William Silverberg, psychoanalyst in the tradition of Freud combined with Sullivan, concurs:

> The other important contribution[2] made by Sullivan lies in his insistence that the central, nuclear factor in human psychology is self-esteem. (165, p. 6).

Carl Rogers

Carl Rogers is well-known as the developer of non-directive or client-centered psychotherapy. The purpose of this is to help the client discover and accept his true feelings and desires. The therapist provides a warm, accepting, non-critical presence to encourage the client in this discovery of his true feeling. Rogers is a proponent of the "third force" in psychology, that is, humanistic psychology, as distinguished from Freudian and behavioristic psychology.

Rogers adopts the basic axiom proposed by Kurt Goldstein (1878-1965), i.e., the human being has only one motivation—the tendency to actualize oneself. Rogers mentions that "ideas similar to this proposition are being increasingly advanced and accepted by psychologists and others. The term 'self-actualization' is used by Goldstein to describe this one basic striving." (154, p. 489) For a fuller statement of his position Rogers uses the formulation offered by psychologists Syngg and Combs: "The organism has one basic tendency and striving—to actualize, maintain and enhance the experiencing organism." (154, p. 487). "Maintain" means to retain those excellences which the person now has; "enhance" means to add to those excellences; "actualize" means to realize the person's full potential, which in essence is the same as enhancement.

And what is this experiencing organism, this self, that is being actualized, maintained and enhanced? The self is the sum total of the perceptions that the "organism" has about itself, i.e., its self-

---

[2]The previously mentioned contribution was the idea that the human personality is essentially a social product.

image. Commentators Melvin Marx and William Hillix sum up Roger's notion of the self:

> To Rogers, the self is a structure compounded out of the experiences which the individual is able to attribute to his own body or to the results of his own behavior; the self, then, is a self-picture, or self-awareness. The experiences come with value tags attached; that is, some aspects of the picture are positive, while others are negative. The self regulates behavior, for behavior that is not consistent with the self-picture either does not occur or is not fitted into the self-picture. (127, p. 339).

Thus, in Roger's psychology, the human being's one basic tendency and striving is the urge to maintain, enhance and actualize the self-image.

Donald Snygg and Arthur Combs

Frequently quoted in self-esteem literature is the book Individual Behavior, by Donald Snygg and Arthur Combs, professors of psychology and clinical psychology at the time the book was written (1949). They develop the thesis that the human desire to preserve and enhance self-concept is the motivating force behind all behavior. Their key concepts are "phenomenal self" and "self-concept." By "phenomenal self" they mean those qualities or things "perceived by a person to be part or characteristic of himself." (170, p. 111). The authors make a distinction between phenomenal self and self-concept, reserving the latter term for those elements of the phenomenal self "which the individual has differentiated as definite and fairly stable characteristics of himself." (170, p. 112). Thus their "phenomenal self" corresponds to what in common usage would be called the self-concept, and their "self-concept" corresponds to the most salient and influential features of the self-concept.

The basic motivation in human behavior is the need to preserve and enhance the phenomenal self, which process the authors equate with "what the layman calls 'boosting self-esteem.'"(170, p. 70).

From birth to death the defense of the phenomenal self is the most pressing, most crucial, if not the only task of existence. Moreover, since human beings are conscious of the future, their needs extend into the future as well, and they strive to preserve not only the self as it exists but to build it up and to strengthen it against the future of which they are aware. We might combine these two aspects into a formal definition of the basic human need as: the preservation and enhancement of the phenomenal self. . . . When each act is seen as an attempt to preserve or to fortify the individual's concept of himself, behavior becomes meaningful . . . .

When we see this child as he sees himself, his behavior becomes understandable. While we might analyze his behavior in terms of many specific needs all these become a function of the one dominant aspect—the need to protect and enhance his own self-concept.(170, p. 58).

All human needs are a function of the need to protect and enhance self-concept—this, in essence, is the Snygg/Combs theory. It is the same as that developed in this present book, with the exception that the Snygg/Combs theory, just as the Adler theory, seems to have implicitly subsumed sense pleasure motivations totally under the drive to preserve and enhance self-concept.

George J. McCall and J. L. Simmons

The theory of human behavior developed in the book _Identities and Interactions_ is almost identical with the Snygg/Combs theory, but expressed in different terms. The authors' principal thesis is that we human beings are constantly, in both our thoughts and actions, attempting to maintain and enhance our "identity." Each of us has a multi-faceted concept of self, which is our "identity." (118, p. 94). For this self-concept the authors also use the terms "role" and "role-identity." Each of us has a glamorized and over-blown concept of himself, which reality is constantly threatening to tarnish, with the result that our main concern and motivation is to "legitimize" our role-identity, that is, to preserve our glowing self-image from being dimmed by harsh reality.

> Because role-identities are idealized and rather idiosyncratic conceptions of oneself, the realities of life are constantly jarring them, raising difficulties and embarrassments for them. As a consequence of this jarring, we are always having to devise perspectives that allow us to <u>maintain</u> these views of ourselves, at some level, despite contradictory occurrences. As a creature of ideals, man's main concern is to maintain a tentative hold on these idealized conceptions of himself, to <u>legitimate</u> his role-identities. (118, p. 71).

Among the most important ways we seek to legitimate our role-identity is through "role-support." This means testimony from others which helps to convince us that we do indeed have the role-identity that we cherish.

> This outcome leads to an consideration of what we call role-support, which is the expressed support accorded to an actor by his audience for his claims concerning his role-identity. This support is not <u>simply</u> for his claim to the right to occupy the social position in question or for the conventional rights and duties of the accompanying social role, although role-support includes these points as a minimum. Nor is role-support to be equated simply with prestige, status, esteem, or social approval of one's conduct in a given social position.

> It is instead a set of reactions and performances by others the expressive implications of which tend to confirm one's detailed and imaginative view of himself as an occupant of a position. Role-support is centrally the implied confirmation of the specific <u>contents</u> of one's idealized and idiosyncratic imaginations of self. These

expressive implications of others may be expressions "given" or expressions "given off," that is, intended or unintended. The unwilling cries that escape the lips of a victim thus support the self-conceptions of the inquisitor as directly as do the flattering pleas of more pliable victims. (118, p. 72).

This "role-support for role-identity" says, once again, that we seek testimony from others to bolster our self-esteem, that is, for "confirmation of the specific contents of one's idealized and idiosyncratic imaginations of self." This support from others for our self-concept is important, but even more important is the support we give to our own role-identity:

Nonetheless, all things being equal, each of us is his own most important audience, for, unlike other audiences, this one cannot be escaped. In the end, it is ourselves that we have to live with, and the role-support that we accord ourselves is most important. (118, p. 74).

We are engaged in a constant battle to maintain and enhance self-esteem:

Because of imperfect role-performances and the instability of role-support, then, identities are continually in need of legitimation. As proposed above, one of man's most distinctive motives is the compelling and perpetual desire to acquire support for his idealized conceptions of himself. (118, p. 75).

In a variety of ways we legitimate our role-identity (maintain and enhance self-esteem). We are forced to this legitimation because role-support (support for our self-esteem coming from reality and from the testimony of others) seldom measures up to our role-identity. The various strategies we use to legitimate our role-identity are referred to by McCall/ Simmons as "mechanisms of legitimation." Among these is "selective perception."

In general, the person is able to pay most attention to a selected fraction of his own actions and the complementary actions of others, that fraction that is most favorable to his self-conceptions.
(118, p. 96).

Related to the selective perception mechanism of legitimation is the selective interpretation mechanism. Here the individual interprets audience reaction in the manner most favorable to his self-concept. A variety of other mechanisms are used by the individual to protect and enhance his self-concept, mechanisms we will only mention by name, inasmuch as these are usually self-explanatory: leaving the interaction; enactment of another role-identity; rationalization; scapegoating; disavowal of an aspect of role-identity; rejecting the audience; reducing investment in a threatened role-identity; and, as an ultimate "solution," suicide.

The authors stress self-deception as a mechanism of legitimation and quote Erving Goffman in support:

Whatever his position in society, the person insulates himself by blindness, half-truths, illusions, and rationalizations. He makes an "adjustment" by convincing himself, with the tactful support of his intimate circle, that he is what he wants to be and that he would not do to gain his ends what the others have done to gain theirs.
(193, p. 230).

In summary, the authors' theory of man's continual struggle to maintain and enhance his role-identity is very similar to the self-esteem theory developed in this present book, except that, like Adler and Snygg/Combs, they do not give any independent role to the sense pleasure motivation.

Ernest Becker (1926-1975)

Becker, cultural anthropologist and prolific author, received the Pulitzer prize for his book Denial of Death.[1]

Becker has a penetrating realization that the desire for self-esteem is the fundamental motivation in human behavior.

> The main reason that the great Alfred Adler is still contemporary is that he broke with Freud[2] very early on this problem, when he very clearly saw and strongly proclaimed that the basic law of human life is the urge to self-esteem. Once you make this break with Freud, stand up for it openly, and build your theories and clinical interpretations around it, a whole new world of understanding opens up to you. After all, you have laid bare man's motive, which is what Freud himself set out to do. This is why the clinical theories of Adler, as well as Sullivan, Rank, Fromm, Horney, and a growing number of young and undogmatic Freudians, give us such rich and true explanations of what really makes people act the way they do—what they are really upset about. (19, p. 66).

Becker has at least three beautiful insights in the above paragraph: self-esteem is the "basic law of human life"; this was the core of Adler's psychology, a fact that even Adlerians sometimes fail to mention; and the realization that a psychology of self-esteem opens up a whole new world of understanding.

---

[1] In this book Becker presents the thesis that fear of death is a principal source of man's activity. The apprehension that death is an imminent nothingness for the person stimulates man to assert his being for now and for posterity.

[2] This emphasis on self-esteem as the "basic law of human life" is not as much a break with Freud as it might seem. Actually Freud had fleeting insights that pointed to this same conclusion, although he did not develop them. Some later Freudians (notably Fenichel and Symonds) have developed the clues left by Freud into a psychology in which the drive for self-esteem plays a major role.

A further honest and penetrating insight is Becker's account of the "inner newsreel" that we run almost constantly in our own minds. This inner newsreel is a stream of consciousness (and subconsciousness) in which we reassure ourselves about our idenity and worth. The contents of this inner newsreel are sometimes conversations we have had, or hope to have, or sheer fantasy conversations, in which we brilliantly impress (enthrall, amuse, defeat, etc.) our audience; or the newsreel may consist of Walter Mitty adventures in which we rescue (and, alas, seduce) fair maidens, smash enemies, perform incredible athletic feats, or build financial empires, etc.; sometimes the newsreel is a factual recounting of our real successes and good qualities. In Becker's excellent description:

> . . . we get our vital sense of inner worth by repeating "I am a good doctor. . . lawyer. . . engineer. . . Look at the operation I performed, the business deal I pulled off, the way that beautiful girl looks at me. . . " and so on. Almost all of one's inner life, when he is not absorbed in some active task, is a traffic in images of self-worth.

> If our first reaction is to shrug at this as an exaggeration, let us try to be honest and admit to ourselves what we do most of the time. We run what I like to call an "inner-newsreel" that passes in constant review the symbols that give self-esteem, make us feel important and good. . . .

> Everyone runs the inner-newsreel, even if it does not record the same symbolic events. Always it passes in review the peculiar symbols of one's choice that give him a warm feeling about himself: the girl he seduced, the money he has made, the picture he directed, the book he published, the shrewd put-down at the cocktail party, the smooth ordering from the menu in the chic restaurant, the beautifully executed piano suite and so on and on. All day long we pass these images in review, and

most of us even in our sleep.
(19, pp. 68-9).

In this manner with untiring energy and ingenuity we seek to convince ourselves of our own personal excellence. But often in the depths of our minds we have an uneasy and unadmitted feeling that all this is a charade, that the beautiful garments of excellence with which we have clothed ourselves are in reality nothing but filthy rags.

> But while we are asleep the ego is not working, it has no conscious control over the messages we send to ourselves about our sense of worth. Our deeper experience may have on record that we really feel worthless, helpless, dependent, mediocre, inadequate, finite: this is our unconscious speaking, and when the ego cannot oppose any positive images to counteract these negative ones, we have the nightmare, the terrible revelation of our basic uselessness. (19, p. 69).

Becker does not dwell further on that sombre note, and we will follow his example. Nor does he deal with a variant of the self-glorifying inner newsreel—the self-deprecating inner newsreel. Sometimes people find themselves rehearsing humiliating scenes from their past, and excoriating themselves: "What a fool I am!" "What a total idiot!" This sort of inner attitude and the reasons for it—its hidden ego payoffs—we have dealt with in the section "Self-Deprecation and Self-Hatred."

When people are no longer able to maintain their self-esteem and see no possibilities of regaining it, they simply lose their will to live. Self-preservation no longer has any value. Becker has discovered this in his studies of anthropology:

> If there were any doubt that self-esteem is the dominant motive of man, there would be one sure way to dispel it; and that would be by showing that when people do not have self-esteem they cannot act, they break down. (19, p. 75).

Data from anthropology support this funda-
mental place of self-esteem in human ac-
tion. It seems that nowhere in this once-
vast globe has man been able to act unless
he had a basic sentiment of self-value.
Unless the individual feels worthwhile, and
unless his action is considered worthwhile,
life grinds to a halt. Whole cultures have
begun to expire in this way: Melanesians,
Marquesans, reservation Indians, and, for a
time after 1929, the world of Wall Street.
(17, p. 113).

Loss of self-esteem, or fear of that loss, may be
the clue to psychosomatic illnesses. More than one
medical researcher recently has advanced the theory
that even cancer is psychosomatic—this does not mean
that the entire cause of cancer is psychological, but
that the body's resistances just give up the fight in
certain times of psychological crisis, most especially
when a cherished dream or life's hope has irretriev-
ably collapsed. Becker hints at this:

Anthropologists have long known that when a
tribe of people lose the feeling that their
way of life is worth-while they may stop
reproducing, or in large numbers simply lie
down and die beside streams full of fish:
food is not the primary nourishment of man,
strange as that may sound to some etholo-
gical faddists. So seriously do we take
self-esteem since Adler, that for over a
generation we have been working toward
theories of disease based on self-esteem.
(19, p. 76).

Self-esteem as integrating principle in a science of man

Psychologists and philosophers have long dabbled
with attempts to discover a basic principle for per-
sonality typology, that is, a useful basis for divi-
ding human beings according to different types. Many
schemas have been advanced—introvert vs. extrovert,
neurotic (in all its variations) vs. normal, stoic vs.
epicurean, liberal vs. conservative, sanguine-choleric-
melancholic-phlegmatic, etc. Becker sees self-esteem
as the basic principle for a personality typology:

various life styles and personality types flow from
different dominant ways of seeking self-esteem. He
does not develop such a typology, but mentions it in
passing as part of a larger theme, namely that the
self-esteem motive is the key to a true science of
human nature. Here at last is a basic integrating
principle that can transform psychology into a science
on a par with physics and chemistry. What Newton's
laws were to physics, the self-esteem principle can be
to psychology. Despite all our discoveries about man,
one thing was lacking for a true science of man:

> I mean, of course, the single unifying
> principle that would form an integrated and
> firmly centered science. For those readers
> whose thought tends to theory and whose
> organism is soothed by the vision of an
> elegant and simplified intellectual struc-
> ture, this part of our story is perhaps the
> most exciting of all. . . .

> The principle which explains the law of
> human character development is the Princi-
> ple of Self-Esteem Maintenance. . . . The
> various styles of human character (or life
> styles) which result from this early train-
> ing can then be considered as variations in
> modes of self-esteem maintenance. Thus in
> the most brief and direct manner, we have a
> law of human development and its explana-
> tory principle.

> I do not think it would be possible to
> overestimate the magnitude of this achieve-
> ment for the science of man. It is a uni-
> versal principle for human action akin to
> gravitation in the physical sciences. In
> other words, we have arrived at a Newtonian
> maturity two hundred years after Hume and
> Hartley, but in a way that permits our
> science to be anything but mechanistic.
> The fundamental datum for our science is a
> fact that at first sight seems banal, or
> irrelevant: it is the fact that—as far as
> we can tell—all organisms like to "feel
> good" about themselves. Or, put in terms
> of existential ontology, self-feeling is at
> the heart of Being in nature. Need we say

that, for a science of developing life, this central fact is anything but banal or irrelevant?

Furthermore, like the principle of gravity—or any viable principle—our principle must explain apparently contradictory phenomena—which is exactly what it does: it explains the most disparate life styles as variations around the single theme of self-esteem maintenance. Just as gravity explains both the northward course of the Rhine and the southward course of the Rhone, so the principle of self-esteem maintenance "explains" both schizophrenia and depression, sadism and masochism, hypersexuality and homosexuality, passivity and aggressivity, and so on. Not, of course, "all by itself," but with a properly elaborated theoretical structure. Given the achievement of this very structure in modern times, we have a perfect synthetic and deductive principle for our science.

Finally, and not least, it is—like gravity—an irreducible primary property. Just as innate attraction and repulsion are the irreducible primary properties of matter, self-esteem is the irreducible primary property of behaving organisms. There is no need at this time to seek further for a valid, nonreducible unifying principle. (18, p. 328).

Becker then poses the question as to "why such a simple and fertile principle had not been discerned previously." His answer: it had been.

As we know, the role of self-esteem in human action was a basic part of the seventeenth- and eighteenth-century theories of human nature. There were literally a host of writings on the love of fame, glory, approbation as principal motive powers of human conduct. (18, p. 328).

Here Becker shows an accurate realization that we desire fame, glory and approbation—i.e., esteem from others—in order to boost our self-esteem.

It seems to the present writer that in the above paragraphs (already cited in the introduction to this book) Becker with his incisive genius has made a discovery which could usher in a new era in psychology, and have a profound impact on sociology, history, education, indeed on any discipline which centers around human behavior. This is precisely the message of the present book, with this qualification: self-esteem maintenance is not the "single theme" of human behavior, although it is the overwhelmingly dominant one. For a complete understanding of behavior we must also take into account another independent motivation, the desire for sense pleasure. (Those who accept traditional Christianity will see a vital, if statistically miniscule, role played by the supernatural motivation, the desire that God be glorified.)

CHAPTER IV

FREUD REVISITED: SELF-ESTEEM
DOMINANT OVER SEX

Introduction

Freud seems a most unlikely witness to call in support of the supremacy of the self-esteem motive. He would have indignantly rejected such an idea. Freud's most cherished theory was the supremacy of the id, with its urges toward sexual expression and aggression. "This oldest portion of the psychical apparatus remains the most important through life. . . The power of the id expresses the true purpose of the individual organism's life." Jung tells us that Freud solemnly begged him to promise that he would always be faithful to the supremacy of sexual libido in the human psyche. "My dear Jung, promise me never to abandon the sexual theory. That is the most essential thing of all. You see, we must make a dogma of it, an unshakable bulwark." (200, p. 50).

Yet Freud in his genius has given us several insights from which a self-esteem psychology can be built. Some of Freud's followers (notably Otto Fenichel, Percival Symonds and Heinz Kohut) have seized upon these clues and developed them into psychological systems which are still recognizably Freudian, but in which self-esteem is a most frequently recurring concept. We hope to show in this chapter that several of the key concepts in Freud's writings are at root matters of self-esteem. The consuming eagerness of the ego to measure up to the ego-ideal, that is, to win the approval of the superego, is a drive for self-esteem. Narcissism, seen by Freud as so important a force in the life of even the normal adult, is primarily a matter of self-exaltation, i.e., of self-esteem in excelsis.[1] Freud's explicit treatment of the topic of self-regard bears out the above points. The relations of the ego with the id are strongly

---

[1]It may be apropos here to point out once again that by the term "self-esteem" we mean to include not only a well-founded self-respect, but also an unjustified self-inflation.

characterized by the ego-defense mechanisms, which are gambits to protect the individual's self-esteem.

Also we will offer evidence from Freud's writing to support the contention that he implicitly acknowledged the self-esteem drive to be stronger than the sex drive.

The question naturally arises, if all this is true, why did Freud not make more of this human motivation for self-regard, instead of merely mentioning it in passing as if it were something peripheral. As we know, Freud was throughout his life revising his theories; his adoption of the idea of a destructive instinct, after years of vigorously resisting such a concept, is one example. When a secretary was laboring over the correct translation of a small nuance in his The Ego and the Id, she reports him as remarking "Never mind, it will be obsolete in thirty years anyway." He did not see his theories as something fully finalized, to be engraved in stone forever. We suggest that his openness to further development might have led him, granted a few more years of creative work, to expand upon the drive for self-esteem, a concept that already lay in germine in his writings.

Ego Strives to Please Super-Ego

The relationship between the ego and the super-ego, very important in the Freudian dynamic, seems to amount to a quest for self-esteem. Preliminary to developing this thesis we will consider what Freud intends by the use of the terms id, ego, and super-ego.

The Id

Freud's descriptions of the id contain the notes of an unconscious part of the psyche, a seething cauldron of sexual and hostile impulses, totally non-moral, and without regard for external reality.

> The id, to which we finally come back, has no means of showing the ego either love or hate. It cannot say what it wants; it has achieved no unity of will. Eros and the death-instinct struggle within it; we have seen with what weapons the one group of

instincts defends itself against the other.
It would be possible to picture the id as
under the domination of the mute but power-
ful death-instincts, which desire to be at
peace and (as the pleasure-principle de-
mands) to put Eros, the intruder, to rest;
but that would be to run the risk of valuing
too cheaply the part played by Eros. (56,
p. 234).

From the point of view of morality, the
control and restriction of instinct, it may
be said of the id that it is totally non-
moral, of the ego that it strives to be
moral, and of the super-ego that it can be
hyper-moral and then becomes as ruthless as
only the id can be. (56, p. 231).

Moreover, the ego has the task of bringing
the influence of the external world to bear
upon the id and its tendencies, and endea-
vors to substitute the reality-principle for
the pleasure-principle which reigns supreme
in the id. In the ego perception plays the
part which in the id devolves upon instinct.
The ego represents what we call reason and
sanity, in contrast to the id which contains
the passions. (56, p. 215).

Despite this not too attractive picture of the
id, Freud considers it the most important part of the
psyche. In his Outline of Psychoanalysis, published
posthumously, he says in a footnote: "This oldest
portion of the psychical apparatus remains the most
important throughout life; moreover, the investiga-
tions of psychoanalysis started with it."
(201, p. 16 n).

Indeed, Freud presents the satisfaction of the id
as man's true purpose in life, with the ego serving as
handmaiden in this endeavor:

The power of the id expresses the true
purpose of the individual organism's life.
This consists in the satisfaction of its
innate needs. No such purpose as that of
keeping itself alive or of protecting itself
from dangers by means of anxiety can be

attributed to the id. That is the task of
the ego, whose business it is also to dis-
cover the most favourable and least perilous
method of obtaining satisfaction, taking the
external world into account. The super-ego
may bring fresh needs to the fore, but its
main function remains the limitation of
satisfactions. (201, p. 19).

The Ego

The ego can be described as the executive agency
in the human psyche. It is primarily conscious, al-
though parts of it are unconscious. As we have seen
in previous quotes describing the id, the ego's func-
tion—one of them—is to insure the fullest possible
satisfaction of the id's desires consistent with real-
ity, reason, and the strictures of the super-ego.

The ego fears offending the super-ego (con-
science):

> On the other hand, we can tell what
> lies hidden behind the ego's dread of the
> super-ego, its fear of conscience. The
> higher being which later became the ego-
> ideal once threatened the ego with castra-
> tion, and this dread of castration is pro-
> bably the kernel round which the subsequent
> fear of conscience has gathered; it is this
> dread that persists as the fear of con-
> science. (66, p. 47).

In the above paragraph we see Freud's identifica-
tion of super-ego, ego-ideal, and conscience. Some-
times he distinguishes between them to the extent that
the ego-ideal is seen as the normative part of the
super-ego (commanding the ego, "you must do such and
such"), and the conscience is the critical agency of
the super-ego (rebuking the ego, "you have failed to
live up to my principles in this matter").

The ego is eager to win the approval of the
super-ego, that is, to measure up to the ego-ideal:

> The fear of death in melancholia only
> admits of one explanation: that the ego
> gives itself up because it feels itself

hated and persecuted by the super-ego, in-
stead of loved. To the ego, therefore,
living means the same as being loved—being
loved by the super-ego. . . .(66, p. 48).

The ego is presented as serving three masters,
the id, external reality, and the super-ego. The ego
is desirous of satisfying the desires of the id, but
without flouting reality and thus bringing disaster
upon itself, and further, it seeks to win the love of
the super-ego:

. . . we see this same ego as a poor crea-
ture owing service to three masters and
consequently menaced by three several dan-
gers: from the external world, from the
libido of the id, and from the severity of
the super-ego. (66, p. 46).

The Super-Ego

As noted previously, Freud uses the terms super-
ego and ego-ideal interchangeably:

The considerations that led us to assume the
existence of a differentiating grade within
the ego, which may be called the ego-ideal
or super-ego, have been set forth else-
where. . . . (66, p. 18).

The super-ego is the "part" of the psyche which
is formed through identification with authority fig-
ures (parents, society, church, etc.) and "introjec-
tion" (internalization) of the values expounded by
these authority figures. Thus it is the individual's
internalized moral code.

For that which prompted the person to
form an ego-ideal, over which his conscience
keeps guard, was the influence of parental
criticism (conveyed to him by the medium of
the voice), reinforced, as time went on, by
those who trained and taught the child and
by all the other persons of his environ-
ment—an indefinite host, too numerous to
mention (fellow men, public opinion). (56,
p. 118).

The super-ego is not merely the individual's internalized code of values (ego-ideal), but also it carries out a function of observing the ego and criticizing it for failing to live up to the code of values. This is the "conscience" function of the super-ego, arousing a sense of guilt in the ego:

> An explanation of the normal conscious sense of guilt (conscience) presents no difficulties; it is due to tension between the ego and the ego-ideal and is the expression of a condemnation of the ego pronounced by its criticizing function. (56, p. 229).

> . . . how is it that the super-ego manifests itself essentially as a sense of guilt (or rather, as criticism—for the sense of guilt is the perception in the ego which corresponds to the criticism). . . . (56, p. 231).

The super-ego, as Freud uses it, is not merely the individual's code of values, but more especially, his code of _moral_ values. Freud seems to envision it as embodying a set of _traditional_ moral values, and does not deal with cases where the individual's code of values may be such as "do the other guy before he does you," "grab all the gusto you can get," "money is a man's best friend," all the sexual prowess and physical prowess connotations of the _macho_ code, and a variety of other values commonly entertained which cannot be classified as "traditional morality."

> The super-ego applies the strictest moral standard to the helpless ego which is at its mercy; in general it represents the claims of morality, and we realize all at once that our moral sense of guilt is the expression of the tension between the ego and the super-ego. (59, p. 61).

Finally, Freud sums up the functions he has ascribed to the super-ego:

> But let us return to the super-ego. We have alloted it the functions of self-observation, of conscience, and of [maintaining] the ideal. (59, p. 66).

110

Ego Strives to Please Super-Ego

Freud portrays the ego as eager for approval by the super-ego. The following passage conveys the impression that this desire for approval by the super-ego is the ego's most basic desire:

> The fear of death in melancholia only admits of one explanation: that the ego gives itself up because it feels itself hated and persecuted by the super-ego, instead of loved. To the ego, therefore, living means the same as being loved—being loved by the super-ego . . . (56, p. 233).

For the ego to be loved by the super-ego means, in Freud's terms, that the ego is measuring up to its ego-ideal, (or at least that the individual feels this is the case), that is, that the individual feels he is living up to his code of values. Or, in other words, he feels that he possesses those excellences which he considers to be ideal. An awareness of possession of excellence is our definition of self-esteem. Therefore, "to the ego, living means being loved by the super-ego" translates as "for the self, living means having self-esteem." Or, equivalently, the individual's most important desire is for self-esteem.

But measuring up to the ego-ideal is only one of the many ways in which we acquire self-esteem. As we noted previously, in Freud's description of the super-ego he is talking primarily, if not exclusively, of a traditional moral code. The awareness of living up to such a moral code is but a part of our total sense of self-respect. Other sources of self-respect are, of course, the acceptance, regard and love that others show us, our feeling of competence in this or that area, our financial status, etc. Thus, correspondence of the ego with ego-ideal (ego being loved by the super-ego) is self-esteem, but only a part of our total self-esteem picture.

Freud himself sometimes uses the term self-esteem for this gratification which the ego feels when it measures up to the ego-ideal:

> On the other hand, if the ego has successfully resisted a temptation to do something

which would be objectionable to the super-
ego, it feels raised in its self-esteem and
strengthened in its pride, as though it had
made some precious acquisition.
(201, p. 63).

This sense of heightened self-esteem he also
describes as a "feeling of triumph":

There is always a feeling of triumph
when something in the ego coincides with the
ego ideal. And the sense of guilt (as well
as the sense of inferiority) can also be
understood as an expression of tension be-
tween the ego and the ego-ideal.
(202, p. 200).

The above passage also indicates that a discre-
pancy between ego and ego-ideal means a lack of self-
esteem in the form of feelings of guilt and inferior-
ity.

Freud recognizes that this measuring up of the
ego to the ego-ideal, this approval of the ego by the
super-ego, is not the total source of self-esteem:

Part of the self-regard is primary—the
residue of childish narcissism; another part
arises out of such omnipotence as experience
corroborates (the fulfillment of the ego-
ideal), while a third part proceeds from
gratification of object-libido.
(56, p. 121).

The two other sources of self-esteem mentioned in
the above paragraph we will consider in the section of
this chapter concerned with Freud's use of the term
"self-regard."

In summary, Freud recognizes the vital importance
to the ego of approval by the super-ego. "To the ego,
living means being loved by the super-ego." Further,
he says that pleasing the super-ego causes the ego to
feel "raised in its self-esteem and strengthened in
its pride." Also, he states that the individual's
self-regard comes in part from fulfillment of the ego-
ideal, an expression synonymous with pleasing the
super-ego. Thus we see the message in Freud, explicit

and implicit, that the ego's eagerness to please the super-ego (fulfill the ego-ideal) is a quest for self-esteem.

Narcissism

Narcissism has become a leading topic of research in psychoanalytic circles, and one of the most common diagnoses. "You used to see people coming in with handwashing compulsions, phobias and familiar neuroses," says Clinical Psychologist Sheldon Bach. "Now you see mostly narcissists." (Time, Sept. 20, 1976, p. 63).

"Every age develops its own peculiar forms of pathology, which express in exaggerated form its underlying character structure," writes social critic Christopher Lasch. He and others have said that ours is an age of narcissism. . . ("Why Some People Can't Love", Linda Wolfe, Psychology Today, June, 1978, p. 55).

Although Havelock Ellis is credited with being the first to apply the term narcissism to the human condition of self-infatuation, probably it was Freud's writing on narcissism that sparked the interest in it that has blossomed in the last few years. Freud's concept of narcissism "was potentially one of his greatest discoveries," says Erich Fromm. (46, p. 69). Once the idea of narcissism has been liberated from the narrow, confining sexual connotation once placed upon it, states Fromm, it is one of the most important concepts for the understanding of man. Fromm feels (1966) that narcissism has not been given substantial attention because it was used too exclusively in reference to children and psychotics.

Fromm's view that narcissism has a place in the psychology of the normal person is echoed by Heinz Kohut, author of The Analysis of the Self and The Restoration of the Self. Narcissism as a human tendency to self-glorification is a normal and inevitable part of the human condition; narcissism as pathological is the tendency to seek this self-esteem in ways that are excessive and out-of-touch with reality. Kohut sees the therapist's task as aiding in the trans-

113

formation of pathological narcissism (grandiosity and exhibitionism) into a more realistic self-esteem.

> I think that the overcoming of a hypocriti-
> cal attitude toward narcissism is as much
> required today as was the overcoming of
> sexual hypocrisy a hundred years ago. We
> should not deny our ambitions, our wish to
> dominate, our wish to shine, and our yearn-
> ing to merge into omnipotent figures, but
> should instead learn to acknowledge the
> legitimacy of these narcissistic forces as
> we have learned to acknowledge the legiti-
> macy of our object-instinctual strivings.
> We shall then be able, as can be observed in
> the systematic therapeutic analysis of nar-
> cissistic personality disorders, to trans-
> form our archaic grandiosity and exhibition-
> ism into realistic self-esteem and into
> pleasure with ourselves. . . (106, p. 365).

Freud himself offered suggestions that narcissism is a part of the normal personality. "We postulate a primary narcissism in everyone," and "he (human beings in general) is not willing to forgo his narcissistic perfection," and "what is fine about humor is the triumph of narcissism, the ego's victorious assertion of its own invulnerability." Freud did not consider narcissism as necessarily either abnormal or undesirable.

Although Freud sometimes uses the term narcissism to mean a sexual love directed toward self, more frequently he uses narcissism to mean either the desire for self-esteem or self-esteem itself. For instance:

> In literature, indeed, even the great crimi-
> nal and the humorist compel our interest by
> the narcissistic self-importance with which
> they manage to keep at arm's length every-
> thing which would diminish the importance of
> their ego. It is as if we envied them their
> power of retaining a blissful state of mind—
> an unassailable libido-position which we
> ourselves have since abandoned.
> (56, p. 113).

Here, the terms "self-importance" and "importance

114

of their ego" correspond to self-esteem more closely than to self-directed sexual desire.

In the following passage we see much more than a mere sexual connotation to the word narcissism:

> To this ideal ego is now directed the self-love which the real ego enjoyed in childhood. The narcissism seems to be now displaced on to this new ideal ego, which, like the infantile ego, deems itself the possessor of all perfections. As always where the libido is concerned, here again man has shown himself incapable of giving up a gratification he has once enjoyed. He is not willing to forgo his narcissistic perfection in his childhood; and if, as he develops, he is disturbed by the admonitions of others and his own critical judgment is awakened, he seeks to recover the early perfection, thus wrested from him, in the form of an ego ideal. That which he projects ahead of him as his ideal is merely his substitute for the lost narcissism of his childhood—the time when he was his own ideal. (56, p. 116).

The term ideal ego in the passage above signifies the sort of person the individual would like to be, and feels he should be. The "self-love which the real ego enjoyed in childhood" is, as the next sentence reveals, "the infantile ego deeming itself the possessor of all perfections." Or, as Freud equivalently states it elsewhere, the "oceanic sense of omnipotence" that the infant feels. Thus, the self-love of narcissism is here identified as an ego deeming itself possessor of perfections, which is a good definition of self-esteem.

The narcissism of childhood, i.e., the ego deeming itself possessor of all perfections, is, as the person matures, "displaced on to this new ideal ego." That is, the person has now an image of the sort of person he wishes to be, and is attempting to develop in that direction. He is "not willing to forgo his narcissistic perfection in his childhood," and he "seeks to recover the early perfection." How? By measuring up to his ideal ego. This striving to measure up to his own ideal is a striving to regain the original sense of being "possessor of all perfection," i.e., a striving to maximize self-esteem.

Freud explicitly recognizes that this striving to measure up to the ideal ego is a matter of self-esteem. In describing why two men, both tempted to immoral conduct, react in different ways, one gladly indulging in the immoral conduct and the other rejecting it with "utmost indignation," Freud says that the latter has an ideal ego which is inconsistent with the immoral conduct, which ideal leads him to repress such conduct or even thoughts thereof. Such "repression, as we have said, proceeds from the ego; we might say with greater precision: from the <u>self-respect</u> of the ego" (56, p. 116). (Emphasis ours.)

In the conclusion of the lengthy paragraph quoted above, Freud uses the expression "when he was his own ideal." By this he means, as the context shows, the condition when the infant was not striving for perfection but already "deemed itself the possessor of all perfection." Thus, "when he was his own ideal" signifies the state of having self-esteem in excelsis. In a later passage Freud recognizes that this state is man's happiness, the goal he strives to attain.

> The ego-ideal has imposed several conditions upon gratification of libido through objects, or, by means of its censorship, it rejects some of them as incompatible with itself. Where no such ideal has been formed, the sexual trend in question makes its appearance unchanged in the personality in the form of a perversion. As in childhood, to be his own ideal once more, also where sexual tendencies are concerned, is the happiness that man strives to attain. (56, p. 121).

In the above paragraph Freud is saying that the individual will reject (presumably, he means "will as a rule reject") such sexual conduct as is incompatible with his ideal self-image. If the person has not internalized such a prohibiting self-image, then "the sexual trend in question makes its appearance unchanged in the personality in the form of a perversion." "To be his own ideal once more, also where sexual tendencies are concerned, is the happiness that man strives to attain." Not a happiness, but the happiness. To regain that original state of self-esteem in excelsis, that "sense of oceanic omnipotence," is man's goal in life. "Also where sexual tendencies are concerned," i.e., even the powerful sexual tendencies must conform to the ideal self-image. Even sex must take a back seat to this drive for self-esteem.

Other references in Freud indicate that he customarily uses the term "narcissism" not to connote sexual love for oneself but rather to connote a sense of one's possession of excellence, i.e., pride, self-esteem, self-regard, self-respect, etc. For instance, in praising the ability to laugh at oneself he says:

> Obviously, what is fine about it [humor] is the triumph of narcissism, the ego's victorious assertion of its own invulnerability. It refuses to be hurt by the arrows of reality or to be compelled to suffer. It insists that it is impervious to wounds dealt by the outside world, in fact, that these are merely occasions for affording it pleasure. (54, p. 1).

Again using narcissism and self-love in the sense of self-esteem Freud says:

> After this introduction I propose to describe how the universal narcissism of men, their self-love, has up to the present suffered three severe blows from the researches of science. (203, p. 139).

The first of these, the discovery that the earth is not the center of the universe but rather revolves around the sun, is a blow to man's "inclination to regard himself as lord of the world." "The second, the biological blow to human narcissism," came from Darwin's discovery that man "is not a being different from animals or superior to them." Freud's own discoveries constitute the third blow to man's narcissism, self-love, self-esteem:

> But these two discoveries—that the life of our sexual instincts cannot be wholly tamed,

and that mental processes are in themselves unconscious and only reach the ego and come under its control through incomplete and untrustworthy perceptions—these two discoveries amount to a statement that <u>the ego is not master in its own house</u>. Together they represent the third blow to man's self-love, what I may call the <u>psychological</u> one. No wonder, then, that the ego does not look favourably upon psychoanalysis and obstinately refuses to believe in it. (203, p. 143).

We might add that the present study offers the basis for a fourth blow to man's narcissism, for few things are more offensive to man's self-esteem than the suggestion that even in his most prized actions he is seeking self-esteem. Sly Voltaire compared the drive for self-esteem with the penis—highly prized but must be kept hidden. In the case of the drive for self-esteem, hidden even from ourselves.

Other writers have recognized the close ties, even the quasi-identification, of the concepts of narcissism, self-love, ego strength, and self-esteem. Symonds says:

> Narcissism or self-love also helps to strengthen the ego. It has already been pointed out that ego strength is coordinate with self-respect, self-esteem, and self-confidence. One of these feeds into the other, and as the child is helped to become successful and is praised for his efforts his ego gathers strength. (177, p. 125).

> It should be noted in passing that any process which damages the ego and renders it less effective at the same time hurts the self and valuation placed in the self. As the ego becomes less effective, narcissism is also hurt and the individual feels less adequate and there is loss of self-esteem. (177, p. 155).

Otto Fenichel, author of <u>The Psychoanalytic Theory of Neurosis</u>, remarks:

The individual's experiences connected with omnipotence lead to a most significant need of the human mind. The longing for the oceanic feeling of primary narcissism can be called the "narcissistic need." "Self-esteem" is the awareness of how close the individual is to the original omnipotence.

The primitive methods of the regulation of self-esteem arise from the fact that the first longing for objects has the character of a longing for the removal of disturbing displeasure, and that the satisfaction by the object removes the object itself and revives the narcissistic state. The longing for the return of omnipotence and the longing for the removal of instinctual tension are not yet differentiated from each other. If one succeeds in getting rid of an unpleasant stimulus, one's self-esteem is again restored. The first supply of satisfaction from the external world, the supply of nourishment, is simultaneously the first regulator of self-esteem. (49, p. 40).

In summation of this section, as Freud frequently uses the term narcissism he refers to a self-love which "deems itself the possessor of all perfections," i.e., self-esteem to the nth degree. Also, he says that man seeks to recover this high degree of self-esteem, experienced in infancy, by striving to live up to his ego-ideal.

Freud's Explicit References to Self-Esteem

Freud's most explicit consideration of the self-esteem motivation is contained in his work On Narcissism: An Introduction. As the context shows, he follows common usage in equating the terms self-regard and self-esteem. He introduces the subject:

At this point we may enter upon a discussion of the self-regarding attitude in normal persons and in neurotics.

First of all, the feeling of self-regard appears to us a measure of the ego; what various components go to make up that

measure is irrelevant. Everything we pos-
sess or achieve, every remnant of the primi-
tive feeling of omnipotence that experience
has corroborated, helps to exalt the self-
regard. (56, p. 119).

The meaning of his comment that self-regard is a
measure of the ego is not immediately evident.   It
might mean that self-regard is the raison d'etre of
the ego, the thing that the ego desires most of all.
This interpretation would seem to be born out by his
remark in The Ego and the Id that for the ego, living
means being loved by the super-ego, i.e., having self-
approval, self-regard.   The editor of Abstracts of his
works offers another interpretation when she states:
"Self-regard appears to be an expression of the size
of the ego." (204, p. 92).   In this interpretation
high self-regard is a large enriched ego, while low
self-regard is a weak impoverished ego.   This inter-
pretation harmonizes well with the raison d'etre in-
terpretation, inasmuch as the ego desires most of all
its own enlargement and enrichment.

In the above passage Freud notes that our self-
esteem is exalted by our possessions, by our achieve-
ments, and by our "primitive feeling of omnipotence."
By "primitive feeling of omnipotence" Freud refers to
the feeling aroused in the infant by having all his
needs immediately satisfied by the mother.   Equiva-
lently, he says that the infantile ego "deems itself
the possessor of all perfections." (56, p. 116).   Inas-
much as self-regard is exalted by possessions, etc.,
it seems plausible to infer that this is why the ego
wants possessions, achievements, and a feeling of
omnipotence, i.e., to exalt the self-regard.

Freud enlarges on the various sources of self-
esteem:

Part of the self-regard is primary—the
residue of childish narcissism; another part
arises out of such omnipotence as experience
corroborates (the fulfillment of the ego-
ideal), while a third part proceeds from
gratification of object-libido.
(56, p. 121).

"Childish narcissism" would seem to refer to an

earlier comment noting the "self-love which the real ego enjoyed in childhood," and the fact that "the infantile ego deems itself the possessor of all perfections." (56, p. 116). This "deems itself the possessor of all perfections" equates with our definition of self-esteem as "awareness of excellence possessed by self." Thus by childish narcissism Freud means the child's self-esteem. Of course, in his concept of narcissism Freud sometimes includes the note of a sexual love for one's own body, but such an aspect of narcissism seems to have minimal significance in the self-esteem of the normal adult, of which Freud is here speaking. Of broader significance for the normal adult would be the residue of his infantile "deeming himself the possessor of all perfections."

The second aspect of self-esteem that Freud mentions is "such omnipotence as experience corroborates." The original infantile feeling of "oceanic omnipotence" is corroborated in the adult ego to the extent that the ego succeeds in measuring up to the ego-ideal (succeeds in winning the approval of the super-ego). This fulfillment of the ego-ideal we have previously seen to be one aspect of self-esteem.

The third aspect of self-esteem "proceeds from gratification of object-libido." By "object-libido" Freud means the external object of sexual desire. And by gratification of this he means success in attaining that object, not merely in a crude physical possession, but in the sense of being loved in return. He says:

> Love in itself, in the form of longing and deprivation, lowers the self-regard; whereas to be loved, to have love returned, and to possess the beloved object, exalts it again. (56, p. 121).

Although Freud here is using the term love primarily in its sexual meaning (he uses the term "erotic cathexis" in this context), he distinguishes between self-regard exaltation from physical possession of the beloved object and exaltation from the psychological gratification of having love returned.

What does he mean by the statement that love in the form of longing lowers self-esteem? Here he is referring to unrequited love ("deprivation"), and probably everyone is aware of the depressing effect that this can have on the ego. As Freud says, "where the erotic life is concerned not being loved lowers the self-regarding feelings, while being loved raises them." (56, p. 120).

Ego Defense Mechanisms

In this section we intend to develop the thesis that the ego defense mechanisms, so important in psychoanalytic literature, are attempts by the psyche to protect itself from admitting into consciousness knowledge that would lower its self-esteem.

By "ego defense mechanisms" Freud means stratagems the ego uses to avoid "unpleasure" and threats of unpleasure.

> . . . the ego makes use of various methods of fulfilling its task, i.e., to put it in general terms, of avoiding danger, anxiety and unpleasure. We call these devices de-fense mechanisms. (64, p. 338).

Danger is an imminent unpleasure, and anxiety is a vague apprehension of possible unpleasure, as well as being in itself a form of unpleasure, so it seems fair to say that in the defense mechanism the ego is seeking to avoid unpleasure.

And that unpleasure which it is seeking to avoid is some perception of reality:

> The psychical apparatus is intolerant of unpleasure and strives to ward it off at all costs and, if the perception of reality involve unpleasure, that perception—i.e., the truth—must be sacrificed. (64, p. 339).

The perception of reality the ego is seeking to avoid is a knowledge (about its own urges, desires, thoughts) which is incompatible with the ego-ideal, i.e., which would cause a lowering of self-esteem:

> The patient's ego had been approached by an idea which proved to be incompatible, which provoked on the part of the ego a repelling

force of which the purpose was defense
against this incompatible idea. . . . I
recognized a universal characteristic of
such ideas: they were all of a distressing
nature, calculated to arouse the affects of
shame, of self-reproach and of psychical
pain, and the feeling of being harmed; they
were all of a kind that one would prefer not
to have experienced, that one would rather
forget. From all this there arose, as it
were automatically, the thought of defence.
(61, p. 269).

As Freud points out in the above paragraph, the
ideas the ego defends against are "all of a distress-
ing nature, calculated to arouse the affects of shame,
of self-reproach, and psychic pain." Shame and self-
reproach are expressions of lowered self-esteem, and
psychic pain is the generic term for those feelings
and others of the same nature.

Explicit recognition by Freud that at least one
of the ego-defense mechanisms, repression, is defend-
ing against loss of self-esteem is contained in the
following passage:

Repression, as we have said, proceeds from
the ego; we might say with greater preci-
sion: from the self-respect of the ego. The
very impressions, experiences, impulses, and
desires that one man indulges or at least
consciously elaborates in his mind will be
rejected with the utmost indignation by
another, or stifled at once even before they
enter consciousness. . . . The one man has
set up an ideal in himself by which he mea-
sures his actual ego, while the other is
without this formation of an ideal. From
the point of view of the ego this formation
of an ideal would be the condition of re-
pression (Emphasis ours.) (56, p. 233).

As we see in the above paragraph, one man has
formed an ego-ideal which causes him to repress cer-
tain "impressions, experiences, impulses and desires"
because they are inconsistent with his ego-ideal. In
other words, admitting them to consciousness would
cause tension between ego and ego-ideal, which tension

we have already seen in a previous section means a loss of self-esteem. More precisely, this tension between ego and ego-ideal is by definition a lack of self-esteem to the degree that the tension exists. Tension between ego and ego-ideal means the individual is aware that he does not possess excellences that he should have. Awareness of lack of proper excellences is lack of self-esteem, at least in the area in question.

In other writers we find recognition of the fact that ego defense mechanisms are strategems for the protection of self-esteem. Ernest Hilgard, in his presidential address to the American Psychological Association in 1949, said:

> Another way of looking at the mechanisms is to see them as bolstering self-esteem through self-deception. . . . If self-deception either by denial or by disguise is accepted as characteristic of a mechanism, the problem still remains as to the source of or reasons for the self-deception. The obvious interpretation is that the need for self-deception arises because of a more fundamental need to maintain or to restore self-esteem. Anything belittling to the self is to be avoided. (89, p. 376).

Gardner Murphy recognizes that the defense mechanisms operate to exclude information that would injure the individual's self-image:

> The device for selecting and filtering, structuring and unifying the system of defenses hardly ever operates in the rather mechanical fashion that was suggested up to the point at which the self entered the picture. The exclusion of information is in very large part guaranteed by another central device—the building up of a picture of the self, to be forever enhanced and defended. (137, p. 44).

Nathaniel Branden, in his book The Disowned Self, sees ego defense mechanisms as attempts to disown a part of self that is humiliating to the self-esteem:

When a person represses certain of his
thoughts and memories, because he regards
them as immoral or humiliating, he disowns a
part of himself—in the name of protecting
his self-esteem.

When a person represses certain of his
desires, because he cannot tolerate the
anxiety of wondering whether or not he will
attain them, an anxiety that makes him feel
helpless and ineffectual, he disowns a part
of himself—in the name of protecting his
self-esteem.

When a person represses certain of his
emotions, because they threaten his sense of
control or conflict with his notion of
"strength" or "maturity" or "sophistica-
tion," he disowns a part of himself—in the
name of protecting his self-esteem.
(22, p. 88).

In summary, Freud has both explicitly and impli-
citly recognized that the ego-defense mechanisms are
attempts to protect self-esteem. First, explicitly,
in that he notes that the mechanism of repression
proceeds from the self-respect of the ego. Then im-
plicitly, in that he sees the defense mechanisms as
defending against ideas and impulses which are incom-
patible with the ego-ideal. Add to this his statement
that the individual's self-regard derives in part from
a fulfillment of the ego-ideal, meaning that a failure
to fulfill the ego-ideal causes a fall in self-regard,
and we are left with the conclusion that the ego de-
fense mechanisms are attempting to protect the ego
from a fall in self-regard.

Is Self-Esteem Dominant Over Sex in Freud's Theory?

It seems hardly likely that Freud would agree
that the self-esteem drive is stronger than the sex
drive. To the end he stoutly maintained the supremacy
of the id, the home of the sex instincts, in man's
psychic life. As Hall and Lindzey put it:

Although Freud regarded the ego as the
executive of the total personality, at least
in the case of the healthy person, he never

granted it an autonomous position; it always remained subservient to the wishes of the id. In what was to be his final pronouncement on psychoanalytic theory, Freud (1940) reiterated what he had said so many times before, "This oldest portion (the id) of the mental apparatus remains the most important throughout life." The id and its instincts express "the true purpose of the individual organism's life." There is no question as to how Freud felt regarding the relationship of the ego and the id: the id is the dominant member of the partnership. (84, p. 62).

It takes considerable chutzpah to suggest the heinous heresy that a case can be made, from Freud's own words, for exactly the opposite position, namely, that the self-esteem drive is indeed dominant over the sex instincts. Yet, timidly and tentatively, that is precisely the suggestion we will try to substantiate in this section. The case we will present does not argue to a triumph of self-esteem over sex instincts in every situation, but to a general dominance of the former when engaged in a confrontation with sex instincts.

First, let us consider Freud's statement that the ego is prepared to refuse the demands of the sex instincts (and aggressive instincts) when the ego sees these demands as endangering its own interests:

> When the Id makes an instinctual demand of an erotic or aggressive nature on a human being, the most simple and natural response for the Ego, which governs the apparatus for thinking and muscle innervation, is to satisfy this by an action. This satisfaction of the instinct is felt as pleasure by the Ego, just as not satisfying this instinct would undoubtedly become a source of discomfort. Now, it may happen that the Ego eschews satisfaction of the instinct because of external obstacles—namely, when it realizes that the action in question would bring in its course serious danger to the Ego. (60, p. 148).

Here we see the ego quite ready to accede to the demands of the id, <u>until its own interests are threatened.</u> Then it shows its dominance and "eschews satisfaction" of the id instincts. Here Freud is speaking of external obstacles to id satisfaction, for instance, a man renounces an opportunity to have an appealing sexual affair because of danger of discovery and resulting humiliation and loss of public esteem. Thus self-esteem (as we have seen, self-esteem derives in large part from public esteem) has dictated a refusal to the gratification of the sex instinct.

On some occasions refusal to gratify the sex instinct may be made for what Freud calls internal reasons, that is, by the ego's desire to live up to the ego-ideal, i.e., please the super-ego:

> While, however, instinctual renunciation for external reasons is only painful, renunciation for internal reasons, in obedience to the demands of the Super-ego, has another economic effect. It brings besides the inevitable pain a gain in pleasure to the Ego—as it were, a substitutive satisfaction. The Ego feels uplifted; it is proud of the renunciation as of a valuable achievement. . . . When the Ego has made the sacrifice to the Super-ego of renouncing an instinctual satisfaction, it expects to be rewarded by being loved all the more. The consciousness of deserving this love is felt as pride. (60, p. 149).

Here the ego finds pleasure in its dominance over erotic and aggressive urges, pleasure which Freud describes as pride, i.e., self-esteem. Thus, whether renunciation was made for external or internal reasons, the ego has had a confrontation with the id and has proved dominant. Of course, the ego never completely conquers its ever-present opponent/ally, and there are occasions when the id wins the day. Then the organism wakes up hating itself.

Another passage indicates the dominance of self-esteem over sex:

> The ego-ideal has imposed several conditions upon the gratification of libido

through objects, for, by means of its censorship, it rejects some of them as incompatible with itself. Where no such ideal has been formed, the sexual trend in question makes its appearance in the form of a perversion. As in childhood, to be his own ideal once more, also where sexual tendencies are concerned, is the happiness that man strives to attain. (56, p. 121).

Here we see the ego-ideal in the driver's seat, imposing conditions on the subservient sex instinct and forbidding its expression in certain circumstances. How does the ego-ideal impose conditions on the sex drive? The ego is eager to measure up to the ego-ideal, for by this it obtains its self-regard, as Freud points out in passages we have cited previously. To measure up to his ego-ideal, even when sexual tendencies pull in the opposite direction, is the self-esteem, the happiness that man strives to attain.

The dominance of self-regard over the sex instincts in the human motivational economy is again implicitly conceded by Freud in his description of the normal development of the girl child:

Analyses of the remote phallic period have now taught me that in girls, soon after the first signs of penis-envy, an intense current of feeling against masturbation makes its appearance, which cannot be attributed exclusively to the educational influence of those in charge of the child. . . . I cannot explain the opposition which is raised in this way by little girls to phallic masturbation except by supposing that there is some concurrent factor which turns her violently against that pleasurable activity. Such a factor lies close at hand in the narcissistic sense of humiliation which is bound up with penis-envy, the girl's reflection that after all this is a point on which she cannot compete with boys and that it would therefore be best for her to give up the idea of doing so. (58, p. 190).

Freud poses this development not as an occasional thing, but as the regular, normal mode. Little girls

show an "intense current of feeling" against sex plea-
sure in the form of masturbation and "violently" re-
ject it. What has so intensely and violently domina-
ted her id urges? Self-esteem, as Freud points out.
Masturbation humiliates her, reminding her of her
organ inferiority to the little boy. The point here
is not whether Freud is right in his analysis of the
little girl's psychology; the point is that he has
implicitly conceded once again that self-regard has
dominated the sex instinct.

In Freud's analysis of hatred we find additional
evidence in the same vein:

> The ego hates, abhors, and pursues with
> intent to destroy all objects which are for
> it a source of painful feelings, without
> taking into account whether they mean to it
> frustration of sexual satisfaction or of
> gratification of the needs of self-preserva-
> tion. Indeed, it may be asserted that the
> true prototypes of the hate-relation are
> derived not from sexual life, but from the
> struggle of the ego for self-preservation
> and self-maintenance. (56, p. 84).

The thought in this passage is admittedly complex
and its meaning is not appreciably clarified by the
context. However, one thought is evident: the ego,
when wounded, sweeps aside sexual considerations in
its intent to destroy that which has wounded it. The
ego's struggle for self-preservation and self-mainte-
nance exerts an imperious supremacy which will brook
no interference from sexual desires. And let us re-
call what Freud means by the self-preservation of the
ego: "for the ego, living means being loved by the
super-ego." That is, living means self-approval.

In summation, Freud has pointed out that the ego
customarily refuses to allow satisfactions to the id
when the ego's own interests would be threatened by so
doing. He also states that desire to live up to the
ego-ideal will lead the ego to refuse the demands of
the id. He cites the usual development of the little
girl in which the ego instinct to avoid humiliation
leads her to give up the sex pleasure of masturbation.
Finally, he points out in the analysis of hate, that
to avoid "ego pain," the ego will forego sexual satis-

faction. All these facts support the contention that the ego instincts are the senior partner in their uneasy alliance with the sex instincts.

Summary of Chapter IV

We have seen that certain concepts of key significance in the Freudian system are at root an expression of the drive for self-esteem. The relation between the ego and the super-ego, in which the ego strives to please the super-ego, or in other words, to fulfill the ego-ideal, is a quest for self-regard, self-respect, to use Freud's words. He frequently uses narcissism in the sense of the psyche's original state of deeming itself possessor of all perfection (having self-esteem to the nth degree) and states that the course of development of the ego is an attempt to regain that original state of high self-esteem. This is the "happiness that men seek." The important ego-defense mechanisms are strategems to protect the ego from unwelcome knowledge about itself, knowledge which would lower self-esteem.

Finally, we have seen evidence in Freud's writings that when the self-esteem drive and the sex drive come into conflict, customarily the self-esteem drive is victorious. The organism "indignantly rejects" sexual urges which conflict with the ego-ideal.

Certainly Freud did not explicitly maintain the dominance of self-esteem motivations over the sex drive. Such a conclusion would be quite alien to his explicit doctrine. However, as we have developed in this chapter, from clues in his writings a case can be made for just such dominance. We do not consider our conclusion as definitive, but hope that it will spark further study in this direction.

CHAPTER V

KANT AND NIETZSCHE: APOSTLES OF SELF-ESTEEM

Introduction

"Immanuel Kant was the foremost thinker of the Enlightenment and one of the great philosophers of all time . . . He inaugurated a new era in the development of philosophical thought." Thus does the staid Encyclopedia Brittanica laud Kant. Kant's voluminous writings on the theory of knowledge and on ethics have had a profound impact on subsequent theological and philosophical trends.

"Friedrich Nietzsche, a 19th century German philosopher, was one of the most influential thinkers of modern times . . . Almost all 20th century German philosophers, as well as the greatest German poets, novelists, and psychologists, are profoundly indebted to him." This assessment of Nietzsche's influence is again from the conservative Encyclopedia Brittanica. Sigmund Freud "paid lavish tribute to his psychology and often remarked that Nietzsche had a more thorough self-knowledge than any other man had had or ever would have." Coming from the great grey eminence of psychology this is praise indeed. Freud marveled that Nietzsche had arrived by intuition at insights that it took Freud years of clinical study to attain.

Generations of preachers and theologians had perceived the self-esteem motive as ubiquitous and denounced it as iniquitous. Kant and Nietzsche see the ubiquity of the same motive and glorify it. Kant perceives it as our desire for "a sense of worth and dignity," and glorifies it under the rubric of moral autonomy, the exalted worth and dignity of each individual who is the supreme arbiter in matters of right and wrong. Nietzsche perceives it as our desire for a "feeling of power," and glorifies it under the rubric of "will to power." Only the superman, by fullest use of his faculties of reason and sensuality, is successful in attaining the fullest possible sense of power—i.e., self-actualization. We present Kant and Nietzsche for their insights that a sense of personal worth is what human beings do seek above all. Evaluation of their position that this is also what human beings should seek above all would require another volume.

This present study is concerned with how people do behave, not with how they should behave. With regard to the self-esteem motive, ubiquity, yes; iniquity, no comment.

Equally dedicated apostles of self-esteem, Kant and Nietzsche differed, like Peter and Paul, in their attitude toward the "gentiles," in this case, the common man. Influenced by Rousseau's glorification of the common man, Kant abandoned his former elitist views of self-esteem coming primarily through intellectual attainments, and proposed a system by which the common man could attain to the fullest possible self-esteem. Valid personal worth and dignity comes only through moral autonomy, that is, stepping into one's rightful role as supreme arbiter of right and wrong, standing supreme over influence from tradition, society, or God.

Nietzsche heartily concurred with the moral autonomy and the individual supremacy aspect of Kant's theory, although he had no sympathy for its populist predilection. His superman, exulting in his personal excellence, is the epitome of individual self-esteem. His individualism is voiced in his thunderous "Superman, yes! Mankind, no!"

Kant's "Duty for Duty's Sake"

Individual's Worth and Self-Esteem Depend Upon Moral Behavior

Immanuel Kant's pervasive influence on modern philosophy and on liberal theology makes mandatory our consideration of a theory of motivation he has proposed which does not seem to fit the theory we have been developing in this book. Kant's famous principle of morality dictates that the only moral acts are those done purely out of reverence for the moral law, abstracting from any desire for reward or personal gain or advantage. "Duty for duty's sake," is the terse and austere formulation of his principle of morality. In enunciating this principle he proposes an irreducible motivation of human nature which seems quite apart from self-esteem or sensual gratification, a motivation that can be described as "desire to do one's duty strictly for duty's sake," or alternately, "desire to obey the moral law." Kant's phrasing "duty

132

for duty's sake" and "reverence for the moral law" does not have much appeal for the modern mind, conveying overtones as it does of a Prussian Junker code of obedience. However, Kant's idea finds its modern expression in the philosophy, "I believe in doing what is right, just because it is right, and never mind any idea of reward." Thus our consideration of Kant's "reverence for the moral law" has relevancy for its modern equivalent, "doing what is right just because it is right."

Kant sees the individual's personal worth, dignity and self-esteem resting entirely on his disposition to live according to the moral law, from the motive of reverence for the moral law. Thus, if a person were to be closely obedient to the moral law from some other motive, e.g., desire for happiness, a natural sympathy for his fellow man, desire for social acclaim, desire for Divine approval, such a "heteronomous" motive would offer no valid basis for moral goodness, nor for personal worth and self-esteem. Not that Kant is opposed to such motivations, indeed, he sees that doing good to others from such motives is a "very beautiful thing," but such motives still fall short of the pure reverence for the moral law in itself, and thus cannot confer moral goodness on actions done.

> . . . but the latter (morality), moral worth, can be placed only in this, that the action is done from duty, that is, simply for the sake of the law.

> It is of the greatest importance to attend with the utmost exactness in all moral judgements to the subjective principle of all maxims, that all the morality of actions may be placed in the necessity of acting from duty and from respect for the law, not from love and inclination for that which the actions are to produce.

> No other subjective principle must be assumed as a motive, else while the action might chance to be such as the law prescribes, yet, as does not proceed from duty, the intention, which is the thing properly in question in this legislation, is not moral.

> It is a very beautiful thing to do good
> to men from love to them and from sympathe-
> tic good will, or to be just from love of
> order; but this is not yet the true moral
> maxim of our conduct. (219, p. 325-6).

The moral law both checks and promotes self-
esteem: it promotes an exalted self-esteem consisting
in reverence for the moral law, and checks propensi-
ties to self-esteem arising from other sources. The
moral law has both a humiliating and an exalting ef-
fect on the individual's self-esteem. It humiliates
in two ways: it makes the subject aware of how far
short he is falling from pure obedience to the stern
call of duty, and second, it makes him aware of the
worthlessness of his claims to self-esteem from sour-
ces other than duty done out of reverence for the
moral law. Kant, speaking of this humiliating effect
of the moral law, says:

> Since it is so far only a <u>negative</u> effect,
> which, arising from the influence of pure
> practical reason, checks the activity of the
> subject, so far as it is determined by in-
> clinations, and hence checks the opinion of
> his personal worth (which, in the absence of
> agreement with the moral law, is reduced to
> nothing); hence, the effect of this law on
> feeling is merely humiliation.
> (219, p. 324).

However, much more important that this negative
effect of the moral law on self-esteem is its positive
influence in exalting self-esteem. Dedication to
following the moral law gives the individual a sense
of both his supremacy and his nobility. His supre-
macy, in that now he is following the dictates of his
own moral reason, and is not subject to laws (in his
moral life) from external sources, not from society,
not from sages, not from God. The individual is, as
Kant says, the supreme law-maker. In his supremacy as
law-maker the individual is now lord of the moral
universe. Secondly, the moral law confers a sense of
nobility upon the individual who strives to live ac-
cording to it. To that extent he is rising above the
urgings of his "inclinations," by which Kant refers
disparagingly to our desires for material gain and
sensual gratification.

> Duty! Thou sublime and mighty name . . . a
> law before which all inclinations are dumb .
> . . a root to be derived from which is the
> indispensable condition of the only worth
> which men can give themselves.
> (219, p. 328).

"Automony" in Kant

Kant's doctrine that the dignity and worth of the individual, and therefore, any valid claim to self-esteem, depends solely upon actions done out of reverence for the moral law, does indeed seem bleak and austere. But its severity is considerably mitigated by Kant's statement that the individual himself makes that moral law which he must reverence. The individual does not receive the moral law from society's codes, nor from any Divine law, nor from his own inclinations and desires, but from the perceptions of his own "pure practical reason." The individual is the supreme law-maker for himself.

> . . . although in the concept of duty we
> think of subjection to the law, yet we also
> at the same time attribute to the person who
> fulfills all his duties a certain sublimity
> and dignity. For it is not so in so far as
> he is subject to the law that he has sublim-
> ity, but rather in so far as, in regard to
> this very same law, he is at the same time
> its author and is subordinated to it only on
> this ground. (217, p. 107.)

> Reason thus relates every maxim of the will,
> considered as making universal law, to every
> other will and also to every action towards
> oneself: it does so, not because of any
> further motive or future advantage, but from
> the Idea of the dignity of a rational being
> who obeys no law other than that which he at
> the same time enacts himself.

> But the law-making which determines all
> value must for this reason have a dignity—
> that is, an unconditioned and incomparable
> worth—for the appreciation of which, as
> necessarily given by a rational being, the
> word "reverence" is the only becoming ex-

pression. <u>Autonomy</u> is therefore the ground of the dignity of human nature and of every rational nature. (217, p. 102-3).

The cynic might remark "ah, this is great. I make up the rules of the game as I go along. I am the judge and jury in my own case." But Kant replies that arriving at the moral law is not a matter of one's own whims or desires, rather it is a work of pure practical reason, honestly applied. The moral law thus arrived at is not idiosyncratic, but is one and the same for all rational beings. And it does not require laborious and careful reasoning; instead it is evident to all rational beings. In response to a critic who maintained that the precepts of the moral law are sometimes difficult to determine, Kant says that "they are graven into the human soul in the crudest, most legible script." (220, p. 287). The moral thing to do in any particular case is arrived at by following the "categorical imperative." "There is therefore only a single categorical imperative and it is thus: <u>'Act only on that maxim through which you can at the same time will that it should become a universal law.'"</u> (217, p. 88). Critics note that the application of this principle to particular cases is not always as self-evident as Kant seems to maintain, and that there is considerable leeway for self-favoring biases.

A further softening of the concept of "duty solely out of reverence for the moral law" is Kant's concession that other motives, such as desire for personal happiness, may indeed be influencing the individual, provided that reverence for the moral law is the determining factor, sufficient in itself to produce the act.

As Kant frequently stresses, the ground of human worth and dignity is the individual's freedom to be obedient only to those laws which he himself makes. This concept of human worth and dignity is the keystone of Kant's moral system. He finds the basis for this dignity in three things: doing duty for duty's sake, in the freedom of the will from all laws not of the person's own making, and in triumphing over one's less noble motivations. His "Idea of Autonomy" sums up these elements.

Is Moral Behavior Actually Possible?

How do we know that human beings actually have this ability to subordinate their desires for personal happiness, gratification and gain, and to determine their behavior by reverence for the moral law? A frequent charge by critics of Kant is that such an idea is unrealistic, that it simply does not happen in the real world. Kant himself admits the difficulty of showing that anyone has ever actually done an act of duty for duty's sake. Even though a person's behavior may seem to be motivated by stern devotion to duty and reverence for the moral law, yet the actual motive may be "some secret impulse of self-love." Neither observation of the behavior of others nor introspection into one's own behavior can establish with certainty that such "reverence for the moral law" behavior actually exists.

> In actual fact it is absolutely impossible for experience to establish with complete certainty a single case in which the maxim of an action in other respects right has rested solely on moral grounds and on the thought of one's duty. It is indeed at times the case that after the keenest self-examination we find nothing that without the moral motive of duty could have been strong enough to move us to this or that good action and to so great a sacrifice; but we cannot infer from this with certainty that it is not some secret impulse of self-love which has actually, under the mere show of the Idea of duty, been the cause genuinely determining our will. We are pleased to flatter ourselves with the false claim to a nobler motive, but in fact we can never, even by the most strenuous self-examination, get to the bottom of our secret impulsions; for when moral value is in question, we are concerned, not with the actions which we see, but with their inner principles, which we cannot see. (217, p. 74).

Kant seems to be undermining his entire system of ethical philosophy by such admissions that the only thing which gives worth and dignity to the human being, the only act which is truly virtuous, namely, duty for duty's sake, is an act "of which the world has perhaps hitherto given no example."

"Proof" That Moral Behavior Is Possible

Kant is not troubled by his conviction that no evidence can be offered, either from observation or introspection, for the actual performance of truly moral acts, by anyone at any time. He continues serenely confident that such an act can be done, that is, that the will can be determined by reverence for the moral law. And such a conclusion is of course the keystone of his moral philosophy. How does he arrive at such serene confidence? His answer is summed up in the famous quote attributed to him: "Thou canst because thou shouldst."* We are aware, says Kant, that we should rise above all clamors of self-interest in order to be obedient to the call of duty, simply out of a reverence for duty. This realization that we should act solely out of reverence for the moral law would be a mockery unless it were possible. Therefore it is possible. The ancient theological dictum "God does not command the impossible" is thus paraphrased by a Kantian "pure practical reason does not command the impossible."

> Still, duty commands him unconditionally; he ought to remain true to his resolve; and thence he rightly concludes that he must be able to do so, and that his will is therefore free. (221, p. 45n).

> For when the moral law command that we ought now to be better men, it follows inevitably that we must be able to be better men. (221, p. 46).

Another "proof" that some human beings are effectively motivated by reverence for the moral law is implicit in Kant's thinking. Human dignity and worth

---

*Concerning this quote often attributed to Kant, Lewis Beck in his commentary notes: "One of Kant's most famous 'statements'—'Thou canst because Thou shouldst'—does not exist in this neat form . . . But statements that express this inference less succinctly abound." (A Commentary on Kant's Critique of Practical Reason, Lewis Beck, p. 200).

are entirely dependent upon acting out of reverence for the moral law. If such conduct were not to exist in reality, then human dignity and worth would be non-existent. But such a monstrous situation is unthinkable. Therefore human behavior determined by reverence for the moral law must indeed actually occur.

How Does the Moral Law Motivate Us?

Kant is admittedly mystified as to how such a stern and selfless code as "duty" could possibly move the human will. When, in the hypothetical case that a person does an act of duty for duty's sake (i.e., out of reverence for the moral law), his will is being moved by the "universal validity of the maxim." The categorical imperative states "act only on those maxims which you could will to be universal law for all rational beings," and it is precisely this "universal moral law" aspect which moves the will. Reverence for the moral law depends upon this aspect of universal applicability. If a proposed moral maxim were to lack this universal applicability to all rational beings, its claim to acceptance would have to lie in some aspect appealing to the person acting (appealing to him either as an individual or as a member of some group) and thus would lose its transcendant nobility, becoming instead the means of personal gain or advantage.

But how such an abstract concept as universal validity can move the human will, so oriented toward its own personal interests, is, as Kant confesses, a mystery. "Hence for us men it is wholly impossible to explain how and why the universality of a maxim as a law—and therefore morality—should interest us." (217, p. 128). By "interest us" Kant means "move our will." "An interest is that in virtue of which reason becomes practical—that is, becomes a cause determining the will."

Another way in which Kant expresses this impossibility of understanding how the will can be moved by the concept of duty: "but reason would overstep all its bounds if it undertook to explain how pure reason can be practical, which could be exactly the same problem as to explain how freedom is possible." (217, p. 127). "Pure reason" is the exercise of reason in arriving at an understanding of the moral law; being "practical" means moving the will to action. The problem of how pure reason can be practical is the problem of how reverence for the moral law can move the will. Which, in turn, is the problem of how freedom is possible. These are not separate problems, but merely synonymous phrasings of the same problem. Remember, for Kant, the concept of freedom of the will (equated with "Idea of freedom," "morality," "Autonomy," "Idea of Autonomy") is not merely the ability to choose this or that, but is a fuller concept, embracing freedom from all laws not of one's own making, freedom to rise above motives of sensuality or personal advantage, and freedom to determine one's will by reverence for the moral law. And how the moral law can thus motivate us is impossible to explain, says Kant.

This conclusion he states in several ways. "The subjective impossibility of explaining freedom of will is the same as the impossibility of finding out and making comprehensible what interest man can take in moral laws; and yet he does in fact take such an interest." "But how this presupposition in itself [the Idea of freedom] is possible is never open to the insight of any human reason." (217, p. 128-9).

Even the ever-present human desire for happiness cannot explain the compelling power of the moral law:

> But on this basis we can as yet have no insight into the principle that we ought to detach ourselves from such interest [desire for happiness]—that is, that we ought to regard ourselves as free in our actions and yet to hold ourselves bound by certain laws in order to find solely in our own person a worth which can compensate us for the loss of everything that makes our state valuable. We do not see how this is possible nor consequently how the moral law can be binding. (217, p. 117-8).

Not only is it impossible to understand how the moral law can motivate us, we cannot offer any examples to show that it actually does motivate us:

> For how it is possible that the bare idea of conformity to law, as such, should be a

stronger incentive for the will than all the incentives conceivable whose source is personal gain, can neither be understood by reason nor yet proved by examples from experience. (221, p. 56).

In his concluding note to the Critique of Practical Reason Kant sums up his position regarding the impossibility of understanding how reverence for the moral law can move the person to action. He notes that human reason by its very nature seeks for basic principles, and ultimately, for an unconditioned basic principle underlying all others. In the realm of moral behavior, that basic principle is reverence for the moral law. To ask how this can move the will is to ask for a more basic principle underlying the most basic principle, which is a contradiction in terms. Further, bringing in some interest (self-interested motive) to explain the moral imperative would destroy its morality and freedom. (As we have seen, for Kant both morality and freedom involve rising above motives of personal advantage. Indeed, he uses morality and freedom as synonyms.) Therefore, there is no way of comprehending how reverence for the moral law can move the will.

Desire for Self-Esteem is the Motive Behind Morality

We propose that the answer to the "insoluble mystery" of why reverence for the moral law moves the will is hinted at repeatedly by Kant: what moves the will is the increased sense of worth and dignity to be gained from acting in accord with the moral law. Already we have seen Kant's oft-repeated statement that human worth and valid self-esteem depend totally on moral behavior. "Morality is the indispensable condition of the only worth which men can give themselves," and, "all claims to self-esteem which precede agreement with the moral law are vain and unjustifiable."

In the following sections we will explore further Kant's implicit doctrine that there is indeed a further motive underlying the attraction that the moral law has for the person's will, that further motive being the desire for a sense of inner worth and dignity. This conclusion will be approached from several directions, all suggested by Kant's writings. First, his writings reveal that the motivating principle for the most important element of morality, duty to self, is the desire for self-esteem. Second, the motive for morality in general is shown to be a desire to feel worthy of happiness. Third, reverence for the moral law is actually reverence for the author and guarantor of that law, that is, self. In summation, we have gathered the most cogent passages from Kant indicating that self-esteem is the motive behind "doing duty and observing the moral law."

Why then is Kant so adamant in proclaiming that there is no further motive for obedience to the moral law other than reverence for the moral law? His reasons for so proclaiming suggest the answer. There can be no further motive dependent upon a source external to the individual's own reason, because this would make him dependent upon that external source, and thus destroy his autonomy, which is the ground of his worth and dignity. Thus ruled out is any motive deriving from physical nature, from sense, or from the will of other rational beings, including God. But the self-esteem motive is not ruled out, because, as Kant admits, it is a function of the individual's pure a priori reasoning. When based upon moral behavior, as he says any valid self-esteem must be, it does not involve dependence upon any external source. It thus does not interfere with the person's autonomy; it does not fall into the category of those motives excluded by Kant's reasoning. Therefore, an assertion that the desire for self-esteem motivates observance of the moral law is quite in accord with Kant's reasoning, and in accord with so many of his statements. Kant's dictum that there is no other motive for observance of the moral law (other than pure reverence for the law) must be understood as "no other motive that would interfere with autonomy."

Self-Esteem is the Motivating Principle of Duty Toward Self

Kant expresses sharp disagreement with philosophers who consider the moral life to consist primarily in our relations with other persons. They hold the view "that man should give a thought to himself only after he has completely fulfilled his duty towards others. All moral philosophers err in this respect." (216, p. 117). In contrast, Kant sees, duty toward

142

self as being most important. "Far from ranking low-
est in the scale of precedence, our duties towards
ourselves are of primary importance and should have
place of pride . . . he who has transgressed his duty
towards himself, can have no inner worth whatever."
(216, p. 117-8).

As examples of failure in duty toward self Kant
cites drunkenness, lying, sycophancy, "vices of the
flesh," and suicide. Such persons "degrade their
manhood," "throw away the worth of their manhood," and
'fail to reverence humanity in their own person." In
short, they fail in self-esteem.

Our duties toward self are based on the principle
of self-esteem; a proper reverence for self demands
that we express that reverence in our habitual beha-
vior. "Not self-favour but self-esteem should be the
principle of our duties towards ourselves. This means
that our actions must be in keeping with the worth of
man." (216, p. 124). (By "self-favour" Kant refers
to our inclinations toward sensual gratification and
material advantage.)

Man's basic duty to himself, and thus the most
important of all duties, is to have a valid self-
esteem.

> Just as law restricts our freedom in our
> relations with other men, so do our duties
> to ourselves restrict our freedom in dealing
> with ourselves. All such duties are grounded
> in a certain love of honour consisting is
> self-esteem; man must not appear unworthy in
> his own eyes; his actions must be in keeping
> with humanity itself if he is to appear in
> his own eyes worthy of respect. To value
> approbation is the essential ingredient of
> our duties towards ourselves.
> (216, p. 125).

This repeated emphasis on the necessity of self-
esteem is a frequently recurring theme in Kant's writ-
ings on morality and ethics. As we see here, self-
esteem is the "ground" and "essential ingredient" of
the most vital duties, duties toward self.

The Motive of Morality is "Worthiness to be Happy"

Kant frequently repeats the theme that the motive and aim of morality is the individual's consciousness of his worthiness to be happy. He has ruled out happiness as the aim of morality because happiness is a product not only of moral behavior but also of circumstances over which the individual has no control, such as good health, good fortune, etc. Therefore if happiness were the goal of moral behavior it would conflict with the essence of human worth and dignity, namely the autonomy of the individual, i.e., his complete moral independence of external influences. However, the same reasoning does not rule our worthiness to be happy as a moral motive. Worthiness to be happy depends only on the person's free behavior, and is therefore not in conflict with his independence of external circumstances. Man's consciousness of his worthiness to be happy is another way of stating his awareness of his dignity and excellence as an observer of the moral law. In either phrasing it is a noble form of self-esteem.

In Religion Within the Limits of Reason Alone we see that the "object of our maxims" (aim of our moral principles) is worthiness to be happy:

> Yet by this same nature of ours (if we wish in general so to term that which is innate), as beings endowed with reason and freedom, this happiness is far from being first, nor indeed is it unconditionally an object of our maxims; rather this object is worthiness to be happy, i.e., the agreement of all our maxims with the moral law. (221, p. 41-2 n).

In the Critique of Pure Reason Kant poses two questions basic to reason's "practical interest." The first is "what ought I to do?" and the second is "what may I hope?" (The answer to the second, incidental to our present interests, is that I may indeed hope for an eternity of happiness "only on the assumption that the cause of nature is a supreme reason, which governs according to moral laws," by which Kant means God.) The answer to "what ought I to do?" is a statement of the moral law—do what will make you worthy of happiness. A little reflection shows that this is an equivalent phrasing of the categorical imperative "act only on those principles you would will to be universal." This categorical imperative derives its validity and nobility from the fact that only in so acting is the individual manifesting and acting upon his supreme freedom from all external influences, which freedom is the source of human worth. And only thus is he acting morally and making himself worthy of happiness. "That is the answer to the first of the two questions of pure reason which relate to its practical interest: Do that which will render thee worthy of happiness." This is a statement of the moral law in terms of its motive: worthiness to be happy.

Everyone seeks happiness, even in every instance of their behavior, Kant admits, but in moral behavior the person must abstract from this desire for happiness, and make his motive the desire to be worthy of happiness:

> The practical law based on the motive of happiness I term a pragmatical law (or prudential rule); but that law, assuming such to exist, which has no other motive than the worthiness of being happy, I term a moral or ethical law. The first tells us that what we have to do, if we wish to become possessed of happiness; the second dictates how we ought to act, in order to deserve happiness. (218, p. 236).

A little further in his Critique of Pure Reason Kant makes a statement that has caused commentators considerable consternation. He seems to deny his celebrated and central thesis "observe the moral law solely out of reverence for the moral law" by admitting that reverence for the moral law is not sufficient to move us. As motives for being moral we need belief in God and in the rewards of a future life:

> Thus, without a God and without a world invisible to us now, but hoped for, the glorious ideas of morality are, indeed, objects of approbation and of admiration, but cannot be the springs of purpose and action. For they do not satisfy all the aims which are natural to every rational being, and which are determined a priori by pure reason itself, and necessary. (218, p. 238).

145

This admission of a "heteronomous" motive for morality, a concept that would be destructive of Kant's entire elaborate system of morality, is generally considered by commentators to be a temporary aberration, committed when his thinking was not fully matured, and not repeated in his later works. It is true that this brief and surprising admission that duty cannot be done just for duty's sake is quite out of harmony with the thrust of Kant's thought. The desire for happiness "in a world invisible to us now" as a "spring and purpose of action" is contrary to his repeated insistence that the desire for happiness must not be the motive for moral action. Instead, the motive is the desire to be worthy of happiness. And as commentators have noted, this latter motive essentially undercuts any need, in his system of thought, for God and immortality, substituting immediate self-esteem reward for a heavenly reward. Commenting on the passage quoted above, Lewis Beck states:

> Yet almost immediately and with no obvious consistency, he denies that the prospect of future happiness makes the moral disposition possible. The moral disposition is one of worthiness to be happy, to which the hope of happiness is added by these "postulates," but the desire for happiness does not generate the moral disposition. The second of these views is the one that is to appear again and again, and the religious eudaemonism of the quoted passage is transcended, never to be asserted again. (224, p. 214-5).

Is the proposed motive for moral behavior the desire to be worthy of happiness, or is it more precisely the desire to consider oneself worthy of happiness? This distinction is not explicitly treated by Kant. However, the individual's desire to be worthy of happiness is satisfied when he honestly feels himself to be worthy of happiness. It is the attainment of this inner conviction of worthiness that satisfies the desire and thus can be considered as the immediate motivating impulse for moral behavior. "The inner applause is a sufficient motive," as Beck puts it.

> But to feel that we are the authors of a state of being worthy of happiness (i.e., to have its a priori condition) is itself a

positive feeling of self-contentment, and
this constitutes the human worth of morality
and is a necessary factor in happiness. The
inner applause is a sufficient motive and is
an "intellectual pleasure" in the enjoyment
of freedom. (224, p. 215).

The use of the somewhat vulgar term "inner ap-
plause" should not obscure the fact that this is a
noble form of self-esteem.

Reverence for the Moral Law is Reverence for Self

What is moral law? It is a code of conduct whose
essence consists in the fact that it applies to all
rational beings, as Kant's imperative points out.
Kant's emphasis that the moral law applies to all
rational beings, not just to human beings, is in har-
mony with his insistence that the moral law transcends
"sensible" (physical) motives. It also transcends any
motives arising from personal gain, or advantage, or
from external authorities (society, wisdom of sages,
God). And herein lies its worthiness to be rever-
enced: it calls the individual to triumph over any
influences external to his own reason, and to follow
only the dictates of his own reason. It is a stern
call—and a glorious challenge—to each person to
assert his nobility and his supreme freedom.

Thus, reverence for the moral law is reverence
for the nobility and freedom it both confers on the
person and evokes from the person. Reverence for the
moral law is reverence for the human being in his most
exalted aspect (as Kant sees it). In reverencing the
qualities of dignity and autonomy and authority in
himself, the person is respecting himself. As Kant
states: "Respect applies always to persons only."

But would it not be possible for a person who
does not keep the moral law to respect it? In doing
so, it might seem that he is not respecting himself,
but is merely respecting a concept. Actually, in this
case he is respecting the moral law for its appeal to
the best in himself, and ultimately his respect is
directed toward his own capacity for nobility and
autonomy.

In the following passage Kant points out that the command (constraint) of the moral law gives us a feeling of self-approbation which has a "special name, that of respect." The source of this feeling of self-respect is the realization that we are subject to no authority but our own reason.

> . . . as this constraint is exercised merely by the legislation of our own reason, it also contains something elevating, and this subjective effect on feeling, inasmuch as pure practical reason is the sole cause of it, may be called in this respect self-approbation . . . whence this feeling obtains a special name, that of respect. (219, p. 324-5).

The will of the individual who performs moral actions is an object of "immediate reverence," and his mental attitude is one of "sanctity," "infinitely above all price." And again we see the note that the individual's reason is the supreme authority.

> Such actions too need no recommendation from any subjective disposition or taste in order to meet with immediate favour and approval; they need no immediate propensity or feeling for themselves; they exhibit the will which performs them as an object of immediate reverence; nor is anything other than reason required to impose them upon the will, not to coax them from the will—which last would anyhow be a contradiction in the case of duties. This assessment reveals as dignity the value of such a mental attitude and puts it infinitely above all price, with which it cannot be brought into reckoning or comparison without, as it were, a profanation of its sanctity. (217, p. 102-3).

It is Kant's core message that the sublime self-esteem that we owe to ourselves is based upon our autonomy, which is our freedom from all laws other than those of our own making. Another aspect of this basic ground of self-esteem is the individual's role as supreme moral law-maker.

> . . . free in respect of all laws of nature,
> obeying only those laws which he makes him-
> self . . . But the law-making which deter-
> mines all value must for this reason have a
> dignity—that is, an unconditioned and in-
> comparable worth—for the appreciation of
> which, as necessarily given by a rational
> being, the word 'reverence' is the only
> becoming expression. <u>Autonomy</u> is therefore
> the ground of the dignity of human nature
> and of every rational nature. (217, p. 103).

Reverence for the moral law is reverence for the
best element in myself, reverence for the activity and
product of my own reason; it is self-esteem in excel-
sis:

> The majesty of the moral law (as of the law
> on Sinai) instils awe (not dread, which
> repels, nor yet charm, which invites famil-
> iarity); and in this instance, since the
> ruler resides within us, this <u>respect</u>, as of
> a subject toward his ruler, awakens a <u>sense</u>
> <u>of the sublimity</u> of our own destiny which
> enraptures us more than any beauty.
> (221, p. 19 n).

And:

> . . . the <u>spiritual</u> feeling of respect for
> moral ideas, which is not one of gratifica-
> tion, but a self-esteem (an esteem for hum-
> anity within us) that raises us above the
> need for gratification . . . (223, p. 539).

In response to critics who would propose that the
moral law arises from some concept or force "bigger
than myself," and that the reverence would then be due
to this other concept or force, Kant replies, speaking
of the moral law as "philosophy":

> It is here that philosophy is seen in
> actual fact to be placed in a precarious
> position, which is supposed to be firm al-
> though neither in heaven nor on earth is
> there anything from which it depends or on
> which it is based. It is here that she has
> to show her purity as the authoress of her

149

own laws—not as the mouthpiece of laws
whispered to her by some implanted sense or
by who knows what tutelary nature, all of
which laws together, though they may always
be better than nothing, can never furnish us
with principles dictated by reason. These
principles must have an origin entirely and
completely a priori and must at the same
time derive from this their sovereign au-
thority . . . (217, p. 93).

In the above paragraph is his oft-repeated posi-
tion that the moral law is not "given to us," neiher
by heaven or anything on earth, nor by any other tute-
lary means, but must be dictated by my own reason. He
is adamant in ruling out any "natural law" concept.
"It is of the utmost importance to take warning that
we should not dream for a moment of trying to derive
the reality of this principle from the special charac-
terisitics of human nature." (217, p. 92). Equally
strong is his rejection of divine authority as a source
for the moral law. Having disposed of "striving for
perfection" (too vague) as a basis for moral law, he
goes on to say that it is at least better than a moral
law derived from divine authority:

. . . this concept none the less is better
than the theological concept which derives
morality from a divine and supremely perfect
will; not merely because we cannot intuit
God's perfection and can only derive it from
our own concepts, among which that of moral-
ity is the most eminent; but because, if we
do not do this (and to do so would be to
give a crudely circular explanation), the
concept of God's will still remaining to
us—one drawn from such characteristics as
lust for glory and domination and bound up
with frightful ideas of power and vengeful-
ness—would inevitably form the basis for a
moral system which would be in direct oppo-
sition to morality. (217, p. 111).

In conclusion, reverence for the moral law speaks
plainly of reverence for the authority which gave the
moral law existence and validity—namely, self, opera-
ting through its reason. A tribute to your finest
characteristics is a tribute to yourself. When in

150

Kant's terms, you esteem your mental attitude as being "infinitely above all price," and attribute to it the quality of sanctity, you are indeed reverencing yourself.

This suggests a further solution to the apparent inconsistency in Kant, the dilemma of his insistence that there is no motive for keeping the moral law other than pure reverence for the moral law, and on the other hand his admission that the desire for self-esteem is the motive for keeping the moral law. The solution lies in the fact that in Kant's system, reverence for the moral law _is_ self-esteem, as we have seen in this section.

Summation of Texts Indicating Self-Esteem as Motive

In this section are assembled some of the more cogent quotes (in several cases, previously presented) from Kant indicating that "duty for duty's sake" is actually "duty for the sake of the sense of worth and dignity that is conferred by doing duty." In other words, actions done "out of reverence for the moral law" are motivated by a desire to increase one's sense of nobility and self-esteem. The same motivation, in its even more compelling negative formulation, is the desire to avoid the devastating self-contempt the person (as Kant envisions him) would feel if he failed to do his moral duty.

From _Lectures on Ethics_:

> It [duty] insists that we must reverence humanity in our own person, because apart from this man becomes an object of contempt, worthless in the eyes of his fellows and worthless in himself. (p. 121).

> . . . he who has transgressed his duty towards himself, can have no inner worth whatsoever. (p. 118).

> Not self-favour but self-esteem should be the principle of our duties towards ourselves . . . . All such duties are grounded in a certain love of honour consisting in self-esteem; man must not appear unworthy in his own eyes; his actions must be in keeping

with humanity itself if he is to appear in his own eyes worthy of inner respect. To value approbation is the essential ingredient of our duties towards ourselves. (p. 124-5)

From The Moral Law (Groundwork of the Metaphysics of Morals) translated by H.J. Paton:

Unmixed with the alien element of added empirical inducements, the pure thought of duty, and in general of the moral law, has by way of reason alone . . . an influence so much more powerful than all the further impulsions capable of being called up from the field of experience that in the consciousness of its own dignity reason despises these impulsions and is gradually able to become their master. (p. 78).

The impersonal phrasing of the above passage does not conceal its message: the desire for self-respect conquers less noble motives and leads the person to obey the moral law.

These principles [of the moral law] must have an origin entirely and completely a priori and must at the same time derive from this their sovereign authority—that they expect nothing from the inclinations of man, but everything from the supremacy of the law and from the reverence due to it, or in default of this condemn man to self-contempt and inward abhorrence. (p. 93).

By "inclinations of man" Kant customarily refers to motives having their origin in sensuality. He does not include "love of honour" or self-esteem in this category.

This fact that Kant implicitly exempts self-esteem when he says that reverence for the moral law transcends motives of personal advantage, gain or inclination, is shown again by the following passage:

Reason thus relates every maxim of the will considered as making universal law, to every other will and also to every action towards

152

oneself: it does so, not because of any
further motive or future advantage, but from
the Idea of the dignity of a rational being
who obeys no law other than that which he at
the same enacts himself. (p. 102).

A sense of personal dignity, transcending "fur-
ther advantage," should be the force moving the will
as it observes the moral law:

And precisely here we encounter the paradox
that without any further end or advantage to
be attained, the mere dignity of humanity,
that is, of rational nature in man—and
consequently that reverence for a mere
Idea—should function as an inflexible pre-
cept for the will . . . (p. 106).

Man finds true self-esteem in moral behavior
alone:

On what do we base the worth we attach to
this way of acting according to the categor-
ical imperative—a worth supposed to be so
great that there cannot be any interest
which is higher? And how does it come about
that in this alone man believes himself to
feel his own personal worth, in comparison
with which that of a pleasurable or painful
state is to count as nothing? (p. 117).

We should consider ourselves bound by the moral
law in order to find solely self-esteem, which is
greater than any good:

. . . we ought to regard ourselves as free
in our actions and yet to hold ourselves
bound by certain laws in order to find sole-
ly in our own person a worth which can com-
pensate us for the loss of everything that
makes our state valuable. (p. 118).

It is proper to human beings to desire to act
nobly, in accordance with the categorical imperative.
This desire, if followed, would result in no satisfac-
tion other than a greater self-esteem:

. . . for from the fulfillment of this wish
he can expect no gratification of his sensu-

ous desires and consequently no state which would satisfy any of his actual or even conceivable inclinations (since by such expectation the very Idea which elicited the wish would be deprived of its superiority); all he can expect is a greater inner worth of his own person. (p. 122).

Is there a distinction between self-esteem and true inner worth? In other words, when Kant says that we get a true inner worth from keeping the moral law, one could say that this is not the same as self-esteem, because self-esteem is the belief that you have worth, whereas Kant is speaking of the actuality of having worth. However, the context of Kant's remarks—and often his explicit words—indicate that he is speaking in terms of the individual's awareness of his inner worth, i.e., of self-esteem. Some of his explicit phrases: "man must not appear unworthy in his own eyes," "to appear in his own eyes worthy of inner respect," "consciousness of its own dignity," "default condemns man to self-contempt," "man believes himself to feel his own personal worth," "self-esteem should be the principle," etc.

Could it be said that in Kant's system self-esteem is not the motive for moral action, but merely a consequence, an unintended bonus. One is tempted to draw this conclusion from Kant's repeated statements that there must be no other motive for moral action other that pure reverence for the moral law. Yet as we have seen, his writings abound in statements that point to the self-esteem motive. Some lines of thought contribute to a solution to the apparent contradiction. First, when Kant excludes other motives from moral behavior, he mentions "inclinations, gain or advantage." And as we have seen in a previous section, he does not include love of honor or self-esteem in such non-moral motives. Second, reverence for the moral law is ultimately reverence for the creator of that law, namely, self. Finally, a sense of inner worth and dignity is not an "unintended bonus," but is, as Kant repeatedly stresses, a supreme good to be actively sought, even at the expense of sacrificing all other inclinations, gain or advantage.

Continuing the same theme, from the Critique of Practical Reason:

> . . . the certainty of a state of mind that
> coincides with this [moral] law is the first
> condition of personal worth (as we shall
> presently show more clearly), and prior to
> this conformity any pretension to worth is
> false and unlawful. (p. 322).

> . . . [the moral law] checks the opinion of
> his personal worth (which, in the absence of
> agreement with the moral law, is reduced to
> nothing) . . . (p. 324).

Submission to the moral law causes an increase in
self-esteem, because it is our own law that we are
obeying, not law imposed on us by some external source:

> On the other hand, however, as this con-
> straint is exercised merely by the legisla-
> tion of our own reason, it also contains
> something elevating, and this subjective
> feeling, inasmuch as pure practical reason
> is the sole cause of it, may be called in
> this respect self-approbation . . .
> (p. 325).

Our desire for self-esteem, motivating us to
follow the moral law, is especially strong in its
negative form, that is, our dread of loss of self-
esteem. Kant is vividly aware of this motive under-
lying our obedience to the call of duty. He remarks
that a man following the moral law will avoid even an
inoffensive lie which would have been of great advan-
tage to himself and his friends. This he will do
"lest he should despise himself secretly in his own
eyes." (p. 328). Man is sustained in his observance
of the moral law by the realization that "he has no
reason to be ashamed of himself in his own sight, or
to dread the inward glance of self-examination." (p.
328). This inner peace is "only the escaping the
danger of sinking in personal worth, after everything
else that is valuable has been lost." For "he cannot
endure that he should be in his own eyes unworthy of
life." Kant sums up these reflections:

> Such is the nature of the true motive
> of pure practical reason; it is no other
> than the pure moral law itself, inasmuch as
> it makes us conscious of the sublimity of

155

> our own super-sensible existence and subjec-
> tively produces respect for their higher
> nature in men who are also conscious of
> their sensible nature . . . (p. 328).

Thus, the moral law moves the individual because it makes him aware of the dignity of his ability to rise above external influences (motives originating from the sensible world). In short, it produces respect for his higher nature—a noble form of self-esteem.

Why does man reverence duty? Because of the pure moral character, rather, the idea of a pure moral character, which is conferred upon him by doing his duty. In On the Old Saw: That May Be Right in Theory, But It Won't Work in Practice Kant says:

> . . . no idea does more to lift the human
> spirit and to fan its enthusiasm than the
> very idea of a pure moral character. Due to
> this idea, man will revere his duty above
> all else . . . this is the revelation of
> divine tendencies within himself deep enough
> to fill him with sacred awe, as it were, at
> the magnitude and sublimity of his true
> destiny. (p. 54).

This moral "self-esteem" Kant describes as one aspect of self-love. He divides self-love into "love of good will" (benevolence) and "love of good plea-sure" (complacence). The "love of good will" (toward self) means desiring to have our natural inclinations satisfied. "Here reason holds but the place of a handmaid to natural inclination." This does not neces-sarily mean hedonism, but includes even a moderate and prudent policy of seeking "each of the components of happiness." This type of self-love is natural to all of us, and in itself "has absolutely no reference to morality," but "when taken as the principle of all our maxims, is the very source of evil."

"Love of good pleasure in oneself" (complacence) Kant again divides into two types. The first is the self-complacence—self-esteem—one feels because of success in satisfying the love of benevolence toward self, i.e., in satisfying natural inclinations. The second is a self-esteem arising from consciousness that one is a moral person (doing duty for duty's sake, acting from reverence for the moral law). This "moral self-love" is "the inner principle of such a contentment as is possible to us only on condition that our maxims are subordinated to the moral law." It denotes an "unconditional respect for the law." This moral self-esteem, moral self-complacence, is proper only to the person "who knows that it is his maxim to make reverence for the law the highest incentive of his will." (Religion Within the Limits of Reason Alone, p. 41).

A problem arises here which we have dealt with previously in slightly different terms: if moral self-esteem is the result of keeping the moral law, how can it also be the cause (motive) for keeping the moral law? The answer is that it is desire for moral self-esteem which is the motive for keeping the moral law. This desire to have the only valid sense of human worth and dignity, and to avoid the self-condemnation arising from moral failure, need not always be explicitly in the person's mind; being sometimes submerged in the subconscious does not lessen the power of its influence.

In Kant's Critique of Aesthetic Judgment we see repeated once again his realization that reverence for the moral law is self-esteem. This is a most logical position when we remember his premise that the moral law is created by self.

> We may, therefore as I conceive, make Epicurus a present of the point that all gratification, even when occasioned by concepts that evoke aesthetic ideas, is animal, i.e., bodily sensation. For from this admission the spiritual feeling of respect for moral ideas, which is not one of gratification, but a self-esteem (an esteem for humanity within us) that raises us above the need of gratification, suffers not a whit— no nor even the less noble feeling of taste. (p. 539).

You Are Supreme!

The individual should seek self-esteem above all.

All of Kant's moral philosophy flows from his conviction that the raison d'etre of the human being is to have a sense of worth and dignity. Ultimately, only this matters, that the individual have a well-founded self-respect. The words dignity and worth (of the person) keep appearing as central features of each of Kant's major concepts—morality, freedom, autonomy, universality of law, categorical imperative, duty, etc. Kant is renowned for having placed duty above all else. He is probably best known for his "duty for duty's sake" dictum. But why is duty so important to him? Because faithfulness to duty increases self-respect, and even more compellingly, failure to do duty deprives a person of self-respect. Self-respect is the ultimate criterion, the ultimate value, the summum bonum.*

Kant's treatment of the most important type of duty, duty toward self, reveals the key to his thinking:

> Self-esteem should be the principle of our duties towards ourselves.
>
> All such duties are grounded in a certain love of honour consisting in self-esteem; man must not appear unworthy in his own eyes; his actions must be in keeping with humanity itself if he is to appear in his own eyes worthy of respect. To value approbation is the essential ingredient of our duties towards ourselves.
>
> He who has transgressed his duty towards himself, can have no inner worth whatever. (216, p. 117-124).

Is there any other goal which can compete with self-esteem as the ultimate aim of human behavior?

---

*Kant defines summum bonum as worthiness to be happy, conjoined with actual attainment of supreme happiness. But as a determinant of behavior, the realization of worthiness to be happy, i.e., the only valid type of self-respect, is the significant factor. Actual attainment of supreme happiness may be a consequence, but must not be a factor in determining conduct.

Kant has ruled out the desire for happiness as a moral goal, inasmuch as its attainment depends upon contingent conditions not completely under control of the individual's reason and will. Thus it is contrary to the principle of autonomy, and cannot be a moral goal. The same reason would eliminate such goals as seeking the welfare of others, establishment of a just social order, doing the will of any other being, seeking rewards here or hereafter, contributing to human progress. All of these—and any goal involving a being other than self, no matter how praiseworthy that goal may be—are in conflict with the principle of autonomy. As heteronomous motives, they cannot be truly moral.

The individual can have _supreme_ self-esteem

The only valid self-esteem is moral self-esteem. The individual is the supreme law-maker in matters of morality. He not only need not, but _must_ not, follow the dictates of any other being in matters of morality. To follow the dictates of another would be a heteronomous motive, destructive of the moral value of the act. Kant's principle of autonomy asserts the supremacy of the individual over the physical world, over his own passions, and over the will of other rational beings. Pointing out the independence of the "will of every rational being" from external influences, Kant states "nevertheless a will which is itself a supreme law-giver cannot possibly as such depend on any interest."

In one sense, the individual's supreme self-esteem is a future possibility, predicated upon his habitual observance of the moral law. But in another sense, supreme self-esteem is offered by Kant as an already achieved reality for the person who accepts Kant's message: "You are the supreme moral authority, subservient to nothing and no one."

Kant's doctrine is a giant step in the direction of the self-deification which is the ultimate aim of the self-esteem motive. As Camus said, "man is the desire to be God."

Every individual can have supreme self-esteem

The _summum bonum_ of supreme self-esteem is subject to no class distinctions. In its attainment no preference or advantage is given to clergy or royalty, to intellectuals or the wealthy. Each individual, no matter how humble his social situation or talents, is supreme in his determination of what he should or should not do, is supreme maker of the moral law. The moral law is clearly evident to even the simplest person. The precepts of duty "are graven into the human soul in the crudest, most legible script."* (220, p. 287). "So sharply and clearly are the boundaries of morality and self-love** that even the commonest eye cannot fail to distinguish whether a thing belongs to the one or the other." "The commonest intelligence can easily and without hesitation see what, on the principle of autonomy of the will, requires to be done." (219, p. 305).

The concepts of <u>supreme</u> self-esteem and supreme self-esteem for <u>everyone</u> Kant seems to owe to Rousseau. Rousseau's ideas exerted a determining influence on Kant's mature thought. In Kant's Spartan and otherwise unadorned study a picture of Rousseau had a prominent place. Kant's regular afternoon walks, so punctual that neighbors could set their clocks by his itinerary, were suspended only for a few days over the course of several years, and during those few days Kant was eagerly digesting the recently arrived copy of Rousseau's <u>Emile</u>.

What could two such different personalities have in common? Kant built his philosophy around reason and its infallible perception of the moral law. Rousseau complained that "reasoning, far from enlightening us, binds us; it does not raise our soul, it enervates and corrupts the judgment, which should be perfect." With Rousseau, "every impulse of the human heart is good," but Kant proclaimed that impulses are the foes

---

*By "graven into the human soul" Kant is not stating that the moral law is given us by nature or God. This he has explicitly rejected. Rather, the individual makes the moral law by his own reason.

**Kant customarily uses the term "self-love" to indicate our desires for pleasures or material goods. Opposed to this is the sense of dignity and worth we get from doing duty. This latter he terms "moral self-love."

of virtue. Kant earned a reputation even in Prussia for his self-discipline and regularity of life; Rousseau earned a reputation even in "Gay Paree" for his lack of self-discipline and his irregularity of life.

Nevertheless, Kant found in Rousseau the ideas that, combined with his own ideas, would produce an exalted philosophy of broad appeal. Kant proclaimed this new philosophy a "Copernican revolution in human thought." Previous to reading Rousseau, Kant had believed that human worth and excellence lay in intellectual pursuits. This of course was an elitist view, relegating the mass of mankind to a state of little worth. Inspired by Rousseau's glorification of the common man, Kant was converted to a new view: the source of human worth and dignity—and thus true self-esteem—lay not in intellectual excellence but in moral excellence. This gave the common man immediate access to exalted worth and dignity, because the prescriptions of the universal moral law are "writ legibly and unmistakably in every mind."

Kant acknowledges his debt to Rousseau:

> By inclination I am an inquirer. I feel a consuming thirst for knowledge, the unrest which goes with desire to progress in it, and satisfaction in every advance in it. There was a time when I believed this constituted the honor of humanity, and I despised the people, who know nothing. Rousseau corrected me in this. This blinding prejudice disappeared and I learned to honor man. I would find myself more useless than the common laborer if I did not believe that this attitude of mine can give worth to all others in establishing the rights of mankind. (224, p. 165).

The "worth to all others" that Kant believes his new philosophy confers is the role of supreme maker of the moral law. The "rights of mankind" are the right to follow the dictates of one's own reason in preference to the commands of kings or hierarchy. Indeed, in preference to the mores of any other persons or groups.

It was _Emile_ which so changed Kant's thought.

His new philosophy of autonomy, which offers supreme self-esteem to every person, may well have been inspired by the profession of faith of the Savoyard Vicar, the mouthpiece for Rousseau's own religious beliefs. The Vicar, like the new Kant, is supreme in matters of morality. Of his principles of conduct, he says:

> I find them in the depths of my heart, traced by nature in characters which nothing can efface. I need only consult myself with regard to what I wish to do; what I feel to be right is right, what I feel to be wrong is wrong.

Kant would not be comfortable with the "traced by nature"; instead, his principles of conduct are made (emphatically, not discovered) by reason. The "feel to be right" is also not Kantian; for him feelings smack of the sensible world, so inimical to virtue. Instead Kant would say "what my reason tells me is right, is right." But this essence, "I need only consult with myself with regard to what I wish to do" is the heart of the Kantian message. This autonomy, Kant proclaims, is the source of all human worth and dignity. This is his message of supreme self-esteem for the common man. The common man of course is not likely to struggle through Kant's morass of verbiage to arrive at this message, but a legion of professors and ministers have eagerly accepted Kant's "declaration of independence," and passed this on to their flocks.

I am supreme!

The central concepts in Kant—morality, moral law, freedom, autonomy, dignity, human worth, duty—are, as he uses them, essentially the same thing. In sum, each embraces a triple proclamation of "I am supreme!" I am supreme over the physical universe. I am supreme over my own "sensible nature." I am supreme over other rational beings. Yes, supreme even over God himself, in the most important sense, namely, deciding what I should or should not do. It is my reason that is the supreme law-maker. It is a case of "my will be done," rather than "thy will be done." Coincidentally, what I proclaim as the moral law is also proclaimed by God as the moral law, just as it is

proclaimed as the moral law by the "commonest intelli-
gence." However, my own proclaiming of the moral law
is in no way dependent upon God's views.

I enjoy this trinity of supremacy because in the
most important aspect of being—deciding right and
wrong—my reason alone is the master. In its deci-
sions it <u>must</u> rise above any claims or suggestions
from any other entity in the universe. This is duty;
this is morality; this is the moral law; this is auto-
nomy; this is freedom; this is the ground of all human
worth and dignity, this is the ground of all valid
self-esteem. Thus Kant.

Friedrich Nietzsche

The Will to Power

All phenomena which are the result of inten-
tions may be reduced to <u>the intention of
increasing power</u>. (235, Bk. III, #663).

<u>The unitary view of psychology</u>. We are
accustomed to regard the development of a
vast number of forms as compatible with one
single origin.

My theory would be: that the will to
power is the primitive force out of which
all other motives have been derived . . .

That all motive force is the will to
power; that there is no other force, either
physical, dynamic, or psychic.
(235, Bk. III, #668).

With these terse statements Nietzsche presents
the heart of his theory of human motivation: the will
to power. All our deliberate thoughts, words and
deeds are a striving for power. Even the most submis-
sive attitude and behavior, even the most passionate
avowal of love, even the most "unselfish" service for
others, is, at root, a disguised striving for power.
The agent need not be aware that this is his basic
motive; indeed he may sincerely and vehemently deny
that he has any such motive, but there is no escaping
this primary law of human behavior. "Life is essen-
tially a striving after more power."

163

The word "power" has a negative taste for most of us. We tend to associate power with manipulation and unfeeling dominance over others, with corruption and brutality. Nietzsche's "will to power," espoused by the Nazis, is associated in our minds with the storm trooper, the blitzkreig, the Drang Nach Osten, the panzer units destroying everything in their path. This however is not fair to Nietzsche. Power, in his philosophy, is something vastly broader than domination over others. Each individual, each organism, is seeking to more fully realize its potential. Today this process has been popularized under the name "self-actualization," or "self-fulfillment." Nietzsche envisions this continuing attempt at self-actualization as overcoming obstacle after obstacle. The obstacles may be other human beings determined to thwart our efforts, or the obstacles may be of our own making—lethargy, fear, ungoverned passions.

In Thus Spake Zarathustra Nietzsche reveals the full scope of his Will to Power. "And this secret spake Life herself unto me. 'Behold,' said she, 'I am that which must ever surpass itself.'" (238, p. 120). Self-surpassing, self-fulfilling, self-actualization: this is N's concept of the will to power. But with the proviso "as the individual perceives it." The Nazis were seeking self-actualization—as they conceived it—in their drive to conquer the world. The pacifist is seeking power, self-actualization, as he conceives it.

Why did Nietzsche choose the word "power" instead of some other term less offensive than power, say, self-fulfillment? First, in the Germany of N's day, power was a prestige term, laden with positive connotations. Admittedly, N had caught the spirit of the times to that extent, and exulted in military power. More basically, he saw the realization of one's potential as requiring power to overcome obstacles. To enjoy life, the superman must be battling against strong obstacles. Certainly N had sufficient of these is his own life—lifelong migraine headaches, poor vision, social rejection.

Disguised Forms of the Will to Power

In support of his thesis that all human behavior flows from the will to power, Nietzsche details some of the less obvious forms of striving for power.

Love, sacrifice, service.

> And where there is sacrifice and service and
> love-glances, there also is the will to be
> master. By by-ways doth the weaker then
> slink into the fortress, and into the heart
> of the mightier one—and there stealeth
> power. (238, p. 120).

The desire for self-preservation. This "will to
life" is a function of the will to power, in that we
can only have power to the extent that we have life.
Self-preservation is <u>not</u> the first law of nature; the
will to increase one's power is the first law of na-
ture.

> Only where there is life, is there also
> will: not, however, Will to Life, but—so I
> teach thee—Will to Power! (238, p. 120).

Freedom. Freedom is a form of power. Here N
mentions, in his terse fashion, "evangelical freedom,"
and "liberty of conscience," with no further elabora-
tion.

Belonging. "Enrollment" is the term used by N.
This enables the individual to satisfy his will to
power by identification with some group.

Submission. Making oneself useful to those in
power is itself an entree to power.

Proclamation of a standard of values other than
social and political power. Here N mentions "Jews:
classical example."[1] He means that the Jews have
given us the ten commandments to be considered as a
standard of more value than social power. This en-
ables the poor and downtrodden, by keeping these com-
mandments, to have "the imaginary consolation of out-

---

[1]Nietzsche has been unfairly associated with
anti-Semitism, due to the Nazi's use of his concepts
of the superman, and will to power. Actually N was
much opposed to anti-Semitism. He mentions that the
Jews have treated him with understanding and tact
which he never received from his fellow Germans. He
makes several disparaging references to anti-Semitism,
and closes a letter to a Jewish friend with the wish-

ranking those who actually possess power." By faithfulness to duty and to conscience a person is seeking the self-conferred power of moral superiority. In the same paragraph he tersely lists "self-condemnation" with no further comment. Based on allusions elsewhere in his writing, N is referring to a Christian tradition of self-condemnation, as exemplified by the parable of the publican and the Pharisee, and by St. Paul's "I am the greatest of sinners." As N envisions it, the Christian is thereby assuring himself of his sincerity and thus conferring upon himself the image of moral superiority, with accompanying moral power.

Praise and gratitude. Praise implies that the one doing the praising has the faculty and right of passing judgment. Thus stepping into the role of judge heightens his sense of power. Gratitude is a form of praise; praising the donor for his goodness. By gratitude we "get even" with the donor. He has given us some benefit, we give him gratitude in return. "Gratitude is a virtuous revenge."

Justice. The strong man wants dominant power, but if this is out of reach, he demands justice, i.e., "the same measure of rights as the ruling type possesses."

Love of mankind; love of the people; love of the gospel; love of truth; sympathy; self-sacrifice. These are the ways chosen by "the strongest, the richest, most independent, most courageous." Identification with a great cause gives the individual a feeling of powerful transcendence of self. "A heightened feeling of happiness and life in also a heightened feeling of power." (236, p. 406-7).

---

ful thought: "I am just now having all anti-Semites shot." In another letter he informs his correspondent that he is becoming alienated from his sister because of her anti-Semitism. However, N does hold the ancient Jews responsible for introducing the ascetic ideal and the altruistic ideal, concepts that reached their full flowering in Christianity, and which N considers as inimical to superman's drive to reach the fullest realization of his rational and sensual powers.

The Will to a Feeling of Power

The will to power is, more precisely and more directly, a will to a _feeling_ of power. Satisfaction and happiness come to the individual with a feeling of power, even when he has not in fact attained power but merely the illusion. Repeatedly Nietzsche used interchangeably the concepts "will to power" and will to a feeling or sense of power.

> Life as an individual case (a hypothesis which may be applied to existence in general) strives after the maximum feeling of power; life is essentially a striving after more power. (235, Bk. III, #690).

> The wealthy in vital strength, the active, want triumph, defeated opponents, and the extension of their feeling of power over ever wider regions. Every healthy function of the organism has this need,—and the whole organism constitutes an intricate complexity of systems struggling for the increase of the feeling of power. (235, Bk. III, #703).

This root drive of every human action is only satisfied, with resultant happiness, when there is a feeling, a consciousness, of having power. "Happiness is only a symptom of the feeling of power attained." (ibid. #688). "The will to an increase lies in the essence of happiness; that power is enhanced, and that this difference becomes conscious." (ibid., #695).

Power, in N's broad use of the term, is not our usual and limited concept, but is personal excellence in its fullest scope. A feeling of power is the individual's feeling of his personal excellence. This is precisely the essence of self-esteem. Nietzsche's "will to power," motivating our every action, is precisely the will to ever higher self-esteem.

Ancient Roots; Modern Fruits

In reading Nietzsche's description of his ideal superman, one has a sense of _deja vu_. "This sounds like Aristotle's description of his great-souled man." Some of the similarities: both are deeply concerned to receive approbation from discerning peers (and these are very few in number), and both have a contempt for the opinions and approbation of the common man. Aristotle's great man is "slow of gait and slow in speech." N's great man is "slow in speech and slow of glance." (Winston Churchill type?) Both envision the great man as absorbed in contemplation of deep truths, and engaged in a search for further truths. Nietzsche does acknowledge an indebtedness to Aristotle.

The similarity between Nietzsche's "single-principle psychology: the will to power as source of all our behavior" and some current psychologies is remarkable. Alfred Adler's Individual Psychology, hailed by Ernest Becker as the most perceptive of modern psychologies, is a single-principle theory, presenting the drive for superiority as the source of all our behavior. Early in his career Adler termed this principle the "will to power," but objections to the term power persuaded him to change his terminology. He adopted, successively, the names "masculine protest," "striving for superiority," and "striving for perfection." Adler sums up the basic principle in his psychology and acknowledges his debt to Nietzsche in the following passages:

> Here is an individual who is striving incessantly from the sphere of insecurity and the feeling of inferiority towards a godlike dominance over his environment, is struggling for his significance, is attempting to force it.

> The actual form of expression and the deepening of this guiding thought could also be designated as <u>will to power</u>. (Nietzsche). (5, p. 244).

> Much of our view of the enhancement of the self-esteem as the guiding fiction is included in Nietzsche's "will to power" and "will to seem." (5, p. 111).

(By "guiding fiction" Adler means the goal toward which the person is striving, even though the goal may be an exalted state impossible to achieve.)

Adler's "striving for perfection" is, like Nietz-
sche's will to power, a self-actualization psychology.
It finds its echo in the "organismic" or "holistic"
psychology of Kurt Goldstein (1878-1965).

> Self-actualization: this is Goldstein's
> master motive; in fact, it is the only mo-
> tive that the organism possess. What appear
> to be different drives such as hunger, sex,
> power, achievement, and curiosity are merely
> manifestations of the sovereign purpose of
> life, to actualize oneself. (84, p. 305).

Carl Roger's psychology is also single-motive
self-actualization. "The organism has one basic ten-
dency and striving—to actualize, maintain, and en-
hance the experiencing organism." (154, p. 487).
Embraced in this self-actualization drive are two
primary needs: positive regard from others, and self-
regard.

To each of these psychologies Nietzsche might
say, "Yes, this is just what I have been proclaiming
to the world. Striving for perfection and self-actua-
lization capture what I meant by will to power."[1]

In brief, Nietzsche sees all deliberate human
behavior as a search for a feeling of power, i.e., a
feeling of having attained the full realization of
one's potentialities. "Become what thou art!" This
awareness of excellence possessed is, by definition,
self-esteem. The superman is he who has achieved what
all are seeking.

---

[1]After Nietzsche's identification in the public
mind with anti-Semitism those who had been influenced
by his writings would be understandably reluctant to
acknowledge any Nietzschean parentage in their theo-
ries. Much of Adler's mention of Nietzsche was writ-
ten before the rise to power of Naziism.

CHAPTER VI

SELF-ESTEEM ROOTS OF SOME BASIC
HUMAN BEHAVIORS AND ATTITUDES

INTRODUCTION

In this chapter we offer the testimony of a variety of thinkers who have independently come to the conclusion that self-esteem is the key factor in a number of human phenomena of crucial consequence. So central is self-esteem to these human concerns that each of them can be defined in terms of self-esteem. Depression, the emotional illness that afflicts all of us at times, lightly and passingly as "the blues," or cripplingly as chronic melancholia, is, in essence, a condition of low self-esteem. Anxiety, the curse of our modern age, casting a pall over the lives of countless millions, is apprehension of impending loss of self-esteem. Neurotic symptoms, the hairshirt that spoils our enjoyment of modern luxuries, "have as their object the task of safe-guarding the patient's self-esteem." (Alfred Adler). Suicide, rising in incidence to become a leading cause of death, is most frequently caused by painfully low self-esteem with no perceived hope of recovery. Anger, the current American mood, according to some social critics, is a desire to restore self-esteem which has been wounded by another person or group. Violence and aggression, on the upsurge throughout the world, have roots in the desire to increase self-esteem at the expense of other human beings. Laughter and the appreciation of humor are expressions of pleasure resulting from a sudden increase of self-esteem. All of the foregoing are conclusions arrived at by thinkers from diverse backgrounds and ideological positions.

The preponderance of negative topics—depression, anxiety, etc.—arises from the fact that these are the ones that psychologists, who comprise the bulk of our witnesses, are most likely to analyze.

The combined insights of these thinkers gives a basic understanding of the nature of these behavioral problems, thus making the most necessary and fundamental contribution to the on-going solution to the problems.

Depression

After Abraham Lincoln broke his engagement to Mary Todd he fell victim to a mental depression that lasted several weeks. He describes his mental torment:

> "I am now the most miserable man living. If what I feel were equally distributed to the whole human family, there would not be one cheerful face on earth. Whether I shall be better I cannot tell. I awfully forbode I shall not. To remain as I am is impossible, I must die or be better. . . ." (75, p. 19).

Similar misery afflicts four to eight million Americans each year, severely enough to send them to a doctor or to keep them home from work for several days. Many millions more experience briefer and less intense feelings of "the blues," or "down in the dumps," or simply, "a low." The American Psychiatric Association names depression as the "most common form of mental disorder." One out of eight persons can expect to experience significant mental depression at some time during his life.

The condition received national publicity after Senator Thomas Eagleton, Democratic vice-presidential candidate in 1972, was revealed to have been hospitalized for treatment of mental depression. Among others suffering from this malady were some illustrious names: U. S. Presidents John Adams, James Madison and John Quincy Adams. Winston Churchill too went through several bouts with the "black dog of depression," with accompanying thoughts of suicide.

Dr. Bertram S. Brown, Director (1974) of the National Institute of Mental Health, describes the feeling of mental depression and its accompanying physical symptoms:

> One of the ways of looking at it that I find illuminating is to say it involves great feelings of helplessness, hopelessness and haplessness . . . . With severe depression, yes, there are physical symptoms and they're fairly well known.

For example, it's rare to have a serious depression without loss of appetite. Sometimes this sneaks up on the victim, so the doctor always asks about weight changes.

Another symptom is a change in sleep patterns. The most common one is when the person wakes up early in the morning for no apparent good reason. Or less often but just as significant, he or she has trouble falling asleep.

A third symptom is that depressed people feel aches and pains and complain about them more. They have chest pains, their head aches, their muscles hurt and their bones creak. (25, p. 37).

Setting the tone for much of the later clinical analysis of depression was Sigmund Freud's classic paper, <u>Mourning and Melancholia</u>. He describes the condition:

The distinguishing mental features of melancholia are a profoundly painful dejection, abrogation of interest in the outside world, loss of the capacity to love, inhibition of all activity, and a lowering of the self-regarding feelings to a degree that finds utterance in self-reproaches and self-revilings, and culminates in a delusional expectation of punishment. . . .   Now the melancholiac displays something else which is lacking in grief—an extraordinary fall in his self-esteem, an impoverishment of his ego on a grand scale. (56, p. 125-7).

Freud's followers have developed his insight that low self-esteem is the core of mental depression. Sandor Rado, one of the first Freudians to appreciate the centrality of self-esteem, sees it as the determining feature in depression, and also sees the inner psychic workings of depression as an attempt to regain self-esteem:

The most striking feature in the picture displayed by the symptoms of depressive conditions is the fall in self-esteem and self-satisfaction. . . .

173

Those predisposed to depression are, moreover, wholly reliant and dependent on other people for maintaining their self-esteem; they have not attained to the level of independence where self-esteem has its foundation in the subject's own achievements and critical judgment. They have a sense of security and comfort only when they feel themselves loved, esteemed, supported, and encouraged. . . .

Thus we come to realize that the process of melancholia represents an attempt at reparation (cure) on a grand scale, carried out with an iron psychological consistence. It is designed to revive the ego's self-regard, which has been annihilated by the loss of love. . .
(147, p. 422, p. 435).

The precise workings of this process are not relevant to our main point here: severely and chronically depleted self-esteem is the essence of melancholy, and the self-revilings of the depressed one are an involuted manuever to regain self-esteem. (In a subsequent chapter we will see that self-deprecation has several ego payoffs.)

Otto Fenichel develops the theme that loss of self-esteem in depression may be due to loss of social approval ("external supplies") or to failure to live up to one's own ideals ("internal supplies"):

In the phenomenology of depression, a greater or lesser loss of self-esteem is in the foreground. The subjective formula is "I have lost everything: now the world is empty," if the loss of self-esteem is mainly due to a loss of external supplies, or "I have lost everything because I do not deserve anything," if it is mainly due to a loss of internal supplies from the superego. (49, p. 391).

Fenichel sums up his analysis by noting that loss of self-esteem is not merely the key factor in depression, but is depression. Depression is depressed self-esteem. "It has been stated that depression is a

174

loss of self-esteem, either a complete breakdown of all self-esteem or a partial one intended as a warning against the possibility of a complete one." (49, p. 396).

Several Freudians have arrived at this same conclusion: "Jacobson adopted and expanded this terminology. She, too, as with Rado, Fenichel, Bibring and others, found that lowered self-esteem represented the core of depression." (132, p. 36).

Anthropologist Ernest Becker develops the same theme in his analysis of the genesis of depression, and cites Freudian Bibring and anti-Freudian Alfred Adler as holding much the same view:

> If the ego is the basis for action, and if a warm feeling of self-value must pervade one's acts, then it is only a step to focusing on the really crucial dynamic of a breakdown in action, namely, the undermining of the individual's sense of self-value. Sap the individual's sense of self-righteousness and he is drained of his life-predication. This is the all-pervasive "slipping-away," the unspeakably, unbelievably "Frightful"— to use an apt word of Binswanger's. Adler very early saw the importance of self-esteem in depression. More recently, Bibring signaled a truly radical break with the older theory in psychoanalysis, by postulating that an undermining of self-esteem was the primary focus in depression, . . . (17, p. 110).

What occasions the loss of self-esteem which constitutes depression? Freud stressed "loss of a love-object," later Freudians emphasize the ego's failure to please an over-demanding super-ego, some commentators mention both causes, and still others make the point—with which we concur—that any loss can trigger depression. That is, loss of money, of love, of health, prestige, etc., or the failure of a movement with which the subject identified, the disparagement of a set of values espoused by the subject— indeed, any imaginable set-back—can be the triggering cause for depression.

175

Does it then follow that any loss or setback will produce depression? Each person need only consult his own experience to answer "no." When faced with a loss or defeat as a fait accompli we customarily and quickly hit upon some saving and consoling consideration——"after all, it's only money, there's more where that came from," "he was promoted instead of me because of his scheming and ingratiating himself with the boss," "I still have my integrity," and an infinite variety of other ingenious face-saving devices. Some are rationalization, but others may be valid transcendant bits of wisdom. Another shield against depression is the emotion of anger. If we see another as having unjustly caused our reversal we feel a surge of determination to "get even." This at least forestalls feelings of depression.

Why is it that the same set-back may produce depression in one person, anger in another, a philosophical "well, you can't win 'em all" in another, and wry amusement in still another? The full——and usually imponderable——answer depends upon many factors: the extent of the individual's ego-involvement in the area (money, let us say) in which the reversal occurred, his estimation of the possibility of a recoup, the depth and variety of his other self-esteem resources, his past life experiences relevant to the current situation, etc. Generally however, the depressive has a self-esteem that is vulnerable because of excessive dependency upon external circumstances, (this paucity of inner resources would be equivalent to a too-weak superego, in Freudian terms), or because of excessive demands upon self (too harsh a superego).

Anxiety

Anxiety seems to be the dominant fact——and is threatening to become the dominant cliche——of modern life. It shouts in the headlines, laughs nervously at cocktail parties, nags from advertisements, speaks suavely in the board room, whines from the stage, clatters from the Wall Street ticker, jokes with fake youthfulness on the golf course and whispers in privacy each day before the shaving mirror and the dressing table.
Time, March 31, 1961

176

In the behavioral and medical sciences, theoretical and empirical interest in anxiety parallels the popular concern. Anxiety is found as a central explanatory concept in almost all contemporary theories of personality, and it is regarded as a principal causative agent for such diverse behavioral consequences as insomnia, immoral and sinful acts, instances of creative self-expression, debilitating psychological and psychosomatic symptoms, and idiosyncratic mannerisms of endless variety. Charles Spielberger, Anxiety and Behavior.

There is no question that the problem of anxiety is a nodal point at which the most various and important questions converge, a riddle whose solution would be bound to throw a flood of light on our whole mental existence. Sigmund Freud, Introductory Lectures on Psychoanalysis

Time magazine finds anxiety to be the dominant fact of modern life, Soren Kierkegaard found it to be the dominant fact of his world of a century ago, and a thousand years ago Arab philosopher Ala ibn Hazm of Cordova, "the greatest scholar and creative genius of Moslem Spain," reports on his observations of human behavior in his day: "no one is moved to act or moved to speak a single word who does not hope by means of this action or word to release anxiety from his spirit." (172, p. 4). Psychoanalyst Karen Horney of 20th century New York agrees with Ibn Hazm of 11th century Spain that the principal human psychic endeavor is to escape anxiety.

It is not difficult to discern the self-esteem roots of anxiety. Anxiety is fear of some impending loss, pain, humiliation, etc. Some psychologists distinguish between fear and anxiety on the basis that fear is concerned with a known, concrete danger, whereas anxiety is about some vague, unknown threat. Generally such is the case, but in common usage anxiety is also applied to situations where the threat is of a definite, known nature. Joe is anxious about the results of his civil service test; the impending loss is quite clear—he may fail and not get that government job, as well as being humiliated. But definite

or vague, the impending disaster means we will lose
some excellence we now possess or hope to possess.
Loss of money, health, friends, prestige, or reputa-
tion means a loss of self-esteem. Loss of future
prospects, such as getting a scholarship to that pres-
tigious university, means a loss of self-esteem.
Mother is anxious about the safety of her vacationing
children; any disaster befalling them is, through her
identification with them, a personal disaster for her.

But are we not also anxious about impending phy-
sical pain, quite apart from any self-esteem consider-
ations? Sometimes we generate a bit of anxiety about
a necessary visit to the dentist, dredging up vivid
memories about that excruciating moment when the drill
hits a nerve. Actually, it is difficult to say how
much of our anxiety is concerned with the physical
pain, and how much is concerned with the possibility
of humiliation should we over-react to the pain. A
screech, a whimper, a jump, would mean a loss of face.
"My six-year old kid can take pain better than that
guy," the dentist later remarks to his beautiful re-
ceptionist.

There seems to be no difficulty in admitting that
in some cases we may develop anxiety over the prospect
of physical pain, apart from accompanying loss of
self-esteem—we have concluded in a previous chapter
that human behavior is motivated by the desire for
sensual pleasure (including its negative aspect, the
desire to avoid pain) as well as by the desire for
self-esteem. However, a few moments consideration of
situations that cause us anxiety will reveal that the
prospect of physical pain plays a minor role.

Several psychologists and psychiatrists have
observed the fact that the essence of anxiety is an
apprehension of some threat to one's self-esteem.
Harry Stack Sullivan, after describing the physical
symptoms of anxiety, remarks that these symptoms seem
to be aiming at the protection of self-esteem:

> They mark the point in the course of
> events at which something disjunctive, some-
> thing that tends to pull away from the other
> fellow, has first appeared or has suddenly
> increased. They signal a change from rela-
> tively uncomplicated movement toward a pre-

sumptively common goal to a protecting of
one's self-esteem . . . (190, p. 378).

Stanley Coopersmith, in his <u>Antecedents of Self-
Esteem</u>, summarizes Sullivan's thought on anxiety:

> The individual is continually guarding him-
> self against loss of self-esteem, for it is
> this loss that produces the feelings of
> distress that are elsewhere termed anxiety.
> Anxiety is an interpersonal phenomenon that
> occurs when an individual expects to be or
> is indeed rejected or demeaned by himself or
> others. (35, p. 32).

Coopersmith adds his own analysis of anxiety,
which is essentially the same as Sullivan's, with the
exception that it is not limited to "interpersonal"
situations:

> . . . the significance of the threat that
> disturbs the individual lies in its negative
> implications for his self-esteem, and the
> attendant experience of anxiety is marked by
> feelings of inadequacy and helplessness. . .
> (35, p. 248).

Carl Rogers too sees anxiety as arising from a
threat to self-esteem:

> He [Rogers] stated that the self-concept
> includes only those characteristics of the
> individual that he is aware of and over
> which he believes he exercises control.
> There is a basic need to maintain and en-
> hance the self. Threat to the organization
> of the self-concept produces anxiety.
> (45, p. 406).

William Silverberg, in <u>Toward a Theory of Person-
ality and Neurosis</u>, notes:

> Actual injury to self-esteem produces the
> emotion of <u>humiliation</u>, the intensity of
> which corresponds to the extent of the in-
> jury. The perception of an impending blow
> to self-esteem produces anxiety, as in the
> case of apprehended somatic danger.
> (166, p. 68).

Camilla M. Anderson, psychiatrist and author of Beyond Freud and Saints, Sinners and Psychiatry, offers the same insight:

> Anxiety is the feeling produced when there is a sensed threat to one's self image, either to his physical self image or to his psychological or grandiose self image. (9, p. 367).

Neuroses

In an investigation into mental and emotional health among persons living in rural settings, psychiatrist Alexander H. Leighton, Cornell University professor, and his team of researchers examined 20,000 inhabitants of the Atlantic coast region of Canada and concluded that only 15% of the people could be considered emotionally well. Another Cornell University survey studied the opposite end of the "population density" spectrum—people living in the heart of New York City—and found the same level of emotional health: about one person in seven could be considered "symptom free." (27, p. 12). The jestingly defiant "we are all a little bit neurotic" may not be far from the truth.

Depression and anxiety are the symptoms that most frequently move people to seek professional help. We have already presented testimony of psychiatrists and psychologists who consider depression and anxiety to be self-esteem problems. Narcissism, "a leading topic of research in psychoanalytic circles," is a character disorder that is sending an increasing number of people to psychiatrists. "Ours is an age of narcissism," says social critic Christopher Lasch. The narcissist operates on the principle of his own personal "divine right of kings," a principle that he would explicitly disavow with the same fervor that he implicitly embraces it. His desires are raised to the dignity of rights, and any person or group which interferes with those "rights" is guilty of lese majeste. Narcissism is the desire for self-esteem, run wild. All of us are would-be narcissists by nature, but the hard knocks of reality have forced us to trim our self-estimates and demands upon others to more modest proportions. The person recognized by psychiatrists as a narcissist has not made such concessions to reality.

Freud characterizes narcissism as "the ego's victorious assertion of its own invulnerability," an attitude to be celebrated as far as harsh reality will permit. The "narcissist" has not learned the limits of that celebration. Pointing out the self-esteem root of narcissism is Otto Fenichel:

> The longing for the oceanic feeling of primary narcissism can be called the "narcissistic need." "Self-esteem" is the awareness of how close the individual is to the original omnipotence. (49, p. 40).

It is currently the vogue among writers on the subject to characterize narcissism as a lack of true self-esteem, indeed as a basic self-hatred. It is true that the narcissist is deficient in self-esteem if self-esteem is understood as a justified high self-estimate. But the essence of narcissism is a promiscuous eagerness for unlimited self-esteem, justified or unjustified.

Ego Defense Mechanisms

Prominent in the Pandora's box of neurotic symptoms are the so-called ego defense mechanisms. Discernment of these protective strategies of the human unconscious was one of Freud's most significant contributions to psychology. Repression, the most important of these strategies, is the refusal to recognize that we are motivated by desires which we consider unworthy. Humiliating experiences might similarly be repressed. Freud recognized that repression is an attempt to protect self-esteem:

> Repression, as we have said, proceeds from the ego; we might say with greater precision: from the self-respect of the ego. The very impressions, experiences, impulses and desires that one man indulges or at least consciously elaborates in his mind will be rejected with the utmost indignation by another, or stifled at once even before they enter consciousness. (56, p. 116).

Some psychologists see the full sweep of ego defense mechanisms as attempts to protect self-esteem. As mentioned in a previous section of this book, Ernest Hilgard, in his presidential address to the American Psychological Association in 1949, voiced this view:

> Another way of looking at the mechanisms is to see them as bolstering self-esteem through self-deception. . . . The obvious interpretation is that the need for self-deception arises because of a more fundamental need to maintain or to restore self-esteem. Anything belittling to the self is to be avoided. (89, p. 376-7).

Percival Symonds, in The Ego and The Self, sees the function of the ego defense mechanisms as not only protecting self-esteem but sometimes also enhancing it:

> The so-called defense mechanisms are really self-defense mechanisms and oftentimes their purpose is as much self-enhancement as it is a defense against those forces which might destroy self-esteem. . . . Repression is necessary for most persons so that they can keep their dignity and self-esteem. Rationalization, denial, and projection all help the individual to avoid facing unpleasant facts about himself. (177, p. 109).

Ernest Becker perceives neurosis as a pattern of self-esteem protecting techniques that restrict one's effectiveness as a person:

> "Neurosis" becomes easily understandable when we consider idiosyncratic socialization. Each individual learns a different style of maintaining his feeling of positive value. . . . Neurosis, then, represents a constriction of action by the rules one has learned for keeping his anxiety to a minimum, and keeping his feeling of warm self-righteousness at a maximum. Neurosis is a constriction of action possibilities by the constitutive modes of maintaining a positively valued self. (19, p. 185).

Some Other Neuroses

The self-esteem roots of paranoia are traced by Becker in his book The Birth and Death of Meaning. A person who feels insignificant and unnoticed can quickly make himself a person of importance, enjoying the limelight on center stage, by believing that he is the object of a conspiracy to "get him."

> Paranoia. . . is a kind of backhanded way of maintaining self-value. . . . Consider an insignificant dweller of New York City who rides the subways unnoticed day after day, and returns home unappreciated night after night. By peopling his world with others who actively hate or dislike him, or who even plan malevolence against him he becomes a center of attention. He comes to exist as a person: "I am someone to reckon with." (19, p. 186).

Compulsive hand-washing makes its small contribution to self-esteem:

> Take the compulsive hand washer. Into his system has been built a series of rules for maintaining a feeling of goodness and cleanliness that he may have violated (say by masturbation), or fear violating. Incessant hand washing becomes a means of protecting his self-esteem (19, p. 186).

Another neurotic symptom, masochism, arises from lowered self-esteem, according to a recent study. Following is the complete report from Time, July 17, 1978:

> What causes masochistic behavior? University of Southern California Psychologist Gary Frieden, 25, thinks he knows the answer: low self-esteem. In a series of tests on college students, he found that lowering self-esteem leads normal people to choose suffering and painful tasks.
>
> Frieden told 40 students they were helping out in a "Patty Hearst simulation" and could choose a simple task (listening to

a propaganda tape) or a more humiliating and painful one (being blindfolded and bound, and given electric shocks). All students were given personality tests. Those whose self-esteem was bolstered by praise for their performance chose the tape. But students who were derided (sample comment: "It's clear you really don't have very good social skills") overwhelmingly chose to be bound and shocked.

In another study, Frieden managed to delude some students into thinking they were masochists. Asked to choose between the tape and the shock, they picked the shock by a significant margin. Three-quarters of the shock group even agreed to eat a dead worm Frieden dangled in front of them. The reason, he thinks, is that they were anxious to learn if they were indeed masochists. In general, Frieden concludes, it is surprisingly easy to push normal people toward masochism. Says he: "When feeling bad about themselves, people actively choose to suffer." The good news is that none of the students received an electric shock or dined on worm. Frieden stopped the test when the newborn masochists made their choice.[1]

But why should people with lowered self-esteem be more likely to "choose to suffer"? In the context of this study, choosing to be bound, shocked, and eat a worm, offered the subject an opportunity to boost his self-esteem by being the center of the stage and, in his own estimation, a small hero in this little drama. Others would gasp in amazement and begrudging admiration at the courage of his choice. An acquaintance of my high school days achieved local reknown for his specialty: bringing a live, wriggling snake to parties and biting it in half before a gasping, giggling audience.

---

[1] A disturbing feature of this study, with far-reaching implications which need not be spelled out for the reader, is the ease with which our level of self-esteem can be manipulated by others, with resultant change in our behavior. To what extent is our behavior already being "engineered"?

Alfred Adler sees all neurotic symptoms in this same vein—as devices to protect or increase the self-esteem of the subject:

> . . . Adler as a psychiatrist, wrote in terms of the neurotic patient; it was the neurotic whom Adler showed as striving for enhancement of his self-esteem or for the safeguarding of it. When he generalized from the neurotic, he described the normal individual as behaving in the same way, only less clearly so and to a lesser degree. (5, p. 101).

Thus the neurotic is the normal individual writ large; his self-esteem ploys are more obvious and exaggerated—and often self-defeating. He is so obsessed with particular strategies for self-esteem protection that he neglects more productive means for increasing self-esteem. Two basic techniques the neurotic uses are depreciation and withdrawal. In the first, the neurotic attempts to prove his own superiority by disparaging or degrading other people. The second technique aims at avoiding any life situation that might prove humiliating. Adlerian psychiatrists Shulman and Mosak sum up Adler's views:

> All symptoms are seen as serving as safeguards for self-esteem or as excuses. One way to accomplish this is through aggression, specifically through: depreciation of others, as in sexual perversion; accusation of others for imagined faults, etc.; and self-accusation and neurotic guilt.
>
> Another way of safeguarding is through "distance" for which four categories are recognized: "moving backward" which includes suicide, agoraphobia, compulsive blushing, migraine, anorexia nervosa, etc.; "standing still" as in psychic impotence, psychogenic asthma, anxiety attacks, compulsions, etc.; "hesitation and back-and-forth" as in all methods of killing time such as procrastination, compulsions, pathological pedantry; and "construction of obstacles," primarily psychosomatic symptoms. (163, p. 80).

185

"Self-accusation and neurotic guilt" are in fact indirect attacks against others, especially parents, even though the parents may be long dead. Thus the neurotic subconsciously aims at exonerating himself from responsibility for his failures, and also gains a measure of revenge——"see what you have done to me!"

Prominent among the forms of neurotic behavior which safeguard the superiority fiction are cursing oneself, reproaching oneself, self-torture, and suicide. This may seem strange, until we realize that the whole arrangement of the neurosis follows the trait of self-torture, that the neurosis is a self-torturing device for the purpose of enhancing the self and depreciating the immediate environment. And indeed the first stirrings of the aggression drive directed against one's own person originate from a situation in which the child wants to hurt the parents or wants to attract their attention more effectively. (5, p. 271).

In short, "all neurotic symptoms have as their object the task of safeguarding the patient's self-esteem. . ." (5, p. 263).

Finally, from psychologist Gordon Allport, additional testimony pointing to the self-esteem roots of neuroses. Allport, "who received virtually every professional honor that psychologists have to offer," says:

The very nature of the neurotic disorder is tied to pride. If the sufferer is hypersensitive, resentful, captious, he may be indicating a fear that he will not appear to advantage in competitive situations where he wants to show his worth. . . . If he is over-scrupulous and self-critical, he may be endeavoring to show how praiseworthy he really is. (7, p. 95).

Suicide

The latest statistics show that suicide is the third leading cause of death among American women between 15 and 29. The rate

in this age group has more than doubled in
the past ten years. No wonder that medical
authorities describe the situation as an
epidemic.
(Harper's Bazaar, June, 1976, p. 68)

There has been considerable publicity and justi-
fiable alarm over the increasing thousands of Ameri-
cans who fall victim to homicide each year, but there
does not seem to be a corresponding realization that
each year suicide claims thousands more victims than
does homicide. These are the reported suicides; those
unreported for fear of family disgrace, and those
which are officially listed as automobile accidents
(researchers offer evidence that suggests that a sig-
nificant percentage of fatalities in automobile acci-
dents are actually deliberate self-destruction) would
run the yearly toll far higher.

It was Freud's theory that the melancholic person
is disposed to suicide because, ironically, he wishes
to kill someone else and that impulse has now turned
in upon himself. His subconscious will not allow him
to admit his hostile feelings toward those others,
usually his closest loved ones, whom he feels are
responsible for his miseries. However these murderous
inclinations must have an outlet and so are directed
toward self. "It is true we have long known that no
neurotic harbors thoughts of suicide which are not
murderous impulses against others redirected upon
himself. . ." (56, p. 133).

The "murderous impulse redirected toward self"
part of this theory is not widely accepted today, and
at best has limited usefulness, inasmuch as in Freud's
view the id in everyone is seething with murderous
impulses. In desire, "we are all murderers," he says.
However, Freud's insight that melancholy, depression,
is a usual pre-condition for suicide is recognized by
almost all writers on the subject. And depression, as
we have seen in a previous section, is a condition of
low self-esteem.

Freud offers further hints that loss of self-
esteem is the necessary cause of suicide. "For the
ego," he says, "living means being loved by the super-
ego." "Being loved by the superego" is self-approval,
self-esteem. When the ego finds that it is not loved

187

by the superego it gives itself up to death. Otto Fenichel develops this Freudian theory more fully:

> From the standpoint of the ego, suicide is, first of all, an expression of the fact that the terrible tension the pressure of the superego induces has become unbearable. Frequently the passive thought of giving up any active fighting seems to express itself; the loss of self-esteem is so complete that any hope of regaining it is abandoned. "The ego sees itself deserted by its super-ego and lets itself die". To have a desire to live evidently means to feel a certain self-esteem, to feel supported by the protective forces of a superego. When this feeling vanishes, the original annihilation of the deserted hungry baby reappears. (49, p. 400).

The same theme of debased self-esteem conducing to suicide is voiced by Joost Meerloo in Suicide and Mass Suicide"

> There exists a subtle relation between over-emphasized prestige, honor and suicidal tendency. The concepts of honor and shame and losing face belong to man's magic thinking. In the magic realm man feels continually judged by his co-citizens. He evaluates himself by proxy. What the other fellow thinks about him burns deeply in his soul. Dishonorable judgment by others has to be met literally with rage or self-destruction. (198, p. 147).

Arriving at the same conclusion on the basis of their experimental research are psychiatrists Howard Kaplan and Alex Pokorny of the Baylor College of Medicine:

> The results were consistent with the view that suicidal responses are attempts to avoid self-devaluing experiences, attack the basis of one's self-rejection, and/or evoke self-enhancing experiences. (104, p. 1213).

According to the above conclusion, suicide is not

only for the purpose of escaping the pain of an intolerably low self-esteem, but also may hold out to the sufferer a hope of positive ego-enhancement. The authors do not elaborate on this aspect, but Alfred Adler has suggested the "positive" values that the victim may see in his suicide—he becomes a center of attention; he exercises a god-like power of life and death, and he gets revenge on those whom he considers responsible for his suffering (they'll be sorry when they see what they've done to me).

> In cases of suicide we can make similar observations. After long training[1] such individuals forego any interest in life and are filled with the thought of attracting general attention through their suicide and of achieving thus, like a murderer, a heightened feeling of superiority. ("I have done what not everyone could do. Formerly nobody took any notice of me; but now. .") To be master over life and death brings them close to God, as it does the murderer who disposes of the lives of others. (5, p. 151).

And the motive of revenge, a form of self-esteem one-up-manship:

> Reduced to its simplest form, the life style of the potential suicide is characterized by the fact that he hurts others by dreaming himself into injuries or by administering them to himself. One will seldom go wrong in determining against whom the attack is aimed when one has found who is actually affected most by it. (6, p. 61).

Several other authors have come to the conclusion that loss of self-esteem is the triggering cause for suicide. Howard Bogard in <u>Collected Thoughts of a Suicidologist</u> says:

---

[1]What Adler means in this context by "long training" is not clear, but in the light of his other comments we assume he means "training in being a spoiled-child type person."

Overinvestment in work, career, or for that matter a love object, always tenuously masks underlying feelings of worthlessness. To feel worthless is to feel unloved and unlovable and, as such, better said by Kierkegaard "we stand denuded and see the intolerable abyss of ourselves." Thus with no self-esteem and with no narcissism, why live? (208, p. 30).

Herbert Hendin in The Cry for Help observes that the suicide potential of a personal disaster depends upon how heavily the subject had invested his ego in the area in which the loss occurred:

. . . when the depression is in reaction to the loss of a person, the relationship often has been a markedly dependent and symbiotic one and one in which the patient's self-esteem was contingent upon the relationship.

I can say something of several recent situations that I have seen where serious suicide attempts followed sudden financial failure. The response to the loss of money was similar to that of the loss of a person in the collapsing effect it had on the self-esteem of these patients. . . . The man who loses a large amount of money and reacts with a suicide attempt thus will often differ from the man who doesn't in that his self-esteem is more dependent on his financial position. (87, p. 184).

Another study brings out two additional points of considerable interest: the suicidal person tends to evaluate other people more highly than does the normal person; and suicide is not likely to occur if the individual has some hope of regaining his lost self-esteem. Dr. Charles Neuringer made a study of males in veterans' hospitals; one group he classified as normal, a second group had psychosomatic difficulties, and the third group had made suicide attempts. None were psychotic. The suicidal patients showed a significantly lower self-esteem than did either the normal or the psychosomatic patients. Also, the suicidal patients rated "other people" significantly higher than did the other two groups, thus exacerbating their own low self-esteem by comparison.

A low self-concept has been one of the axiomatic assumptions of those who speculate about the conditions nurturing suicidal decisions (Farberow, 1950). What is surprising is the extent of the negative self-evaluation. One might expect that the psychosomatic subjects would also have a low opinion of themselves. However, they cannot (in this study) be distinguished from the normal subjects in terms of the level of positiveness of self-appraisal. . . .

It was of interest to note that the suicidal individual tended to perceive other people in a much more positive light than did the psychosomatic and normal subjects. These latter groups did not perceive others as being essentially different from themselves. . . .

The gap of divergency between self and others may be most critical for the conditions leading to suicidal behavior. The suicidal person seems to perceive himself as being constantly "one down" when he compares himself to others. They seem to be ever so better, more active and stronger than he. The possibility of closing this gap (i.e., coming up to their level) may be perceived as impossible, and the suicidal person falls back feeling defeated and hopeless. (138, p. 104).

Neuringer's research suggests an answer to the question "why is it that most low self-esteem persons do not commit suicide?" The suggested answer is quite in accord with common sense: if the severely depressed person sees some possibility of recouping his crushing loss he will not resort to suicide. No matter how depressed, if he can "see light at the end of the tunnel" he will struggle on. Where there is hope, life will continue.

Another possible deterrent to suicide, equally in accord with common sense, is a deep conviction on the part of the desperate person that suicide would not mean an end to his pain but instead would worsen it. Examples of this would be persons who whole-heartedly accept the tenets of certain religions.

191

What we have said thus far about suicide applies to "mental depression" suicide, by far the most common type in modern cultures. Another type, "heroic" suicides—kamikaze actions, common in wartime in some cultures—seems also to be motivated by self-esteem considerations. Gregory Rochlin, professor of psychiatry at the Harvard Medical School, develops the thesis that both the heroic and the despair type of suicide are motivated by the individual's feeling, conscious or subconscious, that his self-esteem interests are best served by his death:

> The common denominator in suicide which the hero shares with the villain is in the wish to quit life. The aim in either case is the sacrifice of oneself. And it is dictated by feeling less worthy than if the self were preserved. What may appear to be a resignation to death, either through suicide or a heroic death, is in actuality a dread of the degradation of self from which there is not expectation of recovery. The need to redeem oneself from ignominy is the compelling and governing wish. (153, p. 15).

"Heroic" suicide aims at avoiding the disgrace of possible defeat for one's own party, or personal disgrace from being considered too cowardly to accept the challenge, and additionally offers the self-esteem boosting prospect of dying a hero.

The usual type of suicide, "despair" suicide, is also self-esteem motivated, according to the consensus of experts we have considered. It is an attempt to escape the excruciating pain of a severely depressed self-esteem, when no possibility of regaining lost self-esteem is seen, and may be additionally motivated by self-esteem "fringe benefits" of notoriety and revenge upon "loved ones."

Anger

The United States has the highest standard of living in its history, and close to the highest standard of living in the world today, but ironically the mood of its people seems to be a rising tide of anger. A New Yorker cartoon captured America's mood: two doting young parents are looking admiringly at their

192

baby in his cradle, "oh darling, he said his first words!" The infant, with gritted gums, is muttering "Kill, kill!" Property owners are angry over sky-rocketing taxes; women's libbers are angry over the past and continuing put-down of women in America; minorities are angry over being treated as second class citizens; conservatives are angry with the trend of social and political events, convinced that their own government is knuckling under to the communists; mainline religions have their liberal and conservative factions who are angry at each other; abortionists and anti-abortionists are angry at each other; ecologists are angry at big industry; rapists, we are told, are motivated not so much by lust as anger; terrorists are angry at almost everything and everyone.

What is the root cause of all this anger? Consider your own moments of anger; is it not true that you can usually trace the source to an insult, a put-down, by someone or by some situation? Whenever someone else says or does something that belittles us we are inclined to get angry. Experience may have taught us to overlook the slight or to control annoyance, but the urge to anger is there. It seems safe to say that any <u>deliberate</u> slight, put-down, insult, disparagement, directed toward us is productive of anger, or the impulse to anger. And what is the nature of a slight, an insult, put-down, etc.? They are all words to describe some action or speech or omission by another that tells us "you are not as worthy of respect as you think you are." I am passed over for promotion and the coveted position given to another—this angers me if I thought myself better suited for the promotion than was the fortunate man. The employer's action has said otherwise—"you are not as worthy as you think you are." This is a threat to my self-esteem.

But isn't there such a thing as just plain outrage at evil conduct, without bringing self-esteem into the picture? Someone may say "I found myself angry when reading of Nixon's shenanigans when he held the highest office in the land—his arrogant use of power, his attempt to obstruct justice, his lying to the American people. Surely I was not angry because of some affront to my self-esteem. Rather, my anger was simply outrage at evil conduct. If you will, righteous anger." In response, we suggest that there were two or three elements in Nixon's conduct which

193

may have affronted the self-esteem of the speaker. First, the "arrogant use of power." An arrogant person is saying, in effect, "you, the public, have neither the intelligence to discover my peccadilloes nor the effectiveness to do anything about it." Second, having someone lie to us is also an affront to our self-esteem. We have been "played for a sucker," taken advantage of, used. Our intelligence has been insulted. Also, a large element in righteous anger is the fact that the offender has flouted a moral code that we consider important, and in so doing he is telling us "your views in this matter are of little value; your judgment in this important matter is erroneous. Further, I have little regard for your opinion of me." Finally, the fact that Nixon seemed to be "getting away with it" was a further affront to many. It pointed up an inequality—"I, or the little people with whom I identify, could not get away with such conduct, why should he?" Inequality, when we come out on the short end of it, is by definition a lack of excellence in ourselves in this particular matter. In the present case, it is a lack of power in the one who could not "get away with it." Awareness of this lack is an affront to our self-esteem.

Why would some people not be angered by the Nixon episode? Possibly they had doubts that Nixon was as guilty as portrayed, or felt that what he did was not really so outrageous, perhaps was even justified under the circumstances. Or perhaps the whole episode touched their lives so tangentially that they had not strong feelings about it. Others might take the prevalent European view: "So what else is new—one expects politicians to behave thus."

The Nixon episode serves to illustrate the source of righteous anger in general: when someone "puts down" a person or group or cause or value with which we identify, he has put us down.

Even though we concede that whenever we are angry, the source has been an affront to our self-esteem, does it follow that any perceived affront to our self-esteem will make us angry? In other words, even though insult is the necessary cause for anger, is it also a necessitating cause for anger? Experience indicates not. We have seen in movies and TV programs the convincing behavior of the victims when

194

bank robbers burst into the bank armed with machine guns and roughly order everyone to lie down on the floor. This callous disregard for the victims' feelings and personal dignity does not arouse their anger but rather fear and eager compliance. The victims realize that any attempt to "strike back" would likely mean death. If anger even becomes incipient, it is smothered in fear. In anger there is always the urge to strike back, to get even and in this situation such a possibility is out of the question. Hence no anger. Of course there are some individuals who would become angry even in this situation, either because of a lack of grasp of the situation, or because they saw some hope of verbally or physically striking back. Relevant here is the remark by Aristotle (Rhetoric, II,2) and Aquinas (Summa Theologica, I-II, Q. 46, a. 1, corp.) that injury arouses anger in the injured party only if he has the desire and hope for revenge.

This element in anger of wanting to "get even" suggests that an accurate definition of anger might be "a surge of determination to repair an injury to self-esteem by injuring the person responsible." Of course this urge may never be carried out, inhibited as it usually is by other considerations. The repair to self-esteem is accomplished by the fact that by injuring the other (physically or verbally) we have to this degree asserted our superiority over him. He is no longer "one up" on us.

Testimony of Others Regarding
Self-Esteem Roots of Anger

Aristotle's definition of anger harmonizes well with the previous discussion:

> Anger may be defined as an impulse, accompanied by pain, to a conspicuous revenge for a conspicuous slight directed without justification towards what concerns oneself or towards what concerns one's friends. (207, Bk. II, ch. 2)

The key element here is "a conspicuous slight." A slight, conveying to the recipient the message "you are not worthy of much respect," is offensive to self-esteem. As Aristotle says, "slighting is the actively entertained opinion of something as obviously of no

importance." Aristotle points out that we are most
angered when insulted in those areas of our heaviest
self-esteem investment; and especially if that heavy
investment is a bit shaky:

> . . . those who are eager to win fame as
> philosophers get angry with those who show
> contempt for their philosophy; those who
> pride themselves on their appearance get
> angry with those who show contempt for their
> appearance; and so on in other cases. We
> feel particularly angry on this account if
> we suspect that we are in fact, or that
> people think we are, lacking completely or
> to an effective extent in the qualities in
> question. (207, Bk. II. ch. 3).

But if our self-esteem is deeply solid, we are
less likely to become angry:

> For when we are convinced that we excel in
> the qualities for which we are jeered at, we
> can ignore the jeering. (ibid).

This explains why we are so eager to deny that
the other person has angered us ("no, of course I'm
not angry," we say testily). Subconsciously we rea-
lize that to be easily angered is an admission of the
shakiness of our self-esteem.

The same analysis of anger is offered by Thomas
Aquinas. He poses the question "whether the sole
motive of anger is slight or contempt?" Here, slight
and contempt are used to translate the Latin parvi-
pensio, "thinking little of," "belittling." Extract-
ing only the most relevant parts of Aquinas' lengthy
treatment:

> I answer that, All the causes of anger
> are reduced to slight. For slight is of
> three kinds, as stated in the Rhetoric,
> namely, contempt, despiteful treatment, that
> is, hindering one from doing one's will, and
> insolence: and all motives of anger are
> reduced to these three. (11, I-II, Q. 47,
> a. 2. corp.).

Also quoting with approval the opinion of Aristotle is a more contemporary witness, former U.S. Attorney General Ramsey Clark. He believes that the universal cause of revolutionary activity is anger aroused by perceived inequality. And inequality, as we have said before, is a threat to the self-esteem of the person or group who see themselves as the victims.

> Aristotle told us that the chief and universal cause of the revolutionary impulse is the desire for equality. I agree with him. What outrages an individual more than a sense of being the victim in inequality, of injustice?
>
> The deprivations which occur in the whole range of subjective and objective activities in society over a long period of time create rage. This anger can manifest itself in a loss of control and thus in a state of lawlessness. (29, p. 320).

Prominent black activists have repeatedly affirmed that the cause of "black rage" is the constant affronts to their human dignity that blacks have suffered in this country. On the scope of black anger we have the testimony of black psychologists William H. Grier and Price M. Cobbs:

> People bear all they can and, if required, bear even more. But if they are black in present-day America they have been asked to shoulder too much. They have had all they can stand. They will be harried no more. Turning from their tormentors, they are filled with rage.
>
> The growing anger of Negroes is frightening to white America. There is a feeling of betrayal and undeserved attack. White people have responded with a rage of their own. . . .
>
> And of the things that need knowing, none is more important than that all blacks are angry. White Americans seem not to recognize it. They seem to think that all the trouble is caused by only a few "extre-

mists." They ought to know better. We have
talked to many Negroes under the most inti-
mate circumstances and we know better.
(82, p. 4).

The core reason for this anger is the affront to
personal dignity offered by inequality and demeaning
treatment. Malcolm X elaborates on this:

She [America] has not only deprived us of
the right to be a citizen, she has deprived
us of the right to be human beings, the
right to be recognized and respected as men
and women. In this country the black can be
fifty years old and he is still a "boy."

All of our people have the same goals,
the same objective. That objective is free-
dom, justice, equality. All of us want
recognition and respect as human beings. We
don't want to be integrationists. Nor do we
want to be separationists. We want to be
human beings. Integration is only a method
that is used by some groups to obtain free-
dom, justice, equality or human dignity.

We have to keep in mind at all times
that we are not fighting for integration,
nor are we fighting for separation. We are
fighting for recognition as human beings.
(122, p. 50).

Also fighting for recognition are women's lib-
bers, with their own share of rage against American
society, according to feminist leaders. And the
source of their anger is the same as that of the black
militants: they feel they have been treated as second-
class citizens. The nitty-gritty of this anger is not
pique at getting less material goods, or jobs that pay
less, or having less power and influence than the male
white. All these things are important, yes, but the
core source of their anger is being considered and
treated as somehow inferior. This constant belittling
of human dignity is what infuriates, and the matter of
jobs, money and power assume importance primarily as
symbols of human worth, value and dignity. The case
is well stated by Ann Nietzke, self-proclaimed femi-
nist, writing in Human Behavior:

The momentum for the women's movement
has come out of our growing sense of self-
worth and dignity and potential, and out of
anger and frustration that our worth as
persons has been so long denied and sup-
pressed. (139, p. 64).

The aggression stemming from feminist anger has
thus far been primarily verbal and at the ballot box,
although the sharp increase in crimes committed by
females may also be a reflection of this anger.

Anger at having been belittled, patronized, and
put down by society may be at the root of many of the
so-called "motiveless" killings we read about. Rele-
vant here is Erich Fromm's observation:

There is extensive clinical material on
this. I refer here to the numerous cases in
the United States, where frequently 17- and
18-year-old people simply go out and stab a
person they don't know at all and then ex-
plain, "That was the greatest moment of my
life, because I saw on the pain-distorted
face of this person that I surely can make
an impression, that I am not completely
nothing." . . .

Hence, it appears to me that the de-
structive tendencies of today are therefore
increasing so quickly because boredom is
increasing, because the senselessness of
life is increasing, because people are be-
coming more fearful, because they have no
faith in the future and no hope. Also not
the least, because they feel themselves
cheated by all promises, by all ideologies,
all parties, by all religions. In this
situation, many people see only one satis-
faction, to destroy life itself, in order to
avenge themselves on the deceivers and on
themselves. (149, p. 23).

Fromm recognizes that the teen-age killers are
acting from anger—"feel themselves cheated," and
"destroy life itself in order to avenge themselves"—
and are acting to increase self-esteem—"I surely can
make an impression, that I am not completely nothing."

Thus we have seen testimony that aggression arising from revolutionary activities, from black militancy, from feminist militancy, and from "motiveless" killings is due to anger. The anger in turn has been caused by a feeling of having been "put down" by society. This wound to self-esteem, so often resulting from perceived inequality, motivates attacks on those institutions and values which are seen as responsible for the humiliations suffered.

Aggression and Violence

> The fateful question for the human species seems to me to be whether and to what extent their cultural development will succeed in mastering the disturbance of their communal life by the human instinct of aggression and self-destruction.
> (62, p. 92).

Thus does Sigmund Freud express his concern over the human propensity for violence. Since these words were written in 1930 their grim forebodings have been confirmed by the death of six million Jews in the Nazi extermination camps, by some fifty million deaths in wars and revolutions, and by today's escalating domestic violence and terrorism. Psychologists have devoted a great deal of research to discover the roots of aggression, arriving at a variety of theories but without a common agreement. Some of their insights and conclusions point in the direction of what could be called a self-esteem theory of aggression.

First, much human aggression and violence is anger motivated. In the previous section dealing with anger we saw the testimony of observers of the human scene concluding that anger is the motivation behind revolutionary activities, terrorism and "motiveless" killings. And underlying anger is the desire to restore wounded self-esteem by asserting dominance (usually by inflicting injury) over the offending persons—or sometimes a convenient scapegoat becomes the victim.

Proposing a self-esteem theory for the full scope of aggression and violence is Gregory Rochlin, practicing psychiatrist and professor of psychiatry at Harvard Medical School. In his book Man's Aggression

Rochlin develops the theme that aggression springs from wounded narcissism. By narcissism he means not some abnormal absorption in self, found only in disturbed persons, but the self-love which dominates the lives of all of us. Rochlin identifies it as "an endless lust for a rewarding self-image." (153, p. 1). Throughout, he equates narcissism with self-esteem. Or rather, with our desire for self-esteem.

When self-esteem is wounded, we are seized with an eagerness to repair the damage, by evening the score with the offender. Aggression is the result.

> What may threaten our accomplishments, imperil our relationships, or deny us rewards risks lowering self-respect—endangers narcissism. In defense against such hazards, and as the instruments of recovery, aggression issues. (153, preface).

> Neither metaphor nor a mere label, narcissism, this love of self, is the human psychological process through which preserving the self is assured. In infancy, childhood, maturity and old age, the necessity of protecting the self may require all our capabilities. And, when narcissism is threatened, we are humiliated, <u>our self-esteem is injured</u>, and <u>aggression appears</u>. (153, p. 1).

Although I can find no formal definition of aggression in Rochlin's excellent book, the various examples he gives suggest that by aggression he means an impulse to injure another. The impulse may be conscious or unconscious, justified or unjustified, carried to fruition or repressed or thwarted.

The psychotic and the normal person operate on the same basic motivation in the arousal of aggressive tendencies:

> In short, the same principle holds true whether in psychosis or in the common course of everyday life: whatever injures self-esteem unconsciously intensifies and generates aggression in its defense. (153, p. 120).

The overwhelming dominance of narcissism——the desire for self-esteem——in our lives is stressed by Rochlin:

> The conflicts of narcissism may isolate us or make us social, keep us egocentric or draw us to be with others. They may hold us to dread change, or they may carry us to be revolutionaries. They may cause us to be charitable and grand, or they may incite us to violence and murder. Narcissism begins its rule in our earliest period and continues its reign to our end. The tyranny of narcissism is the human condition.
> (153, p. 248).

Self-esteem is more important to us than life itself:

> To give up one's life to satisfy one's narcissism on the surface may appear to be a contradiction. But, of the two, it seem narcissism is the more important. The self is best served by maintaining self-regard. If in order to do so, life must be forfeited, the risk to our existence comes from whatever menaces our narcissism.
> (153, p. 15).

Rollo May

Dr. Rollo May, psychoanalyst and author of several popular books, in his Power and Innocence maintains that the violence in our society arises from the individual's search for a sense of potency, that is, a sense of being a worthwhile and effective person. Depersonalization and oppression in our modern world has led large numbers of people to feel that they are considered of little value, and their inability to break out of this situation generates in them a feeling of impotency and insignificance. Seeing no other effective way of asserting their "power," they resort to violence.

> When a person (or group of people) has been denied over a period of time what he feels are his legitimate rights, when he is continuously burdened with feelings of impo-

tence which corrode any remaining self-esteem, violence is the predictable end result. Violence is an explosion of the drive to destroy that which is interpreted as the barrier to one's self-esteem, movement, and growth. (129, p. 182).

The struggle for potency which May sees as being the basic cause of violence is a struggle for self-esteem. May equates sense of potency with self-esteem.

Noteworthy in these violent acts is that often the man who ends up in jail was simply trying, through his act, to defend his self-image or his reputation or his rights. Almost everyone is struggling in some form or other to build up or protect his self-esteem, his sense of significance as a person. Both police and "suspects" are fighting an impotence-potency battle within themselves. . . . But in order to see the roots of violence we must go below these psychological dynamics and seek its source in the individual's struggle to establish and protect his self-esteem. . . .

The need for potency, which is another way of phrasing the struggle for self-esteem, is common to us all. (129, p. 32).

Sigmund Freud

The most prestigious of psychologists, Freud himself, may have provided the insight which led to Dr. May's conclusion that the drive for self-esteem is the root of violence. Freud seems to have summed up the idea in one succinct phrase: "The ego hates, abhors, and pursues with intent to destroy all objects which are for it a source of painful feelings." (56, p.84) Freud concretizes this principle by the anecdote of a little girl who, after being reproved by the family maid, expressed the wish that the maid were dead.

The unbounded self-love (the narcissism) of children regards any interference as an act of lese majeste; and their feelings demand

> (like the Draconian code) that any such
> crime shall receive the one form of punish-
> ment which admits of no degrees.
> (67, p. 288)

Well-known is Freud's view that the desire for
sensual pleasure (the erotic urge) is sometimes the
source of aggression, as in the case of sadism. Not
so publicized is his recognition that aggression also
flows from the ego's desire for a feeling of omnipo-
tence. Speaking of the death instinct, which when
directed outward takes the form of external aggres-
sion, he says:

> But even when it emerges without any sexual
> purpose, in the blindest fury of destruc-
> tiveness, we cannot fail to recognize that
> the satisfaction of the instinct is accom-
> panied by an extraordinarily high degree of
> narcissistic enjoyment, owing to its pre-
> senting the ego with a fulfillment of the
> latter's old wishes for omnipotence.
> (62, p. 68).

The ego's desire for a return to the infant's
primal feeling of omnipotence—Freud's terms—is a
manifestation of its desire for a sense of possession
of excellence, power being one aspect of excellence.
Sense of possession of excellence is by definition,
self-esteem.

Other Authors on Self-Esteem Roots of Aggression

Freud's arch-rival, Alfred Adler, seldom express-
ing explicit agreement with his former mentor, concurs
on this point. Instead of using the term omnipotence,
he uses the equivalent expression of "close to God,"
by which he means being God-like in power:

> In cases of suicide we can make similar
> observations. After long training such
> individuals forego any interest in life and
> are filled with the thought of attracting
> general attention through their suicide and
> of achieving thus, like a murderer, a height-
> ened feeling of superiority. ("I have done
> what not everyone could do. Formerly nobody
> took any notice of me; but now . . .") To

be master over life and death brings them close to God, as it does the murderer who disposes of the lives of others. (5, p. 151).

Thus Adler sees the self-aggressor, the suicide, and the murderer as motivated by the desire for a heightened sense of superiority. Feeling superior to others is one aspect of a sense of excellence possessed, i.e., of self-esteem.

Adler sees the self-esteem motivation also in those who participate willingly in war. Speaking of volunteers he says:

> From then on they felt easier; they had found the desire to escape. Now they were no longer whipped dogs exposed against their will to the rain of bullets, but heroes and defenders of the Fatherland and of their own honor. After all, they themselves had uttered the call to war, and thus they went into the holy battle as defenders of the right in the intoxication of their regained self-esteem. Thus, in the attempt to find themselves again at any price, they were freed by a psychological device from the feeling of deepest humiliation and degradation, and evaded the realization that actually they were but the sorry victims of the power urges of others. They dreamed of self-willed and self-sought deeds of heroism. (5, p. 459).

Some penetrating insights into the problem of aggression are offered in the book Autocracy and Democracy, by White and Lippitt. The reader will perceive that the causes for aggression discovered by the authors are expressions of a desire for a sense of one's own worth.

> The interpretation to be presented here is, in brief, that an impulse to aggression is likely to occur whenever ego needs are specially strong and no other ways of satisfying them are, at the moment, psychologically available. Such aggression is, in a sense, a short cut to a feeling of impor-

tance—a leap, often illusory, into the goal region of triumphant self-assertion. (186, p. 162).

Aggression is a major manifestation, but only one manifestation, of more fundamental ego needs, the goals of which are importance in the eyes of others and an inner sense of power to cope with the environment. . . .

In what sense, now, can their aggression be called a "short cut to a feeling of importance"?

It was a short cut in that, while giving them an immediate and vivid sense of their own power and importance, it did not, in any longer time perspective, increase their actual power or importance at all. It was a quick cashing in on certain kinds of power—the power to insult and hurt and destroy—that they already had. Like a self-glorifying day dream, it gave immediate ego gratification with no realistic thought about the relation of means to ends. . . .

This hypothesis puts the frustration-aggression hypothesis in a new light. Why does frustration so often lead to aggression? One major reason now appears to be that frustration, if it is felt as personal failure, is always a blow to self-esteem. Like being the victim of aggression, then, it mobilizes a need to restore self-esteem, and one way of restoring self-esteem is aggression. (186, p. 164-5).

In the same vein is Konrad Lorenz' "I can lick you" model for the aggressive instinct in man. He views the aggressive instinct in man as a struggle for personal dominance:

So my book should have been titled On Aggressivity, not On Aggression, and certainly not On Violence. Now let's forget that word and refer to it as "I can lick you" behavior

> If you put together two little boys,
> two fish of one species, two roosters, two
> monkeys, they will behave exactly as Mark
> Twain describes a meeting between Tom Sawyer
> and a new boy. The first words Tom says are
> "I can lick you," and the inevitable fight
> ends just as soon as one boy hollers "'Nuff!"
> It's not a drive to kill another person, but
> the drive to lick him into submission. It
> has to do with rank order or territory, and
> not with a killing instinct. (47, p. 89).

Adler, were he able to see this description, would exclaim "Ah yes, a perfect description of the striving for superiority!" Which indeed it is. This striving for rank order, for dominance, for superiority, to lick the other person, can also be considered a perfect example of the striving for self-esteem.

Despite all the testimony proposing self-esteem as the cause of human aggression and violence, some cases of aggression may be due merely to the desire for physical gratification. Stealing to allay the pangs of hunger, or stealing a coat as protection against cold, are cases in point. We have noted in a previous chapter that the desire for sense pleasure, and its corollary, the desire to avoid physical pain, is a basic motivation in the human psyche. However, acts of aggression from this motivation probably represent only a minute fraction of the total aggression and violence on the human scene.

Finally, the theory that aggression has its roots in the human desire for self-esteem has relevance in a much-agitated dispute among students of human nature. This is the so-called nature versus nurture controversy: does the human being have an _innate_ tendency toward violence, or is violence principally the result of cultural factors? The self-esteem theory suggests that there is _not_ an innate urge toward violence as such, but that the innate urge toward self-esteem can easily lead the individual to seek dominance over others by whatever means are available, aggression being one of them. The optimistic bottom line in this picture is the fact that the drive for self-esteem provides the key to channelling and controlling human aggression and violence.

Sex, The Self-Esteem Game

Sex is the human behavior that shows most vividly the duality of the basic human motivations, sensual pleasure and self-esteem. So powerful is the physical pleasure in sex that we are apt to overlook its more subtle self-esteem appeals. However, modern writers on sex are showing increasing awareness that these less obvious self-esteem aspects are actually the dominant factor in determining sexual behavior. Psychoanalyst Heinz Kohut, author of The Analysis of the Self and The Restoration of the Self sees that some people engage in sexual activity "mainly in order to enhance self-esteem," and it would be naive to limit his insight to children, adolescents and Don Juan types:

> Sexual activity, too, ranging from certain kinds of masturbatory practices resorted to by children who are suffering from a chronic narcissistic depletion to the need for the incessant, self-reassuring performance of sexual exploits by certain Don Juan types, has the aim of counteracting a sense of self-depletion or of forestalling the danger of self-fragmentation. Much of the sexual activity of adolescents, who, especially during the later part of this transitional period, are exposed to the revival of the frightening childhood experiences of self-depletion and self-fragmentation, also serves primarily narcissistic purposes; i.e., even relatively stable adolescents undertake it, mainly in order to enhance self-esteem. (210, p. 119).

This saliency of self-esteem considerations in sex is seen also by Leo Madow, chairman of the Department of Psychiatry at The Medical College of Pennsylvania in Philadelphia. Madow, commenting on the female's psychological need to feel that she is loved, says:

> This is not to imply that women do not enjoy sexual relations or that they need to enjoy the physical pleasures of sex any less than men. I am speaking here of the psychological drives associated with the sexual act,

which are probably more important in the
total enjoyment of the experience than the
physical sensation itself. (121, p. 64).

The dominance of psychological over physical in
the sex act is not limited to women. Madow sees men
too as driven by self-esteem considerations in their
sexual life:

Men tend to regard the size of their geni-
talia and their proficiency at sex as true
measures of their worth. . . If the man has
had successful sexual relations with a woman
and she tells him he was a fantastic part-
ner, he is on top of the world, because this
means that he is a sexual superman. . . .
The greatest frustration for a woman is to
be made to feel that she is not lovable,
whereas the greatest frustration for a man
is to be made to feel that he is not a man.
(121, p. 65).

"It is astonishing to what a large extent conduct
seemingly motivated by the sex drive is in reality
fundamentally motivated by the ego drive," says Samuel
Schmalhausen, psychiatrist and author of Humanizing
Education and Why We Misbehave. He continues:

Ego satisfaction in sex adventure has wider
repercussions in self-esteem than the un-
adorned erotic experience. . . . The ten-
dency of certain stereotyped psychoanalysts
to speak of sex as if it were an overwhelm-
ing reality in itself, divorced from the
larger setting of human nature and person-
ality, does violence to the truth about the
subordination of sex to ego-dominance.
(212, p. 52-3).

The dominant role of self-esteem may become more
evident as we consider some of the ego gratifications
that can be associated with sexual behavior. The most
obvious is the exhilarating effect of being loved.
Looking into adoring eyes, hearing tender words, being
granted the ultimate intimacy—all this sends self-
esteem skyrocketing. Someone may say "Self-esteem is
the farthest thing from my mind in a situation like
that." True. Who is so coldly clinical as to say to

himself in such a moment "now I am gaining self-esteem." "Ah, glorious!" "paradise!", or "I'm on cloud nine!" is perhaps as articulate as we get in these moments of exhilaration. These apparently self-transcending ecstasies are supreme moments of glory for self. Theodor Reik, prominent analyst in Freud's Vienna Society, says: "Love is, I think, the most successful attempt to escape our loneliness and isolation. . . . It comes nearest to the ego-gratification we all need in pushing the ego aside." (213, p. 194).

In those sexual encounters where the partners know it is not a matter of love, still there is acceptance from another human being, a temporary release from depressing loneliness. And, ordinarily, admiring words will be spoken, a memory to be fondly cherished. The acceptance and admiring words reassure us of our lovability.

Additional ego gratification flows from "possessing" the partner. Self-esteem is the awareness of possession of something desirable; in the sex act each partner has the feeling of possessing the other, at least for those moments. This ego boost can have several aspects. Quite prosaically, acquiring any new possession gives us a lift, whether it is a new house, a car, a pair of shoes, or a souvenir pencil. Acquiring a lover can rank anywhere on that scale. Also, there is the feeling of having won out over her opposition. "She was no pushover, but who can resist the ol' Bill Gates' charm." Then too there is often the feeling of winning out over competition, of having succeeded where many others have failed, a lovely illusion that both parties carefully cultivate. (Perhaps we should note at this point that not all of the motivations mentioned in this section apply to every example of sexual behavior. The crasser ones are certainly absent from your experience, noble reader.) The self-esteem boost resulting from possession of another is in proportion to the person's estimation of the other's desirability. A certain society columnist radiated in the twice reflected glory of her debutante daughter's affair with Prince Phillip in his bachelor days, "And so my little girl found bliss in the arms of her handsome Prince."

Another family of self-esteem gratifications through sex is generated by dominating the partner. Power is the name of this game. The male feels a sense of being in command, an irresistable force, very much the he-man, muy macho. The female thrills to the fact that she has been able to arouse this tide of passion in the male, a tribute to her power. And for her there is the additional power bonus of being able to "twist him around her little finger"—the amorous male is receptive to her suggestions about the new car or where to go on the family vacation this year. Researchers Abigail Steward (Boston University) and Zick Rubin (Harvard) suggest that "whereas men learn to seek power by means of short term, serial conquests of women (the Don Juan syndrome), women are more inclined to seek lasting relationships with men as power or prestige 'possessions.'" (Human Behavior, April, 1977, p. 37).

The extreme example of seeking a masterful self-image through sex is, of course, rape. Eldridge Cleaver confesses that he set out on a campaign of rape of white women to take revenge upon white society for the wounds it had inflicted on his self-esteem. Boston researchers Groth and Burgess, after a study of 170 men convicted of sexual assault, concluded that rape is a matter of anger and power rather than sex. "The Massachusetts researchers were struck by the apparent lack of sexual motives among the men they've studied. The rapists spoke frequently of anger, control and power; but sex seemed only an expression of these other feelings." (Human Behavior, June, 1978, p. 54).

Still another self-esteem bonus associated with sex is the "liberated" self-image. "I am a mature, free, emancipated person who has risen above the hypocritical taboos that cramped the lives of my parents." Gratifying indeed is the sense of being superior to "the unfortunates whose psyches are withered by sexual taboos," and superior to the institutions that promote traditional sexual codes. Each act of sex becomes, in addition to all else, a Declaration of Independence, an Emancipation Proclamation.

Similar is the aura of glamour associated with sex. We want to be in style, "with it," doing the "in" thing. Movie stars, TV personalities, rock stars, the young beautiful people—their lives set the pattern for glamour and the "in" life style, and rightly or wrongly, we get the impression that abundant sex is the keynote of their lives. An affair gives self-conferred membership in the swinging jet set.

In some sexual behavior there may be an element of revenge. A girl who, consciously or subconsciously, feels that her parents have not given her enough love as a child, or who resents the repressing influence her parents have exerted upon her, may indulge in sex as a way of hurting her parents. Humiliating the parents is a means of "getting even" for the self-esteem wounds they have inflicted upon the child. "Young women sometimes act out their anger against strict parents by becoming sexually promiscuous as a rebellion and not primarily for the sexual gratification at all," says Madow. Julia, only child of the great Emperor Augustus, who gave the world thirty years of peace (still standing as a record?) struck back at her father with the sex weapon. Augustus had been vigorously attempting to get the Senate to pass and enforce strict laws against adultery, and Julia chose to indulge in her adulteries in the Forum and by the very rostrum where the Emperor had delivered his anti-adultery speeches. Of course she did not limit her adventures to these locales. Her strategy was all too effective. "Augustus wrote a letter detailing her crimes and had it read aloud to the Senate, seemingly as self-punishment." He also had Julia banished from Rome and never allowed her to return:

> Merciful and forgiving to many other wrong-doers and enemies, he could never forgive her; perhaps he sensed that she had not merely degraded herself, but used her sexuality as a weapon to strike down her own father. (211, p. 75).

When the author of the above quote speaks of Julia degrading herself it scarcely seems to be an example of "self-esteem through sex." However, Julia did realize her moments of feeling superior to her father, fleeting though those moments were to be. And she was degraded in the eyes of society, but not necessarily in her own estimation. The important point is that sex offers a variety of immediate ego gratifications; there is no guarantee that these self-esteem boosts will be lasting, or ratified by society.

Some sexual episodes seem to offer very little material for ego gratification; the impartial observer might term them sordid throughout. But the participant's fantasy has a Cinderella magic to convert even the most grubby encounter into a frolic with Mary Tyler Moore.

Another in the long list of "self-esteem through sex" motivations is the desire to improve one's personality. Current mystique has it that sex is the necessary entree to becoming a warm, loving, fully rounded person. This "psychic salvation through fornication" theme is not a new one. Two hundred years ago, Lord Chesterfield, apprehensive lest his son's lack of social skills should prejudice the young man's career in the diplomatic service, wrote a letter encouraging the son to enter into a liaison with a married woman, for "nothing so improves a young man's social polish as having a Parisian matron as mistress."

Thus far we have considered self-esteem _increases_ resulting from sexual activity. Actually, an even more powerful motivator may be the eagerness to _avoid negative self-images_ associated with a meager sex life. The desire to avoid the scorn or pity of one's peers, and the correspondingly negative self-image, can be a powerful inducement to engage in sex. "What's the matter? Are you afraid of sex?" "You are really repressed and inhibited!" "Wow, what a mid-Victorian prude!" "Relax, and join the human race." "Time to grow up, kid!" Under such psychological bludgeoning, how many have been "shamed" into sexual activities they had little desire for. We cringe under fear of the peer-image or self-image of being inhibited, frigid, prudish, old-fashioned, etc. Sometimes it seems that people are even more strongly motivated by fear of ridicule or disapproval than they are by love for praise and approval. As psychoanalyst Gregory Rochlin says, "Paradoxically, we seem more compelled to act from what injures narcissism or menaces self-esteem than what comforts it." (153, p. 22). Twenty centuries earlier Cicero had voiced the same sentiment: "Many people despise glory, who are yet most severely mortified by unjust reproach." (214, p. 185). Sex plays a significant role as an ego-defense mechanism.

The several self-esteem enhancements—and protec-

tions——mentioned in this section, plus others which
have no doubt occurred to the reader, give credence to
the conclusion previously quoted: "It is astonishing
to what a large extent conduct seemingly motivated by
the sex drive is in reality fundamentally motivated by
the ego drive."

Laughter and Humor

Sigmund Freud, in his book Jokes and Their Rela-
tion to the Unconscious explains why he feels justi-
fied in devoting considerable study to a topic that
some might criticize as frivolous:

> Is the subject of jokes worth so much
> trouble? There can, I think, be no doubt of
> it. Leaving on one side the personal mo-
> tives which make me wish to gain an insight
> into the problems of jokes and which will
> come to light in the course of these stud-
> ies, I can appeal to the fact that there is
> an intimate connection between all mental
> happenings——a fact which guarantees that a
> psychological discovery even in a remote
> field will be of an unpredictable value in
> other fields. (55, p. 15).

We share Freud's view that a deep analysis of
almost any aspect of human behavior will expose the
common root motivations which underlie other "more
important" aspects of behavior. Certainly humor and
laughter are deserving of serious study; it is a com-

---

*In using the term "laughter" we are referring to
an expression of genuine pleasure. Thus, outside our
scope of consideration are the forced laughter we
sometimes summon up to cover our embarrassment, the
merely polite laughter we affect to save the feelings
of an inept humorist, the bitter, scornful laughter
that seems to have gone out of style along with the
melodrama, and of course laughter induced by chemi-
cals, such as nitrous oxide. Included in our consi-
deration are not only laughter resulting from appreci-
ation of humor, but also laughter of relief from con-
straint, and laughter of sheer joy of living. Accord-
ingly this is a treatment not merely of the motivation
underlying humor, but also of the broader field of
laughter expressing genuine pleasure.

monplace observance that the ability to appreciate humor and to indulge in genuine laughter distinguishes human beings from lower animals—was it Aristotle who defined man as "the risible animal"? As evidence of the widespread interest in the analysis of laughter Freud cites the following quote from a book by one of his contemporaries:

> There is no action that is more common-place or that has been more widely studied than laughter. There is none on which more observations have been collected and more theories built. But at the same time there is none that remains more unexplained. (55, p. 146).

Perhaps the most frequently quoted analysis of laughter is the "sudden glory" theory offered by English philosopher Thomas Hobbes (of Leviathan fame) some three hundred years ago. He sums up his famous theory succinctly:

> I may conclude therefore, that the passion of laughter is nothing else but a sudden glory arising from sudden conception of some eminency in ourselves, by comparison with the infirmities of others, or with our own formerly. (90, p. 31).

Hobbes expands upon what he means by "some eminency in ourselves" by saying that men laugh at "their own actions performed never so little beyond their expectations," at "the infirmities of others," at jests, in which the wit consists in the "elegant discovering and conveying to our minds some absurdity or another," and at "absurdities and infirmities abstracted from persons."

This "sudden glory" theory of laughter can as well be denominated a "sudden self-esteem" theory, for self-esteem is the modern equivalent of what Hobbes means by glory:

> Now, whatsoever seems good, is pleasant, and related either to the sense, or the mind. But all the mind's pleasure is either glory, (or to have a good opinion of one's self), or refers to glory in the end; the rest are

sensual, or conducing to sensuality, which
may be all comprehended under the word con-
veniences. (91, p. 260).

Further illustrating Hobbes' use of "glory" as
meaning self-esteem is the passage:

Joy, arising from imagination of a man's own
power and ability, is that exultation of the
mind which is called glorying: which if
grounded upon the experience of his own
former actions, is the same with confidence:
but if grounded on the flattery of others;
or only supposed by himself, for delight in
the consequence of it, is called vain-glory
. . . . (91, p. 197).

A little reflection reveals the self-esteem ele-
ment in the things which Hobbes says provoke our laugh-
ter. "Actions performed beyond our expectations" is
an obvious boost for self-esteem, as is noting the
"infirmities of others." Even "infirmities abstracted
from persons", when adverted to, makes our own ex-
cellence stand out by comparison. The "elegant dis-
covering and conveying to our mind one absurdity or
another" is a tribute to our mental acuity—"ah, I get
it!" the person sometimes exclaims in triumph. It is
worth noting that Hobbes' theory allows for laughing
at self, for it includes amusement at "our own [infir-
mities] formerly."

Hobbes and the several later analysts of humor
who have espoused the same general theory are some-
times referred to as proponents of the "superiority
theory" of humor, it being the essence of their views
that what makes us laugh is a sudden feeling of super-
iority.

Truly an exponent of the superiority is Hugues
Felicite Robert de Lamennais,[1] quoted in Max Eastman's
Sense of Humor:

---

[1]De Lamennais, a 19th century French philosopher
and cleric, was toward the of his life as eloquent and
influential in his denunciation of the Catholic Church
as formerly he had been eloquent and influential in
its defense. His work quoted above was published near
the end of his life.

216

"Whatever be the cause which provokes laughter," he says, "go to the bottom of it, and you will find it constantly accompanied, whether one avows it or not, with a secret satisfaction of amour-propre, of I know not what malign pleasure. Whoever laughs at another believes himself at that moment superior to him in the aspect in which he views him, and which excites his laughter, and the laugh is everywhere the expression of the contentment which this real or imaginary superiority inspires." (44, p. 147).

His use of the word "malign" is unfortunate, and, it seems to me, quite unnecessary for his superiority theory. A feeling of superiority need not be malign; our good-natured joshing a friend about some small inconsistency or mistake is indeed an expression of a small and temporary superiority over him in this limited matter, but it seems extreme to call this malign. This dark view of the pleasure behind laughter is mitigated by de Lamennais' realization that we can find humorous pleasure in our own weaknesses. In his Esquisse d'une Phlosophie, he says:

"The self," he says, "which discovers the ridiculous in one of the inferior regions of its being, separates itself from that at which it laughs, distinguishes itself from it, and rejoices inwardly at a sagacity which elevates it in its own esteem. Thus pride feeds even upon the sight of certain weaknesses concealed in the folds of the heart, and which it has been able to discover. I am not the dupe of myself—so we say—and we admire ourselves for that." (44, p. 140).

De Lamennais is proposing a self-esteem theory of laughter, but with the added implication—which I believe is not justified—that the pleasure behind laughter is necessarily of an unworthy sort.

A. M. Ludovici (The Secret of Laughter, 1932) is usually listed among the superiority theorists, although he makes the qualification that the sudden burst of self-esteem which underlies all laughter need not spring from a feeling of superiority to others. He says:

> Laughter is self-glory. So we can now under-
> stand why a person can laugh apparently at
> nothing . . . unprovoked by any external
> stimulus. . . . We can now also understand
> all those laughs in which there is definite
> outside provocation; for, although Hobbes
> quite unnecessarily limits the series of
> these external stimuli, those externally
> provoked laughs not mentioned by him are
> . . . implicit in his two words self-glory
> (135, p. 84).

Monro comments on Ludovici's view: "it is a sud-
den access of self-esteem that causes us to burst into
laughter: not a steady sense of superiority." This
precisely sums up the self-esteem theory of laughter.
(ibid.)

Notable among superiority theorists are Henri
Bergson (Laughter, 1914: "In laughter we always find
an unavowed intention to humiliate, and consequently
to correct our neighbor, if not in his will, at least
in his deed. . . ." (44, p. 148); Georg Wilhelm Fried-
rich Hegel: laughter is in general "little more than
an expression of self-satisfied shrewdness; a sign
that they have sufficient wit to recognize such a fact
and are aware of the fact." (144, p. 169); and Charles
Darwin: "something incongruous or unaccountable, ex-
citing surprise and in some sense of superiority in
the laugher, who must be in a happy frame of mind,
seems to be the commonest cause." (209, p. 205).

The great grey eminence Sigmund Freud, although
he did not espouse the superiority theory of humor,
expresses some insights which support that theory.

> Thus a uniform explanation is provided of
> the fact that a person appears comic to us
> if, in comparison with ourselves, he makes
> too great an expenditure upon his bodily
> functions and too little upon his mental
> ones; and it can not be denied that in both
> cases our laughter expresses a pleasurable
> sense of the superiority which we feel in
> relation to him. (55, p. 195).

Further, Freud suggests that the essence of the
comic lies in the "degradation" of the other to the

level of a child. If this be true, the observer derives a feeling of superiority by comparison.

> . . . 'I laugh at a difference in expenditure between another person and myself, every time I rediscover the child in him.' Or, put more exactly, the complete comparison which leads to the comic would run: "That is how he does it—I do it another way—he does it as I used to do it as a child.' (55, p. 224).

The comic degradation of an adult is amusing to a child because it gives him relief from the "oppressive superiority" of the adult, i.e., it enables the child's sense of self-esteem to be suddenly buoyed up.

> There is little that gives children greater pleasure than when a grown-up lets himself down to their level, renounces his oppressive superiority and plays with them as an equal. This relief, which gives the child pure pleasure, becomes in adults, in the form of degradation, a means of making things comic and a source of comic pleasure. (55, p. 227).

Freud clearly perceives that the child laughs from a sudden feeling of superiority when someone "slips and falls" but as to why the adult also may find this amusing he concludes "we do not know why."

> It is probably right to say that children laugh from pure pleasure in a variety of circumstances that we feel as 'comic' and cannot find the motive for, whereas a child's motives are clear and can be stated. For instance, if someone slips in the street and falls down we laugh because the impression—we do not know why—is comic. A child laughs in the same case from feeling of superiority or from Schadenfreude: 'You've fallen down, I haven't.' (55, p. 224).

The answer to his "we do not know why" he has already suggested in a quote from Bergson which he cited earlier:

['Perhaps we should even carry simplification further still, go back to our oldest memories, and trace in the games that amused the child the first sketch of the combinations which make the grown man laugh. . . . Above all, we too often fail to recognize how much of childishness, so to speak, there still is in most of our joyful emotions.'] (55, p. 223).

Other passages from Freud show his insight into the buoyant self-esteem element in humor. (By humor Freud means a person's ability to laugh at himself). He classifies humor as an ego defense mechanism, but it is "the highest of these defensive processes," and indeed is "man's highest psychic achievement." Humor represents a triumph of the ego:

The exaltation of his ego, to which the humorous displacement bears witness, and of which the translations would no doubt be 'I am too big (too fine) to be distressed by these things', might well be derived from his comparing his present ego with his childish one. (55, p. 234).

Freud brings out this "self-esteem victory" essence of humor in another passage:

Like wit and the comic, humour has in it a liberating element. But it has also something fine and elevating, which is lacking in the other two ways of deriving pleasure from intellectual activity. Obviously, what is fine about it is the triumph of narcissism, the ego's victorious assertion of its own invulnerability. (54, p. 2).

Summing up the views we have considered, laughter is an expression of pleasure resulting from "a sudden glory," from "real or imaginary superiority," from "self-glory," from "self-satisfied shrewdness," from a "sense of superiority," from "exaltation of the ego," or as D.H. Monro says in his book The Argument of Laughter, from "a sudden access of self-esteem."

Humility

When we picture the human being as motivated almost entirely (sense pleasure plays a relatively minor role) by a desire to increase self-esteem, it seems that we have ruled out the attitude known as humility. What is humility, actually? We find almost as many definitions as definers. We propose that humility might fairly be called an acceptance of the truth about ourselves. Or equivalently, humility is an accurate awareness, and acceptance of that awareness, of the good possessed by self. This accurate awareness of good possessed by self would of course also mean an accurate awareness of the lack of good possessed, i.e., of one's faults and deficiencies. It seems we must include the word acceptance. Otherwise we would be including in our definition the person who realizes all his deficiencies but bitterly resents that realization. Such a situation would not square with our usual conception of the humble person as being contented, peaceful and accepting.

If humility then is an accurate awareness and acceptance of the good (and lack of good) possessed by self, can this be harmonized with man's desire for an awareness of good possessed by self, i.e., desire for self-esteem? The apparent jarring element is the acceptance of personal deficiencies. But does humility involve an acceptance of personal deficiencies or only an acceptance of the awareness of personal deficiencies? It seems, the latter. Because we picture the truly humble person as honestly and tranquilly facing up to his deficiencies but at the same time working to overcome them, or at least to overcome such of them as he considers significant.

Still, how can a human being, whom we have presented as being avid for awareness of good possessed by self, tranquilly accept an awareness of his lack of good. It seems a contradiction in terms.

Certainly it is a psychic task of the utmost difficulty. The only thing that makes it possible is a bone-deep conviction that increased self-esteem in the long run depends on ruthless devotion to the reality principle here and now.

We all have found that facing reality in its more imperious and obvious aspects is a policy vital to the enhancement of self-esteem. The truly humble person only carries that discovery to its logical conclusion. He faces reality in all its subtle, difficult-to-discover, and humiliating aspects, and accepts it, secure in the confidence that this is the royal road to greater self-esteem.

But have we not here run into another contradiction—the humble person seeking great self-esteem. Ridiculous. Another clash of concepts. It would indeed be a clash of concepts if we define the humble man as accepting his deficiencies. But actually he does not accept his deficiencies, only the <u>awareness</u> of his deficiencies. Meanwhile, he is striving to eliminate those deficiencies. This he does by acquiring more good, and concomitantly, awareness of good possessed, i.e., self-esteem. Finally, we come to the conclusion that the humble person is the one most secure and effective in his search for self-esteem, in that he is most faithful to the reality principle. If a person ignores some aspect of reality—even one of its more subtle aspects—in building his self-esteem, he is playing Russian roulette with his entire psychic structure, exposing it to collapse under stress conditions.

Happiness

What is happiness? Is it not merely satisfied desire, nothing more or less? Consider your moments of happiness—have they not been times of satisfied desire? Of course we are not limiting the term "desire" to something sensual or sexual. Your moments of exaltation at the sight of a beautiful sunset—was it not compounded of satisfaction of your desire for a peaceful state of mind, for a sense of unity with nature, for a vision of beauty? Such desires may be delicate and fleeting, certainly not as clamorous and insistent as some of our other desires, but desires they still are. Your moments of happiness surrounded by your loved ones, feeling their affection and rejoicing in seeing their happiness—is this too not a matter of satisfied desire? Even the mystic in transports of ecstatic prayer, is, by his own accounts, experiencing satisfaction of desire for union with the Beloved.

222

This is of course not to say that in your moments of happiness all of your desires are satisfied. You have experienced some peak periods of happiness when onlookers might say that you seemed to have little to be happy about, since to all appearances your presumed desires were not well satisfied. For instance, in times of economic adversity you may have had some deeply happy moments. Or in times of apparent failure you may have been able to tap some inner resources that gave you a deep sense of well-being and peace. In these cases a very basic desire for a sense of possession of inner excellence was satisfied, even though some more superficial desires were notably unsatisfied.

Granted that each moment of happiness is a moment of satisfied desire, nevertheless in order to equate happiness with satisfied desire we must also establish that the converse is true—that each moment of satisfied desire is a moment of happiness. And here it seems that there are difficulties. Just as in our consideration of pleasure and satisfied desire, so also it seems true that satisfied desire does not always bring happiness, but sometimes disappointment or remorse. If the reader will pardon a personal note, let me describe my boyhood experience of shooting a wild duck. My companions and I were 200 yards away from a small flock of bluebills contentedly sunning themselves on a placid marsh lake. They were too far away to be disturbed by the sound of our .22 rifles. (Illegal rifle for duck hunting, and out of season.) My first shot was short and a foot or so to the right of a white-backed male bluebill. A little spout of water leaped up where the shot hit, but didn't seem to bother the ducks. Adjusting sights, the second shot was on line but still short. The third shot produced a flurry of disoriented flapping that subsided into a drifting inert blob, as the other ducks leaped into the sky. We raced around the lake to retrieve the dead duck. My desire to shoot a duck was satisfied, but as I looked at the glazing eyes and the open beak dribbling blood, instead of happiness I felt a sadness and remorse—what had been a trim, beautiful creature, capable of bringing joy to the beholder, now was a crumpled mass of feathers, never to move again. Why did this satisfaction of desire not bring happiness? Actually, it did bring a brief and superficial happiness—the moment of exultation in success. But

later the action brought unhappiness because it less-
ened satisfaction of desire; my desire to see myself
as an excellent person was frustrated by this con-
frontation with the fact that I was a destroyer of
life and beauty. To the degree that I identify with
the natural world I am diminished by every tragedy in
that world.

Sometimes however it seems that satisfaction of
desire brings not even a moment of happiness but only
disappointment. I desire to bite into a beautiful red
apple and do so, only to find with disgust that it is
dry and mealy inside. Here I suggest that the desire
was for the experience of biting into a crisp, juicy
apple, and this desire was never satisfied, hence not
even a moment of happiness.

Subject to correction by the more enlightened
reader, we suggest that happiness is to be equated
with satisfied desire—the happiness varying in depth
and intensity and duration according to the nature of
the desire and degree of its satisfaction.

Some support for this viewpoint is offered by the
statement by Augustine, "happy is he who has whatever
he desires, and desires nothing amiss." His qualifi-
cation "and desires nothing amiss" is relevant to the
fact that he is speaking of full and lasting happi-
ness, whereas we are speaking of happiness in general,
including that which is fleeting and even that which
is quickly followed by regret.

Further support is found in Aquinas: "He who has
whatever he desires, is happy, because he has what he
desires. . . " (11, I-II, Q. 3, a. 4, ad 5). And,
speaking of perfect and complete happiness, "since
happiness is the perfect and sufficient good, it must
needs set man's desire at rest and exclude every evil."
(ibid., Q. 5,a. 4, corp.)

We have previously developed the equation between
pleasure and satisfied desire, and between awareness
of good possessed by self and satisfied desire. There-
fore all these seem to be terms for one and the same
thing: happiness, pleasure, satisfied desire, and
awareness of good possessed by self. True, many great
philosophers, among them Aristotle, the Stoics, Aug-
ustine, Boethius, and Aquinas, have pointed out that

happiness is not to be equated with pleasure, but on rereading their exposition we find that they are referring to physical pleasure, or in some cases to pleasure in the broader connotation of what are commonly considered to be "pleasureable activities." Of course these philosophers are aware of the fuller intellectual and psychological significance of pleasure, but I do not find them dealing with the question of whether pleasure in this fullest scope can be equated with happiness.

Further, it seems that a fifth term can also be equated with happiness, pleasure, satisfied desire, and awareness of good possessed by self. That fifth term is "sense pleasure and/or self-esteem." Here, by the conjunction "and/or" we intend the meaning that human beings can seek their happiness in a combination of the pleasures of sense and self-esteem, or they can concentrate on self-esteem alone, increasing self-esteem by eschewing the pleasures of sense. It seems psychologically impossible to adopt a lifestyle of putting aside self-esteem gratifications in order to concentrate on sense pleasure. Apparent attempts in this direction are actually on-going alliances between self-esteem and sense pleasure, as in the case of the Epicurean personality, or are a temporary "I'll hate myself in the morning" alliance between sense pleasure and a short-range self-esteem consideration, in conflict with one's habitual self-esteem trends.

Summing the relation of sense pleasure and self-esteem to the other four terms: they are the two ways in which we can become aware of good possessed by self; they sum up the totality of our desires to be satisfied; they are the two basic types of pleasure which embrace all pleasures; and they embrace the various ways in which human beings seek happiness. Happiness then is self-esteem and/or sense pleasure, or for the vast majority of us, simply self-esteem and sense pleasure.[1]

---

[1]The traditional Christian believer may object that happiness is actually union with God. May we point out that Christian tradition is in harmony with the idea that union with God in heaven will entail fullest satisfaction of self-esteem and of the then-existing sense desires.

Self-esteem is essentially a psychological awareness of good possessed by self; happiness is psychological awareness of good possessed by self, plus sensory awareness of good possessed by self.

In view of the above, we should expect researchers to have found a close correlation between the individual's level of self-esteem and his self-reports on his degree of happiness. We would not expect a one-to-one correlation here however, inasmuch as sense pleasure considerations also contribute to the happiness level. We find verifications of this close correlation between happiness (also called "life satisfaction") and self-esteem in Robinson's Measures of Social Psychological Attitudes:

> More direct measures of self-esteem were included in Bachman's et al's (1967) national study of 2,500 tenth-grade boys . . . the correlation between the three-item life satisfaction scale and a ten-item self-esteem scale was .53 for the entire sample . . . It can be seen that again items measuring happiness and satisfaction correlate almost as well with self-esteem items as the self-esteem items do with each other.

> Further evidence for the close interconnection of self-esteem and satisfaction is provided at many points in Wilson's (1967) review. Wilson notes, for example, studies which have demonstrated drops in self-esteem accompanying periods of unhappiness and depression and studies which report correlations in the .40's between unhappiness and discrepancies between real self and ideal self and between need for achievement and actual achievement. (152, p. 27)

However, this correlation between happiness and self-esteem is complicated by various factors. As already mentioned, happiness will also depend partially upon the degree to which the individual's sense pleasure desires are being satisfied, which in turn will have an effect on self-esteem. Also, in measuring self-esteem should we take the individual's absolute level of self-esteem, or should we use the relation of this to the level desired by the individual?

Julius Caesar is a case in point: a man of tremendous self-esteem, by all accounts,[1] and yet he could be miserably unhappy when he compared his achievements with those of Alexander the Great at a comparable age. Are we to measure his self-esteem by his feelings of superiority over his associates, or by his feelings of inferiority with regard to Alexander? Or can we simply say that his happiness correlated well with whichever aspect of his self-esteem was uppermost to his mind at the time? This latter position seems to check well with experience.

Another factor that complicates the self-esteem/happiness correlation is the presence of hope for the future. Joe may measure much the same as John on a self-esteem scale, but have a greater degree of happiness because he sees more prospects for future improvement. However, further analysis, which we shall not attempt at this point, might show that hope for the future raises not only happiness but also self-esteem to the same degree. Despite these complications, our theoretical prediction of a close correlation between happiness and self-esteem is gratifyingly corroborated by Robinson's "it can be seen that items measuring happiness correlate almost as well with self-esteem as the self-esteem items do with each other."

We have maintained that the desire for self-esteem and sense pleasure is the root motivation of all of our behavior, and we have traced an equation between happiness and self-esteem plus sense pleasure. Therefore it follows that the desire for happiness is the root motivation of all of our behavior. At this point our reasoning is corroborated by the opinion of many thinkers, both ancient and modern. Among them, Aquinas maintains that all of man's desires are directed, of necessity, toward his "last end" (the thing

---

[1]When Caesar was captured by pirates and held for ransom, he would call his captors together every day to listen to him read his poetry. Throughout, he assured them that when he was ransomed he would return and hang them all. Presumably they guffawed, "Quite a guy, this Julius! And a great sense of humor." After he was ransomed he assembled a military force, captured the pirates and hanged them.

that he desires most basically), and that this "last end" for all men is necessarily happiness (11, I-II, Q.1.a.6). Aquinas also cites Augustine as holding the same view, that all of our thoughts and actions are motivated by a desire for happiness. (ibid, a.7, sed contra). It is my impression, subject to correction by the more knowledgeable reader, that this same view is widely held in America today, almost as a common sense truism.

Is the Self-Esteem Theory of Human Nature Hedonistic?

Inasmuch as we have stated that self-esteem is a form of pleasure, and that together with sense pleasure it motivates all of our behavior, it follows that we are proposing that pleasure is the root motivation of all of our behavior. Thus it seems that we can be charged with "sheer hedonism," which in some intellectual circles is the ultimate put-down. In response, let us first distinguish between ethical hedonism and philosophical hedonism. Ethical hedonism maintains that the goodness of an action is determined by the degree to which it contributes to "the greatest pleasure for the greatest number of people." It is thus a pleasure/pain calculus of ethics. Our theory is not concerned with ethics, with how people should or should not behave, but rather with how they actually do behave. Therefore our theory cannot qualify as an ethical hedonism. Philosophical hedonism is the view that the desire for pleasure is the basic motivation of all behavior, without going into questions of ethics. But in this context the usual connotation put upon the word "pleasure" is sense pleasure, or at least "fun activities." Thus the hedonist is pictured as being a sensualist, at worst a follower of the Playboy philosophy and at best an Epicurean devoted to "gracious living." Self-esteem pleasures are much broader in scope than this, and thus our theory of human behavior cannot be limited to hedonism in this usual sense. If however, hedonism were taken to embrace even such austere pleasures as that taken in duty well done, as that taken in self-sacrifice for a cause, as that taken in a life devoted to the welfare of others, as that taken in asceticism and virtuous deeds and meditation and scientific research, etc., then our theory of human motivation would qualify as a hedonistic theory. However I have never seen the word hedonism used in such sweeping terms.

CHAPTER VII

SELF-DEPRECATION, SELF-HATRED, AND SELF-DECEPTION

Self-Deprecation

Our theme has been the ever-operative human eagerness to enhance self-esteem. However, there is a frequent type of behavior that seems directly contradictory to that motive. Instead of focusing on and enhancing the good possessed by self, sometimes individuals engage in self-belittling, calling the attention of self and others to the individual's deficiencies and faults. Let's consider some of the forms of self-belittling to discover whether they are opposed to the self-esteem motivation, as they seem to be, or whether actually they are a devious and torturous manifestation of the drive for self-esteem.

The most mild and socially acceptable form of self-belittling is the occasional "modest disclaimer." A shrewd lawyer may affect the bumbling hick exterior and refer to himself as a "poor country boy." An Oscar winner may give all the credit to his writers, director, co-stars, etc. An attractive woman may protest that today she "looks a wreck." Ben Franklin tells us in his autobiography that as a young man he alienated people by the dogmatism of his opinions. He learned that people liked him better and accepted his ideas more easily if he prefaced his opinions with some modest disclaimer—"Perhaps I have been misinformed, but . . ." "Have I erred in thinking that . . . ," etc. We need not belabor the obvious by detailing the ego value of these ploys.

Not so socially acceptable is chronic poor-mouthing of oneself. The type of self-deprecation which is easily seen through as a device for eliciting a reassuring and ego-bolstering denial from the hearers poses no challenge to our theory. However there is a type of self-deprecation that actually carries conviction—the speaker is sincerely lamenting his lack of this or that good quality. If, as our theory states, we are always trying to build up our self-esteem, how can we explain this behavior which seems to be tearing down the individual's self-esteem?

We all indulge in this sort of self-reviling to some extent. We mentally "kick ourselves" at the remembrance of some past stupid behavior of which we were guilty. The man who could have bought Xerox when it first came out has difficulty forgiving himself for muffing the opportunity. The memory of a particularly humiliating social gaffe or moral lapse can wring from us the self-reproach "What a fool!" Even such a minor self-esteem loss as a missed shot in tennis may bring self-excoriations "you clumsy boob," "you complete idiot." Billie Jean King can sometimes be heard sharply reproving herself after a bad shot in a tennis match, a habit which makes her even more human and endearing to the fans.

But this foible ceases to be endearing in those persons in whom it has become an habitual life style. The individual who is constantly reproving himself and running himself down embarrasses us, makes us feel uneasy. Freud mentions this habit as a characteristic of the melancholic:

> The distinguishing mental features of melancholia are a profoundly painful dejection, abrogation of interest in the outside world, loss of the capacity to love, inhibition of all activity, and a lowering of the self-regarding feelings to a degree that finds utterance in self-reproaches and self-revilings. . . . (56, p. 125).

> Now the melancholic displays something else which is lacking in grief—an extraordinary fall in his self-esteem, an impoverishment of his ego on a grand scale. (56, p. 127).

> He [the melancholic] has lost his self-respect and must have some good reason for having done so. (56, p. 129).

Though he does not stress the point, Freud obviously sees self-revilings as the outcry of a wounded self-esteem.

Self-Hatred

When this self-reviling becomes bitter and habitual we refer to it as self-hatred. But, ironically,

self-hatred is a sign of self-love. What is occurring
in self-hatred is the total-self denouncing an aspect,
or several aspects, of the self. A person who finds
his usual social conduct to be painfully awkward,
clumsy, and humiliating will come to hate that aspect
of himself. He hates it because it reflects unfavor-
ably on the total self. It is only because he loves
his total self that he hates the "awkward social be-
havior in a group" aspect of himself. If he did not
love his total self he would be quite indifferent as
to whether his social behavior in a group was polished
or clumsy. The hatred of self can extend to manifold
aspects of self—moral behavior, appearance, intel-
lect, talents—but even the person who is so far sunk
into self-hatred as to proclaim "there is nothing good
about myself, nothing that I like" (if such be possi-
ble), still loves himself. Love is basically two-
fold: a desire for an awareness of good possessed, and
a complacency in good possessed. (We are talking now
about self-love.) The first type corresponds to the
sentiment "I want to be great," and the second to the
sentiment "I am great." Or, in a more modest expres-
sion, "I want to be OK," and "I am OK." Our extreme
self-hater has none of the second type of love, no
complacency in good possessed, because he laments that
he possesses no good. But he still is consumed with
the first type of self-love, that is, a desire to
possess good. It is this type of self-love which is
the motivating force behind his self-hatred of his
negative aspects. The greater the self-love, the
greater the simultaneous self-hatred of those charac-
teristics which reflect unfavorably on the total self.

Thus, self-revilings are the spontaneous out-
pourings of a wounded self-love, of a lacerated self-
esteem. But beyond this, do self-revilings have any
assuaging value for the self-esteem? Is there any ego
pay-off to self-reviling? Adler suggests that there
is:

> Prominent among the forms of neurotic
> behavior which safeguard the superiority
> fiction are cursing oneself, reproaching
> oneself, self-torture, and suicide. This
> may seem strange, until we realize that the
> whole arrangement of the neurosis is a self-
> torturing device for the purpose of enhan-
> cing the self and depreciating the immediate

environment. And indeed the first stirrings of the aggression drive directed against one's own person originate from a situation in which the child wants to hurt the parents or wants to attract their attention more effectively. (5, p. 271).

In Adler's analysis then, the self-reviling in childhood had the self-esteem pay-off of attracting attention, and hopefully the soothing ministrations, of parents, and secondly, of inflicting pain on the parents. Being able to inflict pain on others gives us a corresponding feeling of superiority. The carry-over of the habit of self-reproach into adult life is no doubt motivated by a hope of a similar self-esteem pay-off from (and against) significant others.

Also, there is the lightning rod value of self-criticism in forestalling criticism from others. This too may have been learned in childhood: "Now father, don't be too hard on the poor child. Can't you see he realizes he has done wrong. He is suffering enough already." Even in adult life a self-administered reproach may silence reproaches from others, at least temporarily.

Karen Horney suggests that self-recriminations have two further ego values: they enable the individual to avoid facing his real deficiencies, and they give him leverage to think himself better than others because of his self-honesty.

> With a certainty approximating that of a real instinct his neurotic self-recriminations avoid what are actually the weak points. In fact their very function is to prevent him from facing any real deficiencies. They are a perfunctory concession to the existing goals, a mere means of reassurance that he is not so bad after all and that his very qualms of conscience make him better than others. They are a face-saving device . . . . (94, p. 245).

In summary, we see that self-reviling is the anguished outcry of a self-esteem wounded by realization of the deficiencies of self, and may offer balm to that wounded self-esteem in several ways: wringing

232

some comforting gestures from the hearers, forestalling their criticism, inflicting pain upon others, making self the center of the stage,[1] evading a confrontation with more serious deficiencies, and providing a feeling of noble self-honesty. No doubt this list could be considerably expanded by further analysis.

Resistance to Self-Esteem Increase

Another phenomenon that calls for explanation is the behavior of the person who seems to be making no efforts to raise his self-esteem, but on the contrary resists attempts by his friends and psychiatrist (if he is being treated) to give him greater ego-strength. It is as though subconsciously he preferred to remain in a state which he consciously laments. He is not eager to lose self-esteem, but he does seem motivated by a desire to cling to his present level of self-esteem and resists attempts to improve his self-image. Freud observed some such types among his patients:

> There are certain people who behave in a quite peculiar fashion during the work of analysis. When one speaks hopefully to them or expresses satisfaction with the progress of the treatment, they show signs of discontent and their condition invariably becomes worse. . . . One becomes convinced, not only that such people cannot endure any praise or appreciation, but that they react inversely to the progress of the treatment. . . . There is no doubt that there is something in these people that sets itself against their recovery and dreads its approach as though it were a danger. . . . (56, p. 228).

Freud concludes that a part of such resistance is due to the patient's desire to prove himself superior to the psychiatrist, and to "the various kinds of advantages which the patient derives from the illness," but that a more powerful motivation is an un-

---

[1]La Rochefoucauld says "We would rather speak ill of ourselves than not be spoken of at all."

conscious feeling of guilt on the part of the patient, which is finding atonement in the suffering caused by the illness. Freud adds that it is extremely difficult to convince the patient that this is his motivation in clinging to his illness.[1] Let us see what self-esteem values we can find for the patient in the explanation offered by Freud. First and most obvious is the gratification of a feeling of superiority in resisting the doctor. Among the "various kinds of advantages" might be excusal from activities which have been a source of humiliation for the patient. As for the guilt aspect, what is guilt but an apprehension of future loss (the word punishment is too limiting, implying unnecessarily as it does the concept of an intelligent agent administering the punishment) because of some past blameworthy action (or present blameworthy attitude) on the part of the guilty one. Therefore, by embracing his present illness as his punishment, the person hopes, implicitly, to avoid a greater loss in the future. Thus, his clinging to his illness is, he subconsciously hopes, going to mean a more favorable self-esteem balance in the long-run.

Without challenging the validity of Freud's explanation, we wish to offer an additional explanation for the patient's adverse reaction to praise on his progress, and for his apparent desire to remain in his present low-esteem (tension between ego and ego-ideal) condition. The explanatory principle is this: it is more tolerable to retain a low level of self-esteem than to raise one's self-esteem and then crash back to the same low level. This principle of course is not limited to neurotics; it applies to all of us. We all learn by experience to be wary of inflating our self-esteem too much beyond what reality will support, lest somehow an unavoidable confrontation with reality will be forced upon us, with resultant sharp loss of self-

---

[1]Freud then expresses an insight which has far-reaching implications and which we will discuss more fully in the section on Neurosis and Self-Esteem. He says: "In fact it may be precisely this element in the situation, the attitude of the ego-ideal (condemning the ego for not living up to the ego-ideal), that determines the severity of a neurotic illness." As we will see, he is saying in effect that neurosis is basically a self-esteem problem.

esteem. This end result is more painful than is a realistic, if reluctant, acceptance of our former low level of self-esteem. Thus I hesitate to embrace the delightful and beckoning self-image of being a polished, suave, debonair, charming Beau Brummel, oozing eclat, panache, savoir faire, and whatever. Experience teaches me to draw back from such a self-image, appealing though it is, because it would make subsequent confrontation with reality doubly painful. This is the reality principle in operation. It is an application of William James' useful formula,

$$\text{Self-Esteem} = \frac{\text{Success}}{\text{Pretensions}}, \text{ or, in other words,}$$

$$\text{Self-Esteem} = \frac{\text{actual self-image}}{\text{ideal self-image}}. \text{ The higher I exalt}$$

my pretensions, or ideal self-image, the lower will be my self-esteem when reality forces me to face the gap between actual and ideal self-image.

The folklore of the centuries is replete with this wisdom, if such an elemental and automatic ego-defense can be called wisdom. Aesop's Fables, which have expressed and inculcated folk-wisdom for almost three thousand years, tell us of the jay who tucked some peacock feathers under his wings and strutted about, only to receive a severe pecking from the peacocks for his effrontery; and of the frog who puffed himself up and up, mightily impressing the other frogs, until suddenly he burst. The legends of ancient Greece and Rome are insistent that nemesis follows hubris, disaster follows too-high aspirations. Prometheus has his liver eaten out every day by a vulture, for 30,000 years, the liver growing back each night, as punishment for stealing fire from the gods. For defying the gods, among his other offenses, Sisyphys in Hades strains to roll a huge stone to the top of a hill, whereupon it rolls back down and he has to repeat the performance. Icarus, exulting in his wings of feathers and wax, flew higher and higher until the sun melted the wax and he fell to his death in the sea. His father, Daedalus, flying at a lower altitude, safely made the journey to freedom. Pride goes before a fall. Not an altogether appealing maxim, but one that we all instinctively operate on, realizing that to "get out of our depth," or in this case, to get above our proper altitude, can be disastrous to our self-esteem. We don't want to get up where the sun will melt the wax on our wings. Or to put it in modern terms, we don't want to get to an altitude where our wings will ice over and cause us to crash.

The patients whom Freud observed becoming uneasy when he praised their progress were perhaps instinctively resisting being built up to a point where subsequent relapse would be all the more crushing. Were their resistance vocalized, or even explicitly formed in their own minds, it might run: "thanks a heap, you son of a bitch. You are just trying to get me up there where my wings will ice over and I'll crash, much to the secret gratification of one and all. Thanks, but no thanks." We all operate on this same principle; we differ in the altitude at which our wings ice over. Freud's resisting patients had found that their critical altitude was three feet off the ground.

This same theme is developed by Seymour Epstein in his article "The Self-Concept Revisited." As an alternative to Freud's involved explanation of the self-reviling noticed in the melancholic person, Epstein offers another explanation:

> I would like to suggest a simpler one, which rests on the assumption that a sudden drop in self-esteem is more distressing than a chronically low level of self-esteem. If this is true, then individuals who anticipate that their self-esteem will be lowered by others will tend to chronically devalue themselves in order to prevent a greater discomfort. . . . Further, by retaining his self-evaluation at a low level, he is saved from concern over the greater pain of having it further lowered. This can account for why depressed people resist efforts to increase their self-esteem.
>
> . . . One tendency is for the individual to wish to raise his self-esteem, as high self-esteem feels good. The other is for the individual to wish to avoid a drop in self-esteem, as a drop in self-esteem feels particularly bad. Accordingly, the individual avoids evaluating himself unrealistically highly, as this would expose him to decreases in self-esteem. (45, p. 415).

Cognitive Dissonance Theory

An alternative explanation is sometimes offered for our occasional resistance to a too-sudden or too-high increase of self-esteem, an explanation based on Festinger's "cognitive dissonance" theory. In 1957 Leon Festinger published <u>A Theory of Cognitive Dissonance</u>, which, in its simplest terms, states that we are reluctant to accept "knowledge, opinions, or beliefs" which do not harmonize with our present knowledge, opinions or beliefs. Festinger and others have applied this theory with some success in predicting behavior in certain social situations. The cognitive dissonance theory is also referred to as "consistency theory" (people are disposed to accept only such information as is consistent with their present ideas).

As applied to the resistance occasionally offered by Freud's patients to praise and encouragement, this theory might explain that the words of praise created dissonance with the patient's low self-image, and were therefore rejected. The same explanation applies to the normal person's resistance to a too-high or too-sudden increase of self-esteem.

Certainly there is a wide area in which the cognitive dissonance theory is valid, but we suggest that those cases can be explained more basically by the self-esteem theory. We are indeed reluctant to accept cognitions which are dissonant with any cognitions we now have which enhance our self-image. No one wants to be put down. And we are reluctant to accept cognitions which are dissonant to even our present cognitions which are in themselves neutral in self-image content, e.g., the Panama Canal is due south of New York City, for the simple reason that the dissonant cognition is telling us "you are wrong," which is a threat to our self-esteem, slight or great, depending on the importance of the matter. And we may be reluctant to accept cognitions which elevate our self-esteem considerably, for the "don't ice my wings" reasons we have elaborated in the preceding pages. The mother who is informed that her MIA son is alive and well may hesitate a moment to accept the news—"I was afraid of getting my hopes up"—for fear that the news would turn out to be false.

But cognitive dissonant information which moderately increases our self-esteem we are eager to accept. The student who thought that he got a C in the course is delighted to hear from the professor that is grade was a B. The person who has a self-image of being unlucky is happy with the dissonant information that he has won the office pool on the Super Bowl.

In short, we resist accepting cognitions which threaten our self-esteem. They may do this a) by telling us we do not possess a good we think we possess, b) by telling us that we are wrong in a "neutral" opinion, and c) by offering to raise our self-esteem to a point where it is in danger of a clash with reality. We eagerly accept dissonant cognitions which reasonably increase our self-esteem.

Researchers comparing the consistency theory with the self-esteem theory have focused on behavior of the low self-esteem person. Consistency theory predicts that such a person would welcome derogatory information about himself, inasmuch as it is consistent with his present low self-evaluation. Also, such a person would react unfavorably to praise. The self-esteem theory predicts just the opposite reactions: the low self-esteem person will resent criticism, and perhaps resent it even more than will the high self-esteem person, because the former is more vulnerable in his self-esteem; also, the low self-esteem person will be pleased with receiving praise.

Some recent research on this point supports the self-esteem theory. In "Self- and Interpersonal Evaluations: Esteem Theories Versus Consistency Theories (Psychological Bulletin, 1973) Stephen Jones reports:

> The evidence from experiments which permit a test between these positions provides more substantial support for the self-esteem predictions. Time and again, the unhappy self-derogator seems to glow when praised and glare when censured even more than his self-confident counterpart. (101, p. 197).

"Contrasting Self-Esteem Theory and Consistency Theory in Predicting Interpersonal Attraction" (Krauss and Critchfield, Sociometry, 1975) concludes: "Self-esteem theory alone accounted adequately for the data."

The consistency theory, as used by current advocates, seems to have evolved into a self-esteem theory, thus implicitly conceding the superiority of the latter, according to the authors of "Twenty Years of Cognitive Dissonance: Case Study of the Evolution of a Theory":

> The theory seems now to be focused on cognitive changes occurring in the service of ego defense, or self-esteem maintenance, rather than in the interest of preserving psychological consistency. (79, p. 55).

To summarize, self-derogation is due not to an inherent preference for abasement, nor to a desire to be consistent with a previous low self-evaluation, but is a protective device, conscious or subconscious, to avoid greater self-esteem loss. Self-hatred is, ironically, an expression of self-love: it is hatred not of the total self but of some aspect of self that is causing loss of esteem for the total self.

Self-Deception

Each of us is tender and solicitous in his devotion to the preservation and enhancement of his self-esteem. Much of our good feeling about self consists in frequent and only partially conscious references to our identity in its manifold aspects, each with its self-conferred connotation of good (I am a man, an American, a professor, have a lovely wife and children that I am proud of, have a tidy sum in the bank, my $90,000 home is almost debt-free, I'm one of the better tennis players in my weekend group, etc. etc.), and in the daily little touches of recognition that others give us ("strokes", as the TA people call them), and in our hopes for the future. Much of this self-esteem is valid, that is, an objective observer would testify that we truly do possess these goods that are a comfort to us. However, so avid are we for a high self-regard that we tend to "kid ourselves," even building a million dollar self-image from a $2.98 reality. Conceit, vanity, presumption and pride are a few of the many terms used to describe this endemic over-estimation of our own worth.

The "tails" side of the same coin is our reluctance to admit to ourselves our failings and inade-

quacies. We use the utmost ingenuity to hide our
faults from ourselves, but usually ingenuity is not
necessary—we are willing to be deceived by the most
blatant and patent subterfuges on our own behalf.
Freud's ego defense mechanisms are but one part of
this extensive psychic enterprise.

None of this is new to the reader. Everyone has
seen ample evidence of it operating in others, and
every reflective person has seen the process going on
within himself. It has been a frequent theme in lit-
erature.

Let us consider a few remarks by "observers of
the motions of the human heart" regarding man's pro-
pensity for self-deception. Most of these commenta-
tors regard self-deception as an unmitigated evil.
Certainly the presumption is in favor of the truth,
truth in dealing with others, and a fortiori, truth in
dealing with oneself. But if a defense were to be
made for self-deception one might point out that the
alternative in some cases is crippling depression and
even self-destruction. "It is cruel to rob a man of
his delusions," can apply equally well to robbing self
of self's delusions.

The first witness we will offer regarding man's
inclination to self-deception is Blaise Pascal (1623-
1662), mathematician, philosopher, student of human
nature, and ardent apostle of Jansenism.

> The nature of self-love and of this human
> self is to love only self and consider only
> self. But what is it to do? It cannot
> prevent the object of its love from being
> full of faults and wretchedness: it wants to
> be great and sees that it is small; . . .
> The predicament in which it thus finds it-
> self arouses in it the most unjust and cri-
> minal passion that could possibly be ima-
> gined, for it conceives a deadly hatred for
> the truth which rebukes it and convinces it
> of its faults. It would like to do away
> with this truth, and not being able to de-
> stroy it as such, it destroys it, as best it
> can, in the consciousness of itself and
> others; that is, it takes every care to hide
> its faults both from itself and others, and

cannot bear to have them pointed out or
noticed. (142, p. 347).

A contemporary of Pascal but a very different
sort of person was Francois, duc de La Rochefoucauld
(1613-1680), frequenter of sophisticated salons and
confidant of Anne of Austria in her warfare of in-
trigue and counter-intrigue with her husband Louis
XIII and Cardinal Richelieu. La Rochefoucauld is
renowned for his Maxims, biting and often humorous
aphorisms about human vanity. Among his maxims are
the wry observations:

> We cannot get over being deceived by our
> enemies and betrayed by our friends, yet we
> are often content to be so treated by our-
> selves.

> It is as easy to deceive ourselves without
> noticing it as it is hard to deceive others
> without their noticing it.

> The head is always fooled by the heart.
> (111, #114, 115, 102).

In a similar vein, Samuel Johnson, always percep-
tive in his analysis of human affairs and delightful
in the elegance of his expression:

> If it be reasonable to estimate the
> difficulty of any enterprise by frequent
> miscarriages, it may justly be concluded
> that it is not easy for a man to know him-
> self, for wheresoever we turn our view, we
> shall find almost all, with whom we converse
> so nearly as to judge of their sentiments,
> indulging more favorable conceptions of
> their own virtue than they have been able to
> impress upon others, and congratulating
> themselves upon degrees of excellence, which
> their fondest admirers cannot allow them to
> have attained. (100, No. 28).

Dr. Johnson describes some of the "more frequent-
ly insidious" self-deceptions:

> One sophism by which men persuade themselves
> that they have those virtues which they

really want, is formed by the substitution
of single acts for habits. A miser who once
relieved a friend from the danger of a
prison, suffers his imagination to dwell for
ever upon his own heroic generosity; he
yields his heart up to indignation at those
who are blind to merit, or insensible to
misery, and who can please themselves with
the enjoyment of that wealth, which they
never permit others to partake. From any
censures of the world, or reproaches of his
conscience, he has an appeal to action and
to knowledge: and though his whole life is a
course of rapacity and avarice, he concludes
himself to be tender and liberal, because he
has once performed an act of liberality and
tenderness. (ibid.).

Probably most of us have thus conferred upon
ourselves an image of sterling honesty because we once
returned excess change a cashier had erroneously given
us. And an occasional small donation to charity en-
ables us to preen ourselves on our generosity. John-
son also comments on our tendency to give ourselves
credit for the practice of virtue because we have
occasion to praise it:

There are men who always confound the
praise of goodness with the practice, and
who believe themselves mild and moderate,
charitable and faithful, because they have
exerted their eloquence in commendation of
mildness, fidelity, and other virtues. This
is an error almost universal among those
that converse much with dependents, with
such whose fear or interest disposes them to
a seeming reverence for any declamation,
however enthusiastic, and submission to any
boast, however arrogant. Having none to
recall their attention to their lives, they
rate themselves by the goodness of their
opinions, and forget how much more easily
men may show their virtue in their talk than
in their actions. (ibid.).

A similar device that we all have a propensity to
use is the warm glow of virtue we feel when condemning
evil. When we express moral indignation at the way

the younger generation is behaving, or fulminate against crime in the streets, or at corruption in high places, or express outrage at the behavior of this group or that, we may be expressing valid moral judgments or not, but certainly illusory is our unvocalized feeling that our opposition to the "bad guys" automatically makes us one of the "good guys." Our vigorous condemnation of evil is a self-conferred exoneration from evil, seldom justified. Actually, opposition to vice can be inspired by an incompatible vice as easily as by virtue. We all easily perceive that our opponents are using their moral indignation as an ego ploy ("what stinking self-righteousness," we self-righteously proclaim), but we become doubly indignant when someone questions the validity of our own indignation.

Contemporary with Dr. Johnson, John Adams, our second President, wrote an essay on self-delusion for the _Boston Gazette_. In part:

> There is nothing in the science of human nature more curious, or that deserves a critical attention from every order of men so much, as that principle which moral writers have distinguished by the name of self-deceit. This principle is the spurious offspring of self-love; and is, perhaps, the source of far the greatest and worst part of the vices and calamities among mankind. . . .

> But, if we look abroad, shall we not see the most modest, sensible, and virtuous of the common people, almost every hour of their lives; warped and blinded by the same disposition to flatter and deceive themselves? . . . Insensible of the beams in our own eyes, are we not quick in discerning motes in those of others? Nay, however melancholy it may be, and how humbling soever to the pride of the human heart, even the few favorites of nature, who have received from her clearer understandings and more happy tempers than other men, who seem designed, under Providence, to be the great conductors of the art and science, the war and peace, the laws and religion of this lower world, are often snared by this unhappy disposition in their minds. . . .

Such swarms of passions, avarice and ambi-
tion, servility and adulation, hopes, fears,
jealousies, envy, revenge, malice, and cru-
elty, are continually buzzing in the world,
and we are so extremely prone to mistake the
impulses of these for the dictates of our
consciences—that the greatest genius, uni-
ted to the best disposition, will find it
hard to hearken to the voice of reason, or
even to be certain of the purity of his own
intentions. (1, 3:433-5).

In our own time, Freud has probed most deeply
into the workings of self-deception with his analysis
of ego-defense mechanisms. These we considered in the
previous chapter. Commenting on our endemic tendency
toward self-deception, Freud says in his usual clini-
cal, dispassionate language:

The psychical apparatus is intolerant of
unpleasure and strives to ward it off at all
costs and, if the perception of reality
involves unpleasure, that perception—i.e.
the truth—must be sacrificed. (64, p. 339).

Another contemporary witness is Herbert Finga-
rette, author of Self-Deception:

Were a portrait of man to be drawn, one in
which there would be highlighted whatever is
most human, be it noble or ignoble, we
should surely place well in the foreground
man's enormous capacity for self-deception.

That we deceive ourselves as well as
others was no doubt appreciated of old, but
it has become of quite particular, explicit
interest in recent centuries in the West.
(cf. Peyre, Ch. 8). A Victorian such as
Bulwer-Lytton (Vol. II, p. 189) could al-
ready take it as evident that "The easiest
person to deceive is one's own self." And,
in the mid-twentieth century, Camus, in his
last major work, The Fall, still could place
the theme of self-deception at the centre of
his work:
". . . after prolonged research on
myself, I brought out the fundamental dupli-
city of the human being. Then I realized,

244

as a result of delving in my memory, that
modesty helped me to shine, humility to
conquer, and virtue to oppress. . . ."
(52, p. 1-2).

The basic reason for this "fundamental duplicity
of the human being" is stressed by Nathaniel Branden,
disciple of Ayn Rand ("virtue of selfishness"), ex-
toller of self-esteem and self-proclaimed hater of
humility and altruism:

> So intensely does a man feel the need
> of a positive view of himself, that he may
> evade, repress, distort his judgment, disin-
> tegrate his mind—in order to avoid coming
> face to face with facts that would affect
> his self-appraisal adversely. A man who has
> chosen or accepted irrational standards by
> which to judge himself, can be driven all
> his life to pursue flagrantly self-destruc-
> tive goals—in order to assure himself that
> he possesses a self-esteem which in fact he
> does not have.
>
> If and to the extent that men lack
> self-esteem, they feel driven to _fake_ it, to
> create the _illusion_ of self-esteem—condemn-
> ing themselves to chronic psychological
> fraud—moved by the desperate sense that to
> face the universe without self-esteem is to
> stand naked, disarmed, delivered to destruc-
> tion. (21, p. 110).

This variety of witnesses from different back-
grounds and different ideological positions have ob-
served the constant efforts we make to "put our best
foot forward" in our own estimation, even at the sac-
rifice of self-honesty. The purpose of this self-
deception is to enhance or preserve our awareness of
the good we possess—i.e., to hide our faults (Pas-
cal), to congratulate ourselves upon our excellence
(Johnson), to flatter ourselves (Adams), to have a
positive view of ourselves and reassure ourselves of
our self-esteem (Branden).

CHAPTER VIII

SELF-LOVE, ALTRUISM, AND SELF-ESTEEM

Introduction

We have portrayed human behavior as motivated entirely by self-oriented desires—sense pleasure and self-esteem. Does this mean that human beings are completely selfish in their motivation? Is self-concern and self-love necessarily selfish? How can such a theory explain the many acts of concern for the welfare of others that we see every day? Heroic acts of self-sacrifice, even to the point of death, surely cannot be explained by man's desire for self-esteem? Is such a noble sentiment as "greater love than this no man has, that a man lay down his life for his friend" to be comprehended under the rubric of self-esteem? These relationships between self-love and altruism and self-esteem we will consider in this chapter.

Is Self-Love Selfish?

We picture the selfish person as only concerned for his own welfare, greedily grabbing goodies and callous toward the plight of others. "Hurrah for me and ---- you, Jack!" and its variant "I got mine; ---- you, Jack!" a credo heard among American and British soldiers in World War II, is the heraldic motto of the selfish person. Despite Ayn Rand's best efforts, nothing can be done to re-habilitate the word "selfish"; it always connotes something unpleasant.

Some of this same stigma has rubbed off onto most words that carry the prefix "self." Maslow ran into this difficulty with his term "self-actualization," which he uses to describe man's noblest activities.

> However, besides being clumsy from a literary point of view, this term [self-actualization] has proven to have the unforeseen shortcomings of appearing a) to imply selfishness rather than altruism . . . . This has turned out to be so in spite of my careful efforts to describe the empirical <u>fact</u> that self-actualizing people are altruistic, dedicated, self-transcend-

ing, social, etc. . . . . The word "self"
seems to put people off, and my redefini-
tions and empirical description are often
helpless before the powerful linguistic
habit of identifying "self" with selfish
. . . . (124, p. vi).

The term "self-love" has for centuries shared
this onus. Self-love has had a popular mystique, or
if you prefer, an unpopular mystique, of being equated
with selfishness, conceit and sin. Probably a large
part of this comes from religious emphasis on love for
neighbor as being the ideal, with the corollary that
love for self is the antithesis of the ideal. Gener-
ations of preachers have condemned self-love as the
source of all sin, and as the prime obstacle in the
way of love for God and for neighbor, and as the enemy
of salvation. Erich Fromm in Man For Himself ob-
serves:

Modern culture is pervaded by a tabu on
selfishness. We are taught that to be self-
ish is sinful and that to love others is
virtuous . . . . the doctrine which declares
selfishness to be the arch evil and love for
others to be the greatest virtue is still
powerful. Selfishness is used here almost
synonymously with self-love. The alterna-
tive is to love others, which is a virtue,
or to love oneself, which is a sin . . . .
(68, p. 124).

The doctrine that selfishness is the
arch-evil and that to love oneself excludes
loving others is by no means restricted to
theology and philosophy, but it became one
of the stock ideas promulgated in home,
school, motion pictures, books; indeed in
all instruments of social suggestion as
well. (68, p. 131).

A strange bed-fellow with theology and philosophy
in supporting this animus against self-love is Sigmund
Freud, as Fromm points out. Freud makes no direct
attack on self-love, but his thought presents self-
love as a rival competing against love for others.
The psychic organism has a fixed quantity of libido,
in Freud's view, which means that any libido cathected

toward self (self-love), is not available for cathexis toward an external object (love for others). Self-love and love for others are thus competing for the available energy of the libido; when one flourishes the other diminishes. Fromm spells this out:

> The doctrine that love for oneself is identical with "selfishness" and an alternative to love for others has pervaded theology, philosophy, and popular thought; the same doctrine has been rationalized in scientific language in Freud's theory of narcissism. Freud's concept presupposes a fixed amount of libido. In the infant, all of the libido has the child's own person as its objective, the stage of "primary narcissism," as Freud calls it. During the individual's development, the libido is shifting from one's own person toward other objects. If a person is blocked in his "object-relationships," the libido is withdrawn from the objects and returned to his own person; this is called "secondary narcissism." According to Freud, the more love I turn toward the outside world the less love is left for myself, and vice versa. He thus describes the phenomenon of love as an impoverishment of one's self-love because all libido is turned to an object outside oneself. (68, p. 132).

Joining in the attack on self-love are political systems which demand that the individual submerge his own interests and identity in his devotion to the state, the party, fatherland, cause, etc. Fromm comments:

> The deteriorated meaning of the concept of self-interest which pervades modern society has given rise to attacks on democracy from the various types of totalitarian ideologies. These claim that capitalism is morally wrong because it is governed by the principle of selfishness, and commend the moral superiority of their own systems by pointing to their principle of the unselfish subordination of the individual to the "higher" purposes of the state, the "race," or the "socialist fatherland." (68, p. 142).

Relevant to the above are Mao-era articles in the Peking Review, authoritative voice of the ideology then in power in Peking, which condemn Confucius' doctrine of "self-cultivation" as bourgeois and productive of the counter-revolutionary vice of individualism.

But is self-love necessarily the villain in the human psychic drama? Is self-love necessarily opposed to love for others? Fromm concedes that there is a pro-self-love mystique current in today's culture, diametrically opposed to the anti-self-love attitude described above. There are several varieties of the pro-self-love viewpoint. Basic is the natural reaction of the man in the street: "If you don't look out for #1, nobody will." This attitude, carried to an extreme and raised to the dignity of a philosophy, was proposed by Nietzsche. He glorified the superman who exults in his drive for power, scorning such qualities as altruism, self-sacrifice, self-denial, brotherly love and humility as the refuge of weaklings who were failures in the power struggle. Ayn Rand and Nathaniel Branden are the latter-day apostles of this creed, with the added concept that a policy of "virtuous selfishness" is most effective in promoting the welfare of everyone. "What's good for General Bullmoose is good for the country."

Not so militant but still pro-self-love is the proposition that one finds with increasing frequency in psychological journals and books: a healthy self-love is the necessary condition for a healthy love for others; a healthy self-esteem correlates positively with esteem for others. Erich Fromm espouses this view. He disagrees with the Freudian concept of love as a reservoir of libido which if given to self must necessarily have less to give to others. Instead he sees love as a unitary attitude toward persons, self being one of these persons. The individual who has a loving attitude embraces self and others in this loving attitude. The person who does not have a loving attitude is unloving not only toward others but in reality toward himself as well.

We have now come to the basic psychological premises on which the conclusions of our arguments are built. Generally, these premises are as follows: not only others,

but we ourselves are the "object" of our
feelings and attitudes; the attitudes toward
others and toward ourselves, far from being
contradictory, are basically conjunctive.
With regard to the problem under discussion
this means: Love of others and love of our-
selves are not alternatives. On the con-
trary, an attitude of love toward themselves
will be found in all who are capable of
loving others. Love, in principle, is indi-
visible as far as the connection between
"objects" and one's own self is concerned.
(68, p. 134).

In his use of the term "love," love for self or
for others, Fromm intends care and respect for the
person, with an active striving for the growth and
happiness of the person. He sees selfishness as tot-
ally opposed to self-love. The selfish person, lack-
ing in concern for others, cannot truly respect him-
self and is not, in the truest sense, striving for the
growth and happiness of self. Therefore he does not
truly love himself. "Selfishness and self-love, far
from being identical, are actually opposites."
(68, p. 135).

Self-love is selfish and evil; or, self-love and
selfishness are good, qualities of the strong, authen-
tic man; or, self-love is good and is totally opposed
to selfishness—which of these views has most validi-
ty? With due humility—thus arousing the scathing
scorn of the Nietzsches and Ayn Rands—we will propose
our own view, a view that is certainly not original.

We use the word selfish with its usual connota-
tions: the selfish person thinks only of himself and
has no concern for others. Bad. Self-love has two
aspects: first, desiring good for self; and second,
taking pleasure in perceiving self as the possessor of
good. Once again, by the term "good" we mean anything
that the individual in question regards as desirable.
An example of the first aspect of self-love is the
desire "I want to be financially independent" (or to
marry that girl, or to get a divorce, or to have sup-
per now, or whatever). The second aspect of self-love
is expressed by the attitude "I am now financially
independent. How sweet it is!" If we must make value
judgments, it seems that both these aspects of self-

love can be good or bad, depending on circumstances. (The term "good" as used in a value judgment we intend to mean "praiseworthy"; admittedly imprecise but adequate for our purposes.)

According to these definitions, selfishness is self-love without love for others. But of course self-love is not limited to selfishness: the person who in his self-love desires for himself, and realizes, a sincere concern and dedication to the welfare of others, is not selfish. His desire in its roots is self-oriented, but it is totally opposed to selfishness, as that term is commonly understood. Self-love in its first aspect, that of desiring some good for self, is to be praised or deplored according to the good that is desired, and the attendant circumstances. If the object of desire is, let us say, that I (self) discover a cure for cancer, and circumstances make that desire reasonable, then such an other-oriented self-love is to be applauded. Such a desire, although basically self-oriented, is other-oriented in that it contributes to the welfare of others. Self-love in its second aspect, that is, a pride in the possession of some good, can also meet with general acclaim or with disapproval depending on the good in which pride is being taken. If I have a quiet pride and self-esteem in my worth as a person, it is called self-respect and meets with approval in the common estimation. If, on the other hand, I take an ostentatious pleasure in my possession of knowledge, this form of self-love merits disapproval. "Nobody likes a smart-ass."

Does this "in some cases self-love is good, in some cases it is bad," sum up the situation? Rather, I prefer the formulation "self-love is basically good; its aberrations are bad." Desiring good for self and taking pleasure in self's possession of good is the irreducible basis of our nature. To say that this is bad is to say that self-preservation is bad, it is to say that thinking, talking, breathing, being itself, is bad. It is self-love that motivates us to eat, to clothe ourselves, to avoid pain and to take whatever other steps are necessary to preserve our health and continued existence. It is self-love that motivates us to increase our knowledge,[1] competence, and general excellence. It is self-love which motivates us to seek the approval of our fellow human beings. All of this is good and proper. Neither individual life nor communal life would be possible without self-love. Is self-love selfish? It is the source of our selfish actions; but it is also the source of our benevolent behavior, without detracting from the excellence of that behavior, and it is the source of the remainder of our behavior, which does not qualify as either selfish or benevolent.

Even after 2300 years Aristotle's discussion of this point is so pertinent and fresh that we can do no better, in summation, than to quote him at some length:

> People who use self-love as a term of reproach apply the name to those who take more than their share of money, honors, and bodily pleasures; . . . This is characteristic of the majority of men; whence the term 'egoist' has come to be used pejoratively, from the fact that egoism of the ordinary sort is something despicable. . . . if a man were always bent on outdoing others in acting justly or temperately or in a generally virtuous manner, so that what he tried to get for himself was nobility of conduct, surely no one would call him an egoist nor reproach him. And yet such a man evidently possesses self-regard in the highest degree. At least, he takes for himself what is noblest and most truly good, and it is the sovereign part of himself that he gratifies and obeys in everything. . . . And therefore he who loves and gratifies the sovereign element in himself is in the truest sense an egoist. . . . Hence we must regard him as self-loving in the highest degree, although in another sense from that in which we commonly call a man egotistical: . . .
>
> The 'good man' (agathos) therefore ought to be a lover of self, for by doing what is noble he will at once benefit himself and aid his fellows; . . .

---

[1]"Knowledge for knowledge's sake" is is reality "knowledge for self-perfection's sake."

The 'virtuous man' (spoudaios), again, does many things for the sake of friends and country, and will even, if need be, lay down his life for them. He will sacrifice money and honors and all the other good things for which men compete, receiving the character of nobility in exchange; . . . Those who die for others apparently attain this result; therein choosing for themselves nobility on a grand scale. . . . And in this sense, as we have said, a man ought to be self-loving; not, however, in the sense in which most men (hoi polloi) are so. (12, Bk. 9, sec. 8).

From the one root of self-love, then, spring not only the weeds of selfishness but also the beautiful flowers and fruit of kindness, consideration and love for others. The agent may have many motives for producing this agreeable fruit, not all of them the noblest. Among these motivation, possibly the most irreproachable is consideration of the other as an extended self. This process of identification we will now consider in some detail.

The Principle of Identification

We are all familiar with the feeling of kinship for another human being to the extent that we regard that person as another self, an extended self. This feeling of identification with another person may be a fleeting thing or an enduring thing; it may be deep—"the soul of Jonathan was knit with the soul of David"—or it may be superficial, as a twinge of embarrassment for the man who muffs the punch line of a joke; it may extend to a few persons or it may extend to the whole human race—nihil mihi humanum alienum est. Identification with others is a shifting and relative thing; we identify with our city's winning football team and the town goes wild when we win the Superbowl, but as soon as the team loses three or four games the process of dis-identification begins, reaching almost complete apathy and alienation for the team that has had a few losing seasons. It is no longer "our guys" but "those losers."

We can identify with a person in one aspect and sharply dis-identify with him in another aspect. John and Bill, teenage brothers, have a sharp sibling rivalry that leads them to frequent quarrels. Not much identification evident here. But Bill gets into a fist fight with a bigger boy from the next block and John comes to his rescue——"after all, he is my brother." Two black militant groups may engage in internecine warfare but unite as blood brothers against "The Man."

Identification and competition are mutually opposed. The good possessed by the person with whom we identify we regard as to some extent our own good, and we rejoice in his triumphs and successes. The good possessed by a competitor, in the area of competition, we regard as detracting from our own good, and we are not gladdened by his successes. However, we can feel identification and competition toward the same person, but in different situations. Two players competing for one opening on the Davis Cup tennis team feel sharp dis-identification. But once one of them gains a spot, the other roots for him in international competition. At least such is the expected and usual result. A wife identifies with her husband and rejoices in his successes and proudly lets others know about them, but in their private arguments the feeling of identification has been temporarily replaced by the feeling of alienation. Before, his victory was her victory; now his victory is her defeat. Thus we have ambivalent feelings toward our friends and loved ones: to the extent that we identify with them we are happy in their successes; to the extent that we consider them competitors we feel menaced by their successes. Not only are we afraid of their outgrowing us and leaving us, but even apart from that, their exaltation is our diminishment. A cynic has said that sweet as it is to hear of your enemy's failure, it is still sweeter to hear of your friend's failure. This Schadenfreude arises when we measure our own status against that of our friend.

As a definition of identification, we tentatively propose the following: identification is a feeling of oneness with another organism, arising from a perceived similarity, and leading us to desire that the other possess good, and to regard the good possessed by the other as a good possessed by self, in a diluted sense.

Now to flesh out some of the terms used in the above definition. Some of the terms commonly used as synonyms for this feeling of oneness, in its various manifestations, are: fellow feeling, sympathy, empathy, comradeship, camaraderie, friendship, compassion, love. And the basis for this feeling of oneness seems to be a perceived similarity between self and other. This perceived similarity provides a common bond (it need not be a mutual feeling) without which identification is not possible. The perceived similarity may be remote and generic, resulting in a weak sense of identification: a person may see a tree as "a living creature, like myself," or "one of God's creations, like myself" and have some degree of fellow feeling for the tree. Stronger is our feeling for the rabbit hopping across the lawn, or for the horse at the race track that has fallen: "Is its leg broken? I hope they won't have to kill it." Why the concern? Any money we may have bet on the horse is lost already; we have never seen the animal before and will never see it again, but still we are concerned for its welfare. It is a creature like ourselves in that it can feel pain and suffer.

Our identification with another person may arise from any of a variety of perceived similarities: blood relationship, fellow citizenship, same native language, same race, belong to same organizations, have similar physical appearance, shared experiences, shared attitudes, etc. The more important to us is the quality or attitude we see in ourselves, the deeper the identification with the person we see as sharing that quality or attitude. We feel a deeper kinship with the man who shares our system of ultimate values than we do with a blood brother who has an alien outlook on life. Blood is thicker than water, but shared values are "thicker" than blood. Aristotle tells us that the deepest friendship can only be built upon the common bond of virtue existing in both parties, by which he means that both must have as their ultimate concern a devotion to the search for truth.

By the term "good" in our definition of identification we mean anything that is commonly considered to be desirable—life, freedom, safety, money, pleasure, reputation, etc. Our identification with others leads us to regard the good which they possess as our own, in a diluted sense. We pride ourselves on ancestors

256

that may have achieved distinction; we are only too ready to bring into conversation the names of friends and acquaintances who have some degree of fame or success; parents love to retail the accomplishments of their offspring. The lustre of these "other selves," even when the identification is most tenuous and one which the other would disavow, gives added lustre to our own self-image.

William James describes this feeling of triumph in the success of our friends:

> In its widest possible sense, however, a man's Self is the sum total of all that he can call his, not only his body and his psychic powers, but his clothes and his house, his wife and children, his ancestors and friends, his reputation and works, his lands and horses, and yacht and bank account. All these things give him the same emotions. If they wax and prosper, he feels triumphant; if they dwindle and die away, he feels cast down,—not necessarily in the same degree for each thing, but in much the same way for all. (99, vol. I, p. 291).

Not only do we rejoice in the good possessed by those with whom we identify, but as an almost inevitable corollary, we are ready to contribute to their welfare. Depending upon the depth of our identification, we are concerned for the happiness and success of the other, and are prepared to make sacrifices for him. Herein lies the capacity for nobility in human nature. The man whose sincere sense of identification extends to all human beings, regardless of "sex, creed, or color," and regardless of the much more difficult-to-transcend differences in ultimate values, is a man to be admired; the man whose sense of identification with even a few is so deep as to lead him to great sacrifices for their welfare is also to be admired. The man who combines both that ultimate degree of breadth and of depth in his identification with others truly deserves to be called a great man. Perhaps only he merits the title "great."

The good that such a man does to benefit others is not the result of any calculation of advantage that will accrue to himself. Even if it were evident that

he would not thereby achieve any prestige, reputation
or honor——much less any material advantages——he would
still continue to labor for the welfare of others.
Realistically however, even in the greatest man these
personal considerations are probably felt to be an
added plus, although they are not the prime motiva-
tion. We like to think that such men actually exist,
but in any particular case what solid evidence can we
offer to persuade the impartial observer that the
motivation behind beneficent behavior is this deep
sense of identification, rather than a more direct and
more commonplace desire to live up to the agent's ego-
ideal, that is, to enhance self-respect. Sometimes
the "great identifier" is counterfeited by a benefac-
tor, who, if candid, might admit to the cliche "I love
humanity, it's just people I can't stand." In actual
life we should not expect to find "pure types"; even
the greatest identifier would probably have a smorgas-
bord of other motivations in his benefactions.

Many writers have commented upon the principle of
identification as a source of our benevolent attitudes
and behavior toward others. Freud has a good deal to
say about identification. He describes it as an emo-
tional tie with another, which can arise in two ways:
first, as a substitute for a libidinal object-choice,
and second, as a result of the perception of a quality
in common with the other. The first occurs when a
person's libidinous desires toward another are frus-
trated, either by repression or by loss of the other
(cf. Freud's description of the melancholic person in
Mourning and Melancholia), and the other is "intro-
jected into the lover's ego," that is, identification
is substituted for the libidinous feelings.

> First, identification is the original form
> of emotional tie with an object; secondly,
> in a regressive way it becomes a substitute
> for a libidinal object-tie, as it were by
> means of introjection of the object into the
> ego; and thirdly, it may arise with any new
> perception of a common quality shared with
> some other person who is not an object of
> the sexual instinct. The more important
> this common quality is, the more successful
> may this partial identification become, and
> it may thus represent the beginning of a new
> tie., (202, p. 49).

Freud sees the phenomenon of identification as leading to benevolent behavior toward others:

> Moreover there is still much to be explained in the manifestations of existing identifications. These result among other things in a person limiting his aggressiveness toward those with whom he has identified himself, and in his sparing them and giving them help. . . . (202, p. 53).

> It is obvious that a soldier takes his superior, that is, in fact, the leader of the army, as his ideal, while he identifies himself with his equals, and derives from this community of their egos the obligations for giving mutual help and for sharing possessions which comradeship implies. . . . (202, p. 85).

> It is otherwise in the Catholic Church. Every Christian loves Christ as his ideal and feels himself united with all other Christians by the tie of identification. But the Church requires more of him. He has also to identify himself with Christ and love all other Christians as Christ loved them. At both points, therefore, the Church requires that the position of the libido which is given by group formation should be supplemented. Identification has to be added where object-choice has taken place, and object-love where there is identification. (202, p. 86).

Although Alfred Adler has some disagreements with Freud as to the nature of identification, he agrees that it is the source of our most benevolent actions. He equates identification with empathy, that is, entering into the feelings and thoughts of others.

> We see immediately that this ability coincides in part with what we call identification or empathy. . . . The capacity for identification, which alone makes us capable of friendship, love of mankind, sympathy, occupation, and love, is the basis of social interest and can be practiced and exercised

only in conjunction with others. (5, p. 136).

This recognition that altruistic behavior arises from our sense of identification with others can be found as far back as Aquinas:

> We only love someone insofar as we are one with him. (205, ch. 15, lection VI).

> The love a man has for others arises in man from the love he has for himself. (10, Q. 153, 2).

> Doing good to another may give pleasure. . . inasmuch as through being united to others by love, we look upon their good as being our own, we take pleasure in the good we do to others, especially our friends, as in our own good. (11, I-II, Q. 32, a. 6, corp.).

A contemporary author, Anthony Storr, London psychiatrist, develops this theme more fully:

> Human beings possess the capacity for fraternal feeling towards members of their own group because they are able to recognize others who are close to them as being like themselves, and thus to identify with them. It is on this basis that the interest of the one can be submerged in the interest of the group as a whole: and it is also the capacity for identification which makes self-sacrifice possible. . . . (174, p. 32).

> Men, however, possess the capacity of identification as well as that of projection. They are able to enter into the pain of another, and to imagine what the sufferer feels. Upon this basis of identification with the insulted and injured rests man's charity and altruism: for no one would have been concerned to free slaves or to prevent child-labour unless, imaginatively, he could put himself into the shoes of a slave or an ill-treated child. (174, p. 109).

We will conclude with a paean of praise for iden-
tification as the source of altruistic behavior from
Schopenhauer, not otherwise noted for his glowing
enthusiasms. He sees identification with another as a
partial glimpse of the Hindu and Buddhist monist phi-
losophy to the effect that there is only one reality,
and apparent individuation is an illusion:

> The readers of my Ethics know that with
> me the ultimate foundation of morality is
> the truth which in the Vedas and the Vedanta
> receives its expression in the established,
> mystical formula, Tat twam asi (This is
> thyself), which is spoken with reference to
> every living thing, be it man or beast, and
> is called the Mahavakya, the great word.

> Actions which proceed in accordance
> with this principle, such as those of the
> philanthropist, may indeed be regarded as
> the beginning of mysticism. Every benefit
> rendered with a pure intention proclaims
> that the man who exercises it acts in direct
> conflict with the world of appearance; for
> he recognizes himself as identical with
> another individual, who exists in complete
> separation from him. . . .

> The above mentioned recognition of a
> man's own true being in another individual
> objectively presented to him, is exhibited
> in a particularly beautiful and clear way in
> the cases in which a man, already destined
> to death beyond any hope of rescue, gives
> himself up to the welfare of others with
> great solicitude and zeal, and tries to save
> them. (160, p. 133).

Is identification with others ultimately self-
oriented? When we desire good for others with whom we
identify, is that desire ultimately self-oriented? It
is immediately other-oriented; we have a sincere de-
sire for the welfare of the other. But inasmuch as
the process of identification is regarding the other
as another self, to a greater or lesser extent, can we
not say that the desire for the welfare of the other
is, in that sense, a self-oriented desire? This is
not to detract from the nobility of that motivation.

Identification with others and the resultant interest
in their welfare is universally recognized as praise-
worthy. We suggest that the breadth and depth of a
person's identification with others is the truest
measure of his excellence as a person. There is no
cynicism or implied degradation of the human race then
in Aristotle's dictum that every agent in all its
deeds seeks its own perfection. Nor need we feel put
down by his equivalent statement "Evidently, then,
happiness is something final and self-sufficient, and
is the end and aim of all that we do." (12, Bk. 1,
sec. 7).

Prominent Motivational Systems Are Self-Oriented

As further support for the contention that our
benevolence and benevolences are ultimately self-
oriented—a conclusion that need not be depressing to
those who believe that self-fulfillment and self-
actualization are praiseworthy human goals—let us
consider the fact that the major modern motivational
systems propose motivations that are self-oriented.

It is not our purpose to attempt a judgment as
to which psychological systems of motivation are most
influential today, but certainly among the contenders
are the theories of Freud, Adler and Maslow. The
motivations proposed by each of these systems are
self-oriented, as we shall consider in some detail.
This does not mean that these systems assert that all
individuals are selfish. As we have already noted,
self-oriented is not to be equated with selfish.
Freud, Adler and Maslow all recognize and praise indi-
viduals who are kindly, noble, concerned for the wel-
fare of others, and altruistic, in the sense of being
ready to make sacrifices for others. Adler and Maslow
stress that this attitude is characteristic of the
psychologically mature person with social interest
(Adler), and his Maslovian equivalent, the self-
actualizing B-person. However, this altruism is at
root a matter of self-fulfillment—not always con-
sciously so, of course. Our remarks in this section
are certainly no derogation of the systems considered,
nor of the altruism which springs from the higher
reaches of self-fulfillment.

Freud in his later works maintained that all
human behavior springs from two sets of basic in-

stincts, Eros and Thanatos. Eros comprises the life
instincts. These are two-fold: ego instincts and sex
instincts. The first are concerned with the survival
of the individual, and embrace hunger and thirst, as
well as the ego's concern for its own welfare. Just
what various forms this concern takes is not fully
clear in Freud, but one inescapable aspect is the
ego's desire to win the approval of the super-ego,
that is, the ego's desire to live up to the ego-ideal.
The sex instincts include genital sexuality and the
desire for pleasure in the other "erogenous" zones.
Freud sees man's tenderer emotions toward others as
deriving from the sex instinct. A darker side of our
nature is represented by Thanatos. This is our ever-
operative death wish, inexorably working to bring
about the diffusion of all tension within the organ-
ism, i.e., to bring about death, but in the way and at
the time that the organism unconsciously desires.
When this death wish is directed externally it ex-
presses itself as a destructive instinct seeking to do
damage to others. Frustrated in external expression,
the destructive urge rebounds upon self.

In this system, altruistic behavior is traceable
to the sex instinct. In this context, by altruistic
behavior we mean behavior that contributes to the
welfare of others, regardless of the agent's moti-
vation. Philip Rieff, author of <u>Freud, The Mind of
the Moralist</u>, observes:

> Thus Freud's ideas of sexuality as a general
> energy of the self may be given another
> interpretation: that satisfaction from an
> object is but a devious means of self-love.

> Loving, the body is loved, and thus any
> object is absorbed into the subject; even
> adult loves retain their autistic and self-
> regarding character. That love must serve
> the self or the self will shrink from it,
> that the self may chase love round an object
> back to itself again—this is Freud's bril-
> liant and true insight, reminiscent of La
> Rochefoucauld's keen detection of the ego
> behind the curtain. To care is the polite
> form of desire; the man who desires nothing
> cares for nothing. All loves are unmasked
> as self-satisfaction: from the love of the

child for the parent-provider, to the love of spouses which reincarnates these parent-images, to the parent's "narcissistic" love for his own children. The duplicity of the erotic sentiment is Freud's theme. (150, p. 173).

When we search in our experience for examples of unselfish love, we usually find the purest examples in a mother's tender love for her children. No dewy-eyed sentimentalist, Freud says of this love:

> If we look at the attitude of fond parents towards their children, we cannot but perceive it as a revival and reproduction of their own, long since abandoned narcissism. Their feeling, as is well known, is characterized by over-estimation, that sure indication of a narcissistic feature in object-choice which we have already appreciated . . . . Parental love, which is so touching and at bottom so childish, is nothing but parental narcissism born again and, transformed though it be into object-love, it reveals its former character infallibly . . (56, p. 115).

If we pose to Freud the question "Do you believe that human beings have an innate urge to be kindly and considerate toward fellow human beings?", he gives us the definitive answer:

> The element of truth behind all this, which people are so ready to disavow, is that men are not gentle creatures who want to be loved, and who at the most can defend themselves if they are attacked; they are, on the contrary, creatures among whose instinctual endowments is to be reckoned a powerful share of aggressiveness. As a result, their neighbour is for them not only a potential helper or sexual object, but also someone who tempts them to satisfy their aggressiveness on him, to exploit his capacity for work without compensation, to use him sexually without his consent, to seize his possessions, to humiliate him, to cause him pain, to torture and to kill him.

Homo homini lupus. Who, in the face of all his experience of life and of history, will have the courage to dispute this assertion? As a rule this cruel aggressiveness waits for some provocation or puts itself at the service of some other purpose, whose goal might also have been reached by milder measures. In circumstances that are favorable to it, when the mental counter-forces which ordinarily inhibit it are out of action, it also manifests itself spontaneously and reveals man as a savage beast to whom consideration towards his own kind is something alien. (62, p. 58).

Self-Orientation in Adler

To condense the presentation of Adler's psychology which we offered in Chapter II, recall that he pictures the individual as totally concerned with increasing his own sense of superiority. This drive he variously refers to as the drive for superiority, for perfection, for completion, for power, for security, for self-enhancement, for self-esteem, for overcoming, etc.

Whatever premises all our philosophers and psychologists dream of—self-preservation, pleasure principle, equalization—all these are but vague representations, attempts to express the great upward drive. (5, p. 103).

Yet Adler emphasizes the concept of devotion to the welfare of others, and singles this out as the mark of the mature personality. This is his concept of "social interest." At first sight this "social interest" seems to be an exception to the self-oriented drive for superiority, and indeed a superficial reading of Adler might give the impression that the social interest drive is an independent entity in its own right, not derived from the drive for superiority but existing alongside of it. However, in some passages Adler does make it clear that he considers social interest to be a derivative of the drive for superiority, and its highest expression.

The continuous striving for security urges toward the overcoming of the present reality in favor of a better one. This goal of perfection must bear within it the goal of an ideal community, because all that we value in life, all that endures and continues to endure, is eternally the product of social interest. . . .(5, p. 107). Whether the highest effective goal is called God or Socialism, or, as we call it, the pure idea of social interest, it always reflects the same ruling, completion-promising, grace-giving goal of over-coming. (5, p. 461).

Self-Orientation in Maslow

The motivational system proposed by Abraham Maslow is self-oriented, as his terminology itself indicates. He has reduced motivational components into five categories. Most basic and imperious (prepotent) are physiological needs, sometimes referred to as tissue needs—hunger, thirst, sex, sleep, etc. When these needs are relatively well satisfied, the safety needs assert themselves. The individual is concerned to render secure his possession of life, limb and property and stable emotional world. Having achieved a fair degree of security, the individual can interest himself in the next higher level of needs, belong-ingness and love needs. He is eager for a place in the group, and for love and affection. These achieved, he "graduates" to esteem needs. These include self-esteem, whose source is competency, achievement, mastery, independence and freedom, and esteem from others, in the form of reputation, prestige, appreciation, importance, etc. All the needs up to this point, four levels, are referred to as deficiency needs, that is, these deficiencies must be filled before one can begin to flower into a fully developed human being. The very term "need" signifies some good which the organism must acquire for its well being. In other words, these motivations are by their nature self-oriented.

It is true that among the love needs Maslow includes the need to give love. This however does not constitute an other-oriented motivation in the sense that the organism is concerned that others receive love, but is self-oriented in the sense that self needs to be a loving self. The pleasure, self-expansion and self-development involved in loving is the major concern.

The fifth and highest level in Maslow's hierarchy of needs is also self-oriented. The term need once again indicates something that the organism must acquire for itself and for its own welfare. And the special name for this need is self-actualization, meaning the fulfillment of one's best potentialities. As equivalent terms for self-actualization Maslow has self-realization, psychological health, integration, individuation, autonomy, creativity, etc. (126, p. 123). All these involve a perfection to be achieved by self.

It is true that Maslow speaks of his self-actualizing people as being altruistic, unselfish, and ego-transcending. Indeed he makes quite a point of this because he has been stung, as he admits, by criticism of the term "self-actualizing" as smacking of selfishness. However, such altruism as he attributes to his ideal people must spring from his five levels of motivation, inasmuch as he has given us no other, and these are self-oriented. Such a meaning of altruism is a common and acceptable one, that is, the individual desires no external reward for his benefactions, but only the internal reward of realizing that he is thereby becoming a better person, i.e., that he is actualizing his potentialities. That Maslow intends this meaning of altruism is hinted at by his frequent modifier "relatively" in front of altruistic or unselfish. Additionally, he speaks of the self-actualizing altruistic people as deriving a pleasure reward from their good deeds:

> Only such people uniformly yearn for what is good for them and for others, and then are able wholeheartedly to enjoy it and approve of it. For such people virtue is its own reward in the sense of being enjoyed in itself. They spontaneously tend to do right because that is what they want to do, what they need to do, what they enjoy, what they approve of doing, and what they will continue to enjoy. (126, p. 129).

Of these "relative" altruisms of the self-actualizing people:

. . . Maslow finds that the psychologically
healthy person is both selfish and unsel-
fish; in fact, these two attitudes merge
into one. The healthy person finds hap-
piness in helping others. Thus, for him,
unselfishness is selfish. "They get selfish
pleasures from the pleasures of other peo-
ple, which is a way of saying unselfish."
(76, p. 29).

To take Maslow's own words that the unselfishness
of the self-actualizing person is a source of selfish
pleasure for him implies no derogation of Maslow or
his system. He has used the words "altruistic" and
"unselfish" in a quite acceptable sense. And his
presentation of human motivation as being ultimately
self-oriented is totally in harmony with most of the
great thinkers who have expressed themselves on this
subject.

Behaviorism of B. F. Skinner

B. F. Skinner's ideas can scarcely be classified
as a theory of motivation. He expresses distaste for
the concept of motivations as being something that is
not immediately subject to observation as behavior is.
His concern is to modify behavior, which he has done
with considerable success ("operant conditioning"),
and he considers that he has thus by-passed and ren-
dered obsolete any consideration of motives.

However, we are considering him in this section
both because of his widespread popularity—and unpop-
ularity—and because one can construct what could
fairly be called the Skinnerian theory of motivation
from his choices of effective reinforcers. Skinner
uses the term "reinforcer" to refer to things that
induce us to behave in a certain way.

Good things are positive reinforcers.
The food that tastes good reinforces us when
we taste it. Things that feel good rein-
force us when we feel them. Things that
look good reinforce us when we look at them.
When we say colloquially that we "go for"
such things, we identify a kind of behavior
which is frequently reinforced by them.
(The things we call bad also have no [sic]

common property. They are all negative reinforcers, and we are reinforced when we escape from or avoid them.)(169, p. 98).

Thus, what Skinner calls a reinforcer corresponds to a motivator; it motivates us to "go for" it or avoid it. Skinner's rejection of the term motivation, and his rejection of the notion that these reinforcers are causal antecedents of behavior does not prevent his reinforcers from being de facto what other theoreticians refer to as motivators.

> Thus Skinner employs a set of concepts that might be called dynamic or motivational. These concepts, similar to the motivational concepts in other theories, are employed in order to account for the variability of behavior in otherwise constant situations. (84, p. 488).

Culling from Skinner's writings his citations concerning reinforcers, we will attempt to discover whether his system of "motivation" is self-oriented, as have been the others we have considered thus far.

In addition to his division of reinforcers into positive and negative (aversive), the following passage suggests that he further divides them into "established" or primary reinforcers, such as physical pleasures (caress) and material possessions, and "conditioned" or secondary reinforcers, which include social approval, desirable because it is often associated with the established reinforcers:

> We attest to the value of a person's behavior by patting him on the back, or saying "Good!" or "Right!" or by giving him a "token of our esteem" such as a prize, honor, or award. Some of these things are reinforcing in their own right—a pat on the back may be a kind of caress, and prizes include established reinforcers—but others are conditioned—that is, they reinforce only because they have been accompanied by or exchanged for established reinforcers. Praise and approval are generally reinforcing because anyone who praises a person or approves what he has done is inclined to reinforce him in other ways. (169, p. 41).

Although social approval, "credit" as Skinner calls it, is a conditioned reinforcer, he recognizes its ubiquity and power in a passage concerning the relationship between credit and "control" (conditions which force us to behave as we do, thus minimizing the credit others accord us):

> We acknowledge this curious relation-ship between credit and the inconspicuous-ness of controlling conditions when we conceal control to avoid losing credit or to claim credit not really due us. The general does his best to maintain his dignity while riding in a jeep over rough terrain, and the flute player continues to play although a fly crawls over his face. We try not to sneeze or laugh on solemn occasions, and after making an embarrassing mistake we try to act as if we had not done so. We submit to pain without flinching, we eat daintily though ravenous, we reach casually for our winnings at cards, and we risk a burn by slowly putting down a hot plate. . . . In other words we resist any condition in which we behave in undignified ways. (84, p. 45).

Among aversive reinforcers are not only physical pain and deprivation of freedom, but also the removal of positive reinforcers, such as social approval:

> What we may call the struggle for dignity has many features in common with the strug-gle for freedom. The removal of a positive reinforcer is aversive, and when people are deprived of credit or admiration or the chance to be commended or admired, they respond in appropriate ways. They escape from those who deprive them or attack in order to weaken their effectiveness. (84, p. 50).

The motivation of dominance or superiority he recognizes, as shown by the statement of Frazier, the fictional architect of Skinner's ideal community in Walden Two:

> "We don't use the motive of domination, because we are always thinking of the whole

group. We could motivate a few geniuses that way—it was certainly my own motivation—but we'd sacrifice some of the happiness of everyone else. Triumph over nature and over oneself, yes. But over others, never." (168, p. 112).

From these and other statements in Skinner's writings we find that his implicit theory of motivation is pretty much run-of-the-mill: physical pleasure, money, possessions, social approval, sense of personal dignity, dominance, power, (168, p. 299), winning love (168, p. 300), etc., all self-oriented. He, like Freud, Adler and Maslow, seems to regard pure altruism, that is, behavior solely motivated by a desire for the welfare of others, and with no underlying self-oriented motivation, as a sort of psychological unicorn, quite mythological. His attitude toward apparently altruistic behavior is fairly summed up in his description of the person who sacrifices himself for the community welfare, as symbolized by the hero who saves the village by killing the threatening dragon:

> Suppose, for example, that a group is threatened by a predator (the "monster" of mythology). Someone possessing special strength or skill attacks and kills the monster or drives him away. The group, released from threat, reinforces the hero with approval, praise, honor, affection, celebrations, statues, arches of triumph, and the hand of the princess. Some of this may be unintentional, but it is nevertheless reinforcing to the hero. Some may be intentional—that is, the hero is reinforced precisely to induce him to take on other monsters. The important fact about such contingencies is that the greater the threat, the greater the esteem accorded the hero who alleviates it. The hero therefore takes on more and more dangerous assignments until he is killed. (169, p. 106).

Further expressing his view that apparently altruistic behavior is merely a matter of rewards, or in his terms, "reinforcing contingencies":

271

As organized agencies induce people to behave "for the good of others" more effectively, they change what is felt. A person does not support his government because he is loyal but because the government has arranged special contingencies. We call him loyal and teach him to call himself loyal and to report any special conditions he may feel as "loyalty." A person does not support a religion because he is devout; he supports it because of the contingencies arranged by the religious agency. We call him devout and teach him to call himself devout and report what he feels as "devotion." Conflicts among feelings, as in the classical literary themes of love versus duty or patriotism versus faith, are really conflicts between contingencies of reinforcement. (169, p. 111).

In the same vein:

The "something to believe in and be devoted to" is to be found among the contrived contingencies which induce people to behave "for the good of others." (169, p. 113).

In summary, such diverse systems as those of Freud, Adler, Maslow and Skinner agree that human behavior is self-oriented. None of these famous students of human behavior seems to believe in the actuality of human behavior that, in its most basic orientation, is dedicated solely to the welfare of others.

For those who concede the legitimacy of the wisdom of the ancients, the testimony of Plato and Aristotle also supports the view that all human behavior is self-oriented. As mentioned previously, Plato in the Symposium, speaking through the persona of Socrates, voices his views that the noblest Greeks in their noblest deeds were seeking the "immortality of lasting fame." Socrates presents the view of his preceptress Diotima of Mantineae, with whom he fully agrees:

"Marvel not then at the love which all men have of their offspring; for that universal love and interest is for the sake of immortality."

I was astonished at her words, and said: "Is this really true, O thou wise Diotima?" And she answered with all the authority of an accomplished sophist: "Of that, Socrates, you may be assured;—think only of the ambition of men, and you will wonder at the senselessness of their ways, unless you consider how they are stirred by the love of an immortality of fame. They are ready to run all risks greater far than they would have run for their children, and to spend money and undergo any sort of toil, and even to die, for the sake of leaving behind them a name this shall be eternal. Do you imagine that Alcestis would have died to save Admetus, or Achilles to avenge Patroclus, or your own Codrus in order to preserve the kingdom for his sons, if they had not imagined that the memory of their virtues, which still survives among us, would be immortal? Nay," she said, "I am persuaded that all men do all things, and the better they are the more they do them, in hope of the glorious fame of immortal virtue; for they desire the immortal." (145, p. 167).

We should not be put off by the word "sophist." Plato is applying it to Diotima's skill in address, which he admired in the sophists, and not to her reasoning, which he did not admire in the sophists. Of her sentiments, he says (again speaking through Socrates): "Such, Phaedrus—and I speak not only to you, but to all of you—were the words of Diotima; and I am persuaded of their truth." (145, p. 172).

Aristotle, as we have cited previously, holds that all of our behavior is directed toward the attainment of happiness for ourselves: "Evidently, then, happiness is something final and self-sufficient, and is the end and aim of all that we do." (12, Bk. 1, sec. 7).

Conclusion

In this section we have touched upon the views of some outstanding students of human behavior—Freud, Adler, Maslow, Skinner, Plato and Aristotle. Diverse and opposed though their theories are on many points, they agree in presenting only self-oriented motivations underlying human behavior. Perhaps a fitting conclusion to this section is corroboration from the unlikely agreement of such diverse ideologues as enthusiastic TV preacher Dr. Robert Schuller and acidulous skeptic Voltaire. Voltaire remarks, amusing in his salacious twist:

> Those who have said that love of ourselves is the basis of all our opinions and all our actions, have therefore been quite right in India, Spain, and all the habitable world: and as one does not write to prove to men that they have faces, it is not necessary to prove to them that they have self-love. Self-love is our instrument of preservation; it resembles the instrument which perpetuates the species. It is necessary, it is dear to us, it gives pleasure, and it has to be hidden. (181, p. 200).

And Schuller:

> I strongly suggest that self-love is the ultimate will of man—that what you really want more than anything else in the world is the awareness that you are a worthy person. It is the deepest of all the currents that drive man onward, forward and upward. All other drives—pleasure, power, love, meaning, creativity—are symptoms, expressions or attempts to fulfill that primal need for personal dignity. (161, p. 21).

Some Contemporary Theories of Altruism

Introduction

In the past ten years there has been an upsurge of interest among psychologists and social psychologists in the question of positive social behavior, also referred to as helping behavior or altruism. There has been an increasing realization that the study, prevention and cure of undesirable behavior is only a part of the psychologist's function. Psychology is not complete without a good understanding of why human beings engage in activity benefitting another, even at sacrifice to self. A Harvard professor remarks:

> It is not difficult to see why altruism has captured the interest of social scientists. In view of its practical and theoretical importance, it may well be wondered why the study of altruism has only recently gained popularity. (109, p. 258).

Ironically enough, a triggering factor in this surge of interest in altruistic behavior was a classic case of callous behavior. The Journal of Social Issues devotes an entire quarterly issue to "Positive Forms of Social Behavior," with the following preface:

The Absence of Altruism: The Genovese Case

> On a March night in 1964 at least 38 neighbors in the Kew Gardens Apartments in New York City watched a young woman named Kitty Genovese being stabbed to death by an assaultive maniac. Although it took him more than half an hour to murder her, brutally and in cold blood, not one of the witnesses even lifted the telephone to call the police. The victim's cries of terror and her attempts to fight back left no doubt in anyone's mind about what was going on. It was 3:00 A.M. But no one helped.
>
> A torrent of speculation was loosed several weeks later by a New York Times story about the murder. Conclusions ranged from "moral decay" to "apathy." The witnesses themselves said they were afraid, embarrassed, unsure how to proceed in an emergency. They "didn't want to get involved."
>
> This incident, unusual mainly in its documentation, has received from the public and from psychologists such detailed and continued attention that it has come to be considered a classic case in the annals of human social behavior. (206, preface).

As this case vividly points up, one of the tragedies of modern society is our increasing reluctance to engage in helping behavior. As a first step toward alleviating this malaise, social scientists are concerned to discover what motivates us to helping behavior. We will consider some of their theories about the motives for altruism, to discover what relation these bear to the self-esteem theory.

The term "altruism" was coined in the 19th century by Auguste Comte, the founder of Positivism. Comte's intention was to replace traditional religion with a naturalistic religion of his own devising, whose basic code of morality was devotion to the welfare of others. To this concern for, and contribution to, the happiness of others Comte gave the name altruism. It seems that he did not envision an altruistic act as being entirely devoid of self-interest, for he says:

> When it condenses the whole of sound morality in its law of "Life for Others," Positivism allows and consecrates the constant satisfaction of our several instincts. (32, p. 54).

Herbert Spencer, sometimes cited as an apostle of altruism, shows the same realism:

> Ethics has to recognize the truth, recognized in unethical thought, that egoism comes before altruism. . . . to say that each individual shall reap the benefits brought to him by his own powers, inherited and acquired, is to enunciate egoism as an ultimate principle of conduct. It is to say that egoistic claims must take precedence of altruistic claims. (173, p. 216).

However, sometimes altruism is taken to mean behavior that is totally oriented toward the welfare of others. In this view, if there is an accompanying intention to benefit self, or even an unconscious motivation to benefit self, then the action is no longer to be considered altruistic. For this concept of altruism we will use the term "total altruism." Otherwise we will follow the practice of the contemporary social scientists whose theories we are consid-

276

ering, and use altruism to mean merely "helping behavior," regardless of the motivation behind it.

The "Guilt Theory" of Altruism

When a man brings his wife flowers or candy, on other than a special occasion, observers sometimes banteringly exclaim "Aha! What has he been up to?" This insight that behavior beneficial to others is sometimes motivated by a desire to salve the benefactor's conscience has led to many experiments by social psychologists to test this "guilt theory" of altruism. Sigmund Freud's comments about moral masochism—psychic pleasure in self-abasement—have also given impetus to the guilt theory of altruism.

In the typical experiment, a subject is maneuvered into committing some faux pas, or is led to believe that he has somehow harmed someone, and then later is given an opportunity to engage in helpful behavior. Experimenters have repeatedly found that the persons in the thus-induced guilt condition are more likely to respond favorably to appeals for help than are "non-guilty" persons. This is true whether the person requesting help is the "victim" or is an independent third party.

> A considerable amount of research has demonstrated a strong relationship between transgression and altruism. . . . Over a wide range of operationalizations of transgression (e.g., shocking a fellow-subject, ruining the experimental equipment, knocking over a box of sequenced index cards), such harm-doing is consistently found to increase one's tendency to comply to the requests of another for aid; the nature of this aid has also been quite varied (e.g., donating blood, participating in subsequent experiments without recompense, hand-scoring exam sheets). (28, p. 502).

In an article entitled "Guilt-Edged Giving: The Shame of It All," the authors conclude:

> In these cases of generosity, we found support for theories—relatively recent in psychology—that much charitable behavior is motivated by guilt and shame. (110, p. 50).

This conclusion was the result of an experiment in which students were given a test ostensibly to measure their academic motivation, but which actually was a "laboratory manipulation designed to instill feelings of shame and guilt in some of the subjects." The experimenters distinguish between shame and guilt: "A guilty person reacts to twinges of conscience, but a shamed person reacts to the reactions of others—whether real or imagined." (110, p. 52). Their "shame theory" proposes that the person who has been humiliated is eager to restore his self-image, and is thus likely to accomplish this by favorably responding to appeals for help. The authors attempt to distinguish this "shame theory" from a "guilt theory":

> The theory that one becomes altruistic as a result of causing harm to others—the shame theory—leans heavily on the importance of feedback from others to a person's self-image. The guilt explanations leans on the effect of intrapsychic pain. (110, p. 52).

Actually it seems very much in accord with the findings of the authors to describe their shame theory and guilt theory as two aspects of a "self-image" theory. They recognize that shame leads to the desire to restore the self-image, and, although the authors do not explicitly give cognizance to this, a feeling of guilt also injures one's self-image, and logically leads to a desire to restore that image. Thus, altruism resulting from a feeling either of shame or guilt has the same ultimate explanation:

> This interpretation suggests that people attempt to maintain a realistic level of self-esteem by acting out particular images in front of others. When self-esteem is low, they act out positive images. . . (110, p. 52).

The above explanation of the shame theory becomes an explanation of the guilt theory if, for "in front of others" we substitute "in the forum of one's conscience." One might say the shame theory concerns a loss of image in the external forum, while the guilt theory concerns a loss of image in the internal forum.

Others have proposed this self-image explanation for the guilt theory. Another group of psychologists found that "some people seem to exhibit their own brand of brotherly love best when they're feeling guilt about something," and conclude "harm-doing lowers self-esteem, which leads to altruism in an attempt by the harm-doer to raise his self-esteem." (86, p. 53).

From another source:

> Finally, a number of investigators. . . have suggested that a transgressor tends toward altruistic behavior in a desire to restore his self-esteem. It is assumed that the act of harming another, even unintentionally and in what appears to be an unavoidable accident. . . will result in the lowering of one's self-image. In order to bolster a sagging self-concept, the transgressor will seek to perform good works. (28, p. 504).

Dennis Krebs, in a review of the literature of recent experiments on altruism, concludes:

> In summary, many studies have supported the notion that public transgression, whether intentional or unintentional, whether immoral or only situationally unfortunate, leads to reparative altruism. Reparative altruism would seem to alleviate a negative state associated with lowered self-esteem. When amends cannot be made to the victim, reparative responses are generalized to others; in fact, in some situations reparative responses are made only if they can be directed toward a third party. (109, p. 267).

Several factors suggest that the loss of self-esteem following transgression is largely due to "loss of face" in the public forum rather than to a realization of failure to live up to an internalized code of ethics. That is, the shame factor is more potent in explaining altruism than is the guilt factor. First, as noted in the above quote, the subject's behavior is the same even though his transgression was unintentional. Unintentional transgression should not weigh upon one's conscience, proper, although it may be deeply offensive to one's social sense of shame. That is, unintentional transgression should not produce true guilt, although it does produce shame. Secondly, in some experiments where the subject thought that his transgression was undetected, very little altruism resulted. Had the loss of self-image been a matter of guilt, that is, in the internal forum of conscience, the altruistic behavior should have resulted whether the transgression was detected or not.

> Two final studies suggest that private trans-
> gressions are not as likely to lead to al-
> truistic reparation as public transgres-
> sions. Wallace and Sadalla found that sub-
> jects who broke an expensive machine were
> more likely to volunteer for a painful ex-
> periment than those who did not, but only if
> their transgression was discovered. Silver-
> man failed to find a higher incidence of
> volunteering from children who cheated on a
> task but did not consider themselves caught
> than from those who did not cheat. (109,
> p. 267).

Perhaps this supports Sigmund Freud's statement that most people never develop a super-ego to any significant extent.

The "Self-Esteem Theory" of Altruism

The guilt theory studies show that a person who has committed a recent transgression is more likely to respond favorably to requests for assistance than is a non-transgressor. Taking this as his starting point, David McMillen theorized that self-esteem was lowered by the transgression, and that the subject was there-fore more likely to engage in an altruistic act in order to restore his self-esteem. To test this theory experimentally, some subjects (students) were given an opportunity to cheat on an exam, then after the exam some of the subjects were given a "self-esteem mani-pulation" by showing them a very favorable personality rating (bogus) about themselves. Then all subjects were presented with an optional opportunity to perform a task. Results showed that subjects who had cheated were significantly more likely to volunteer for the helpful task than were non-cheaters, provided that the cheater had not received a self-esteem manipulation following the test. Those who had received such a manipulation were not significantly different from the non-cheaters in their altruism. The author concludes:

> The data suggest that self-image is an important factor in determining if compliance increases following transgression. Evidently, the individual is primarily concerned about how it affects the person transgressed against. The cognition that he has transgressed is inconsistent with his self-image. The compliant request gives the individual an opportunity to bolster his self-image by doing something good. If an incident occurs which restores self-esteem before the compliance request is made, the subject does not need to comply to restore his self-image. (120, p. 176).

McMillen proposes that his theory is an improvement on the guilt theory, offering the previously missing psychic link explaining why guilty persons should be more altruistic.

> The "self-esteem" interpretation of compliance following transgression is a refinement of the guilt interpretation. Transgression theoretically may lead to guilt, but there is no obvious reason why compliance should alleviate guilt. The individual knows he has transgressed, regardless of whether he complies or not. However, if the compliance behavior can function to raise self-esteem, this may compensate for any loss of self-esteem sustained as a result of experiencing guilt. Knowledge of guilt will still be present, but its saliency will be reduced. (120, p. 179).

In his excellent review of experimental studies of altruism, Dennis Krebs offers support for the self-esteem theory:

> The Darlington and Macker (1966), Krebs and Baer (unpubl.), Carlsmith and Gross (1969), and Freedman et al., (1967) studies suggest that reparative altruistic behavior relieves an unpleasant negative state asso-

ciated with lowered self-esteem by supplying
a situation in which a wrong can be righted
and self-esteem elevated. . . .
(109, p. 267).

In summary, many studies have supported
the notion that public transgression, whe-
ther intentional or unintentional, whether
immoral or only situationally unfortunate,
leads to reparative altruism. Reparative
altruism would seem to alleviate a negative
state associated with lowered self-esteem.
(ibid.)

The "Relief of Negative Affect" Theory of Altruism

Cialdini et al. reject the guilt theory of al-
truism, and its corollary, the self-esteem theory of
altruism, because neither seems able to explain the
increase of altruistic behavior among witnesses to a
transgression, who were themselves quite innocent of
the transgression. Certainly, according to Cialdini,
these witnesses should not be feeling guilt nor loss
of self-esteem, and thus have no motivation to indulge
in altruistic acts to repair an injured self-esteem.
How then to explain the fact that such witnesses do
actually show an increase in altruistic behavior as
compared with control groups who did not witness the
transgression? These psychologists propose the fol-
lowing explanation:

In its simplest form this explanation—which
might be called Negative State Relief—
postulates: first, that altruism is one
technique, among many, which people use to
make themselves feel good; and second, that
the sight of another's suffering is seen to
produce a general, negative affective state,
and altruism is seen but as one of several
ways a person might go about relieving that
state. The reason that many studies have
shown altruism to follow transgression is
that the first opportunity the experimenter
affords the subject to restore his affective
positivity is the opportunity to be chari-
table. (28, p. 505).

To test this theory, the experimenters arranged
for some subjects to commit a "transgression" by ac-

cidentally knocking over a box of indexed computer cards. "Oh, heavens, John spent hours arranging these cards. I can't bear to think what he is going to say when he finds what a mess they are in." Other subjects merely witnessed the cards being knocked over. It was theorized that observation of the accident would produce a negative affect in the innocent witnesses, an assumption supported by the testimony of Weiss et al. that "their subjects witnessing another being harmed sweat visibly, frequently express verbal distress, and exhibit other signs of strain." (28, p. 509).

Next, some of the subjects in each group were given a chance to "relieve the negative affect" resulting from causing or seeing the accident. The relief condition was accomplished by giving some of the subjects an unexpected dollar for participating in the experiment, and in other cases by complimenting the subject on his competence in solving a maze. Then, all subjects were asked to help a second experimenter by doing interviews of students by telephone.

As predicted, those subjects who had committed a transgression, or had witnessed it, were much more likely than were the control subjects to offer to help the experimenter. And those who had witnessed or caused the transgression, but had been given a dollar or compliment to relieve their negative affect, were no more helpful than were control subjects. The experimenters conclude:

> Because the Negative State Relief model asserts that one will be altruistic in order to reduce general affective negativity, it should follow that any procedure which induces such a negative mood will increase the tendency to help. Thus, procedures other than transgression which diminish affective tone ought to enhance benevolence as well. A number of studies provide evidence that this is indeed the case. (28, p. 513).

Although the authors of this study have rejected the self-esteem theory of altruism, we suggest that actually the self-esteem motivation can explain their results. They reject the self-esteem theory for two reasons:

First, transgression witnesses who received a compliment, also were no more charitable than a control group. Unless we are willing to maintain that one who observes a harmful act experiences as much self-image damage as one who performs it, this result cannot be explained by employing the concept of self-esteem. Second, the presentation of a monetary payment which was not contingent upon the quality of a subject's task performance produced a benevolence which was identical to that of a performance-contingent compliment. Subjects receiving the payment were made to understand that the same amount of money was automatically given to all experimental participants; thus, it is highly unlikely that they would have experienced a gain in self-esteem as a result. The Self-Esteem Bolstering interpretation, then, cannot account for the lack of helping in subjects who received the monetary payment. (28, p. 512).

To this we will attempt to respond as the authors of the Self-Esteem Bolstering theory might do. In response to the first point, it seems plausible that just as the witness to a transgression feels by empathy a "negative affect," as the experimenters assume, so also the nature of that negative affect will be the same in the witness as in the transgressor with whom he is empathizing. That negative affect is humiliation at his clumsiness in knocking over the cards, that is, he is experiencing a self-esteem loss. That we sometimes experience embarrassment (self-esteem loss) from empathy with another is common experience. We feel mortification when our school football team makes a poor showing; we sometimes cringe in embarrassment when a personality on TV, even someone we have never heard of previously, makes a fool of himself. It seems quite predictable then, that some of the subjects would feel sufficient empathy with the transgressor to share, to a degree, his humiliation and embarrassment.

Cialdini's second point is that the compliment used to alleviate negative affect would also restore self-esteem, but the dollar reward would have no effect in restoring self-esteem because the subject was led to believe that all the subjects were receiving the dollar. This reasoning would be valid if our only source of self-esteem boosts were through comparison with others. However, self-esteem boosts also come from comparison with our former state. Acquisition of the dollar gives the recipient a feeling of superiority, a self-esteem boost, over his former state. To the affluent reader this may seem to be making to much over the acquisition of a pitiful little dollar, but in fact the experimenters found that the dollar meant enough to the subjects to provide "relief of negative affect."

Thus it seems that the objections raised by Cialdini against the self-esteem theory of altruism can be adequately answered, and that the desire to restore injured self-esteem can explain his experimental results. As a matter of fact, the "negative affect" concept which he uses to explain altruistic behavior seems, in the context of their experiment, to be merely injured self-esteem, in the form of empathized embarrassment.

The "Elation Theory" of Altruism

Apparently in flat contradiction to the guilt, shame, self-esteem and negative affect theories of altruism is the elation theory. As we have seen, the former theories amount to an explanation of altruism as an attempt to restore injured self-esteem. The elation theory, in contrast, asserts that an individual is more likely to engage in altruistic behavior when his self-esteem is already unusually high. This idea is very much in harmony with our every-day experience. Mother and the children know that the best time to approach daddy for a favor is when he is in a good mood. It is folk wisdom to ask for a raise only when the boss is in an expansive mood.

Several attempts have been made by social psychologists to provide experimental support for this common sense approach. We will briefly sketch some of these studies and their findings, then attempt an analysis of the human motivation involved. In a 1970 study, the experimenter induced a "warm glow of success" in some subjects by giving a test in "perceptual-motor skills" to a group, half of whom were later given a glowingly favorable report on their success,

285

and the other half of who were told that they had performed poorly. Then all subjects were given an opportunity to donate to a charity. In a later version of the experiment, all subjects were given the opportunity to be helpful to a stranger. In both versions of the experiment, the "success" subjects proved to be significantly more altruistic than were either the "failure" or control subjects. The failure and control subjects did not significantly differ from one another in their altruism, leading the author to reject the explanation that failure-induced hostility would result in lowered altruism. The experimenter concludes that a "warm glow of success" heightens altruism, but she is unable to supply the reasons as to just why this should be the case:

> The warm glow of success hypothesis, however, does not really clear up the matter of why success subjects are more helpful than other subjects. . . . But the nature of this link and the distinguishing aspects of success-induced good feeling (if such there be) remain to be examined and specified. . . . In addition, one might ask whether any kind of feeling good would lead to helping others, or whether there is something unique about the good feeling which results from success. (97, p. 300).

Two possible psychic links between success and altruism are suggested:

> The exact operation of this warm glow could not, of course, be specified, but two possibilities seemed reasonable: one supposed that individuals who have experienced success feel more positive toward others; the second was that such people feel more competent, able to cope with the world and events that might occur, and less in need of clutching all of their resources to themselves. These two descriptions, clearly, are not mutually exclusive. (97, p. 295).

To discover whether increased altruism was due to a feeling of competence at having succeeded, or was due merely to a "good mood," other experimenters have given cookies to subjects or arranged for them to find a dime, then tested their willingness to engage in acts helpful to an independent third party. The subjects thus favored were significantly more helpful than were control subjects, thus giving support to the hypothesis that altruism results from a good mood, even with no change in feelings of competence.

These "cookie and dime" results were reported by Aderman, who also used another approach to inducing moods. He had some subjects read fifty positive mood statements ("I'm full of energy!" "I feel great!," etc.), while other subjects read fifty negative mood statements ("all the unhappiness of my past life is taking possession of me now," "I want to go to sleep and never wake up," etc.), and the controls read neutral statements. His findings:

> The results of the present experiment provide support for the notion that people in a good mood are generally more willing to be helpful than people in a bad mood. . . . The helping differences between the two prior mood groups appear to have been due, in part, to the depression subjects' greater readiness to perceive the requests for help as threats to their behavioral freedom. (4, p. 99).

Aderman also suggests that Adam's Equity theory may be the explanation for his findings. We will consider the Equity Theory in a later section.

A 1974 study supported the conclusion that a good mood (positive affect) increases altruism. Some subjects (second and third grade children) were asked to think about things in their experience that made them feel sad, others were asked to think about things that made them feel happy, and the control group did some simple counting exercises. Then all subjects were presented with an opportunity to help themselves to candies and to contribute money to a fund for needy children. They could do either, both or neither of these. The results: happy children contributed more than did unhappy children or controls. There was no difference in altruism between unhappy children and controls.

An interesting further finding of this experiment is that both happy and unhappy children took more candy than did control children. Thus, contrary to what may be popular opinion, an inclination to be self-rewarding is not necessarily antithetical to altruism. "It is now empirically clear that altruism does not require self-immolation, or even self-denial." (156, p. 551).

Why does positive affect increase altruism? The experimenters explain:

> Negative affect, by definition, increases the psychological distance between self and other. It creates, in Tomkins's (1962) colorful expression, a sociophobe. Quite commonly children in the negative affect condition would think of events that hurt them or made them angry. We suspect that natural tendencies arise to comfort self, by heightening self-reward, and to punish others, by decreasing their reward.
>
> Positive affect, in contrast, decreases psychological distance, making one feel good about the self and others. Again in Tomkins's terms, positive affect creates a sociophile. . . . Because the psychological distance between self and others is decreased, one feels about others as one does about oneself. To the extent that one is generous to oneself, one will predictably be generous with others. (156, p. 550).

Thus, in essence it seems fair to paraphrase the authors' conclusions by saying that positive affect leads us to identify ("one feels about others as one does about oneself") with others, and therefore be more ready to help this extended self.

The fact that the negative affect subjects in this study were less altruistic may seem to contradict the fact that negative affect subjects in the guilt and shame studies proved to be _more_ altruistic. Perhaps the reconciliation lies in the fact that the negative affects in the opposed studies were of different types. In the previous studies, the negative affect was customarily one of embarrassment, loss of face, either direct or empathized. In such a case, doing a good deed would help to regain face. In the latter studies, the negative affect is not so much a loss of face as it is anger or sadness. In the grip of such affects, the subject is not usually motivated to do a good deed to prove that he is a good guy after all, but rather he is motivated to strike out at the perceived source of his disgruntlement, or if that is not possible, to grumble and feel ill-will.

We have seen that the self-esteem theory can explain altruism following transgression, as an attempt to boost injured self-esteem. But how can the self-esteem theory explain altruism following increased positive affect? The Isen study, as we have already quoted, offered two possible psychic links between positive affect and altruism: a more positive feeling toward others, and a feeling of greater ability to cope with life. The Rosenhan, Underwood and Moore study suggests substantially the same two explanations. First, there is an increased sense of identification and empathy with the person in need of help, an increase resulting from positive affect. "Because the psychological distance between self and others is decreased, one feels about others as one does about oneself." (156, p. 550.) The authors hint at the second factor, coping, when they remark that "the more one is touched by negative affect, the more one conserves resources." (156, p. 551). Conversely, the more one is enjoying positive affect, the less one feels the need of conserving resources, because of the feeling "I've got it made."

Actually, it might seem that the self-esteem theory would predict that a person would always seize the opportunity to help others, thus brightening his self-image. However, there are possible self-esteem losses associated with particular acts of altruism—"is he trying to take advantage of me?" "I don't want to get the reputation for being a push-over," "I had to work hard for mine and he gets his the easy way. No thanks," etc. Thus, the fear of these self-esteem losses inhibits our tendency to seek a self-esteem gain from helping others. But in a positive mood, whether induced by success in a task, by a compliment, by receiving a cookie, or by thinking happy thoughts, we are in a condition of heightened self-esteem and thus feel more self-esteem security and are less

threatened and inhibited by the possibility of loss
involved in helping another.

But would not such a condition of heightened
self-esteem, for the very reason of satiety, lessen
our drive to acquire more self-esteem and thus lessen
our altruistic activities? Actually our desire for
self-esteem is insatiable. Satisfaction of desire
here only inflames desire further. As Augustine said
"satisfaction of desire opens wide the jaws of de-
sire." As Goethe said of himself, successes inspire
him to "drive the pyramid of his existence ever high-
er."

It seems we can derive self-esteem from two op-
posite roles, each suited to a different mood. The
person in an elated, expansive mood is prepared to
step into the flattering role of Mr. Bountiful: "Meet
Diamond Jim, the last of the big spenders! Nothing is
too good for my friends, and you, stranger, are my
instant friend. I always say, when you got it, spread
it around!" But in a depressed mood, or perhaps even
in a normal mood, we are more disposed to get ego
gratification by playing the role of Mr. Shrewd, play-
ing his cards close to his chest, looking out for #1,
and not to be taken advantage of by anyone. Natur-
ally, both of these behaviors are automatic, without
any conscious advertance to which role we are stepping
into.

The "Equity Theory" of Altruism

The "equity theory" of personal interchange, most
extensively and explicitly developed by Stacey Adams,
has stimulated considerable research to ascertain its
usefulness in predicting employee behavior. In sim-
plest terms, the theory states that an individual
feels he should get the same proportionate reward from
an interchange as obtained by the others involved in
the "deal." More precisely, the equity theory pro-
poses that in any interchange, each party involved
feels tension unless he perceives that the ratio of
his investment in the interchange to his return is
equal to a similar ratio on the part of the others
involved. The interchange may be any personal inter-
action, but Adams is especially concerned with trans-
actions in the industrial world—hiring, wages, pro-
motions, working conditions, etc. He uses the term

"inputs" to describe the investment that a Person makes in the transaction; this investment includes all the relevant "plus" entities that Person perceives (not as perceived by an unbiased observer) himself as bringing to the transaction. Thus, inputs to a hiring situation might include Person's experience, his personality, competence, connections, and anything else that he subjectively perceives as a relevant contribution to the interchange. Adams uses the term "outcomes" to signify the rewards of various sorts that Person subjectively perceives himself as obtaining from the interchange. In assessing his input, Person will also include perceived negative entities that he brings to the transaction, perhaps lack of experience, poor record on last job, etc. The same is true when he assesses his total outcome; he will include in the picture negative aspects such as monotonous job, long commuting trip, etc. Thus, his total input will be the summation of positive and negative features that he brings to the transaction, as estimated by himself. Similarly, his total outcomes will be the summation of positive and negative results he sees coming to himself from the transaction. Naturally, Person is interested in maximizing the Outcome/Input ratio.

But also, Adams postulates, Person feels uneasy if his Outcome/Input ratio is different from that of the other parties involved in the transaction. The other parties may be the boss, the corporation, fellow workers, his friends in a similar line of work—the Other is not limited to the other parties to the transaction, but may include any others with whom Person is comparing himself. It is a matter of common experience that if Person perceives his Outcome/Input ratio as less than that of Other, he will feel disgruntled. But Adams states that even in the opposite condition, where common sense might predict that Person would feel jubilation over coming out of the deal with a greater Outcome/Input than does Other, Person still feels uneasy, and will be motivated to reduce that inequity, even though the inequity is in his own favor. This conclusion is Adams' derivation from Festinger's cognitive dissonance theory, which we have considered in an earlier section. In a nutshell, the cognitive dissonance theory states that we resist those cognitions which are at variance with our present cognitions. When Person perceives an inequity favoring the Other, this presumably creates dissonance with his previous cognition of himself as a fair and just person.

> . . . two general postulates are presented, closely following propositions from cognitive dissonance theory (Festinger, 1957). First, the presence of inequity in Person creates tension in him. The tension is proportionate to the magnitude of inequity present. Second, the tension created in Person will motivate him to eliminate or reduce it. The strength of the motivation is proportional to the tension created. In short, the presence of inequity will motivate Person to achieve equity or to reduce inequity, and the strength of motivation to do so will vary directly with the magnitude of inequity experienced. (2, p. 283).

Thus, the situation that Person is seeking to maintain or obtain is:

$$\frac{Outcome_p}{Input_p} = \frac{Outcome_o}{Input_o}$$

If Person perceives imbalance favoring either side he is motivated to restore balance. This, Adams offers, can be accomplished in any, or a combination, of the following ways:

1. Person alters his own inputs, outcomes, or distorts them by self-deception.

2. Person leaves the field. (Quits job, backs out of deal.)

3. Person alters the inputs, or outcomes of Other, or distorts them by self-deception.

4. Person forces Other to leave the field.

5. Person changes the object of his comparison. (Well, the company may be getting the best of me in this deal, but at least I'm doing better than Charley.")

Equity Theory Applied to Altruism

Adams' equity theory has been adapted by Walster,

Berscheid and Walster to explain altruistic behavior. They postulate that when Person perceives that a transaction favors himself more than it does Other (this situation they describe as "harm-doing" on the part of Person, regardless of his intent or whether any actual harm was done to Other), then Person feels distress. "We will emphasize two possible sources for the harm-doer's distress: retaliation distress and self-concept distress." (183, p. 181). Thus, Person is motivated to restore equity in order to prevent some sort of retaliation, by Other, or perhaps by God or a Just World; and secondly, to maintain his self-image as being a just and fair person. (Accomplishment of this latter objective will diminish Person's cognitive dissonance.) The authors suggest that Person will seek to restore equity by any of the following ways: Self-delusion (deciding that the victim deserved his fate, denying Person's own responsibility, minimizing the victim's sufferings, etc.); compensation to victim; or self-punishment. Under self-punishment the authors include self-abasement (apologies), self-injury and altruistic behavior toward independent third parties ("altruism" toward the victim would be compensation).

> Several theorists have proposed that after injuring another, individuals will be especially willing to endure costs to perform altruistic acts for the benefit of persons other than the victim. . . . Such altruistic acts do not restore equity directly to the harm-doer-victim relationship. It is possible, however, that the performance of such altruistic acts may be perceived as restoring equity with the "world in general" and, therefore, with the victim indirectly.
> (183, p. 186).

Thus the altruistic act helps to relieve Person's self-concept distress ("I am a good person after all"), and his retaliation distress ("A just fate will now spare me further retribution"). In essence, then, this theory seems indistinguishable from the guilt theory we have already considered. As in the case of the guilt theory, self-esteem considerations explain the whole procedure. Relieving self-concept distress is another way of saying "restoring injured self-esteem." Relieving retaliation distress is forestalling possible future loss of good, i.e., self-esteem loss, and/or sense pleasure loss.

The "Projection Theory" of Altruism

Anna Freud has suggested a form of altruism which she describes as arising from the ego defense mechanism of projection. Projection is the psychic process by which we refuse to admit to consciousness those thoughts and desires which would be offensive to the ego were they admitted, and instead attribute those thoughts and desires to others. Thus, the person seething with inner hostility may deny that fact and instead see the external world as bristling with hostility toward himself. Usually the process of projection is a socially negative force, but Anna Freud suggests that it can have a positive aspect, leading us to attribute some of our socially acceptable desires to others and to work for the fulfillment of those desires in the other. In other words, the process of projection can lead to a concern for the welfare of others:

> The mechanism of projection disturbs our human relations when we project our own jealousy and attribute to other people our own aggressive aims. But it may work in another way as well, enabling us to form valuable positive attachments and so to consolidate our relations with one another. This normal and less conspicuous form of projection might be described as 'altruistic surrender' of our own instinctual impulses in favour of other people. (53, p. 133).

Anna Freud offers an example of this from among her analysands. A young governess, single and childless, unassuming and shabbily dressed, displayed a high degree of what we might call unselfish interest in her friends:

> She might be said to display an unusual degree of concern about her friends' having pretty clothes, being admired and having children. Similarly, in spite of her own retiring behaviour, she was ambitious for the men she loved and followed their careers with the utmost interest. It looked as if

her own life had been emptied of interests
and wishes; up to the time of her analysis
it was almost entirely uneventful. Instead
of exerting herself to achieve any aims of
her own, she expended all her energy in
sympathizing with the experiences of people
she cared for. She lived in the lives of
other people, instead of having any experi-
ence of her own. (53, p. 135).

Through analysis Freud arrived at the explanation
that this young governess by early renunciation of
instinct had developed an exceptionally severe super-
ego which "made it impossible for her to gratify her
own wishes."

But these impulses were not repressed: she
found some proxy in the outside world to
serve as a repository for each of them. The
vanity of her women friends provided, as it
were, a foothold for the projection of her
own vanity, while her libidinal wishes and
ambitious phantasies were likewise deposited
in the outside world. . . . Her super-ego,
which condemned a particular instinctual
impulse when it related to her own ego, was
surprisingly tolerant of it in other people.
She gratified her instincts by sharing in
the gratification of others, employing for
this purpose the mechanisms of projection
and identification. . . . The surrender of
her instinctual impulses in favour of other
people had thus an egoistic significance,
but in her efforts to gratify the impulses
of others her behavior could only be called
altruistic. (53, p. 136).

Freud does not propose that this projection me-
chanism explains all forms of altruistic behavior, but
she does maintain that it has a wide applicability:

Any number of cases similar to those which I
have quoted can be observed in everyday
life, when once our attention has been
called to this combination of projection and
identification for purposes of defense. (53,
p. 139). . . . The surrender of one's own
wishes to another person and the attempt to

secure their fulfillment thus vicariously
are, indeed, comparable to the interest and
pleasure with which one watches a game in
which one has no stake oneself.
(53, p. 140).

Freud cites the case of Cyrano de Bergerac as a
classic example in literature of projection altruism.
Cyrano's love for the beautiful Roxanne being incapa-
ble of fulfillment because of his monstrous nose, he
identifies with the handsome Christian and not only
makes every effort to help Christian win Roxanne's
love, but even risks his own life in battle attempting
to save Christian.

Thus, the projection theory of altruism amounts
to vicarious satisfaction of desire. The individual,
blocked in his satisfaction of some sense pleasure or
self-esteem desires, seeks their gratification through
a substitute self.

The "Transferred Aggression" Theory of Altruism

Anna Freud offers a "transferred aggression" ex-
planation for the Robin Hood type of altruism, in
which the benefactor exerts aggression against the
establishment or against other authority figures in
behalf of the oppressed. This theory has a topical
interest in the light of demands in recent years by
radical kidnappers that the victim's rich relatives
provide "two million dollars worth of free food for
the poor." According to Freud's analysis, some per-
sons who have had renunciation of instinctual gratifi-
cations imposed upon them by parents may build up
feelings of hostility toward the parents. These feel-
ings of hostility may not be overtly expressed toward
the parents but are transferred in adult life to other
authority figures, and overtly expressed, with appar-
ently altruistic motives serving as the justification:

An employee who would never venture to ask
for a rise in salary for herself suddenly
besieged the manageress with demands that
one of her fellow-workers should have her
rights. Analysis of such situations shows
that this defensive process has its origin
in the infantile conflict with parental
authority about some form of instinctual

gratification. Aggressive impulses against
the mother, prohibited so long as it is a
question of fulfilling the subject's own
wishes, are given rein when the wishes are
ostensibly those of someone else. The most
familiar representative of this type of
person is the public benefactor, who with
the utmost aggressiveness and energy demands
money from one set of people in order to
give it to another. Perhaps the most ex-
treme instance is that of the assassin who,
in the name of the oppressed, murders the
oppressor. The object against which the
liberated aggression is directed is invari-
ably the representative of the authority
which imposed renunciation of instinct on
the subject in infancy. (53, p. 141).

Summary of Recent Theories About Altruism

We have seen quite a variety of theories proposed
by modern psychologists concerning the cause of altru-
istic behavior. We will briefly review each and re-
state how in each case the relevant variable can be
traced to a self-esteem or sense pleasure motive. For
clarity, we repeat that by the term "altruism" the
authors customarily mean helping behavior, regardless
of motive.

Anna Freud's projection theory of altruism is a
matter of the altruist identifying with the other, and
desiring sense pleasures and self-esteem gratifica-
tions for this extended self—"vicarious gratifica-
tion," as she terms it. Her "transferred aggression"
theory of altruism is a case of venting hostility
against authority figures in order to benefit third
parties. Robbing the establishment is a tremendous
self-esteem boost for Robin Hood, and his donation to
the poor both serves as justification and gives addi-
tional increments of self-esteem in the form of right-
eous self-image and public popularity. The element of
identification with the poor can also be a factor.

The guilt theory ascribes altruism to an attempt
to salve a troubled conscience. The shame theory
suggests that an attempt to regain face after public
humiliation is a more likely explanation. Both of
these cases are patently matters of wounded self-

esteem, which the agent attempts to restore by his noble deed. In the "relief of negative affect" theory, the negative affect was embarrassment at a social faux pas. Obviously this too is a matter of wounded self-esteem. This theory has the added feature that even a witness to the "transgression" is likely to show altruistic behavior. Common experience shows that we can feel embarrassment in empathy with another, putting the empathizer in the same condition of temporarily ruffled self-esteem, in need of repair.

Positive affect was said to lead to altruism because it decreases the psychological distance between self and others, leading one to feel about others as one does about self. This is a good description of identification. Positive affect also causes the possessor to feel less need to conserve his resources. Both of these factors dispose the agent to step into the flattering role of Mr. Bountiful, jovially dispensing largesse of money, time and good will.

In the equity theory the altruist is seen as motivated by an attempt to restore the balance of benefits after he has received what he considers disproportionate benefits in some social transaction. The proponents see two deeper motivations behind this altruistic urge—retaliation distress and self-concept distress. The latter is the desire to restore the subject's self-image as a fair and just person. The former is his desire to avoid future sense pleasure or self-esteem losses.

All of the foregoing modern psychological theories of altruism explicitly present self-oriented motives on the part of the altruist, and as we have seen, all of them implicitly present self-image or sense pleasure as the root motivating force. Regarding the possibility of "pure" altruism, that is, behaving the possibility of "pure" altruism, that is, behavior beneficial to another with no underlying self-oriented motive, not even the praiseworthy identification motif, the authors make the following comments.

Anna Freud, disagreeing with her father, concedes the possibility that there may be such a thing as pure altruism. However, one feels that in such concession she may be following the advice of her father "Much will be forgiven the author who occasionally makes a low bow in the direction of human nature." She does not seem sanguine about the possibility of pure altruism:

> It remains an open question whether there is such a thing as a genuinely altruistic relation to one's fellow-men, in which the gratification of one's own instinct plays no part at all, even in some displaced and sublimated form. In any case it is certain that projection and identification are not the only means of acquiring an attitude which has every appearance of altruism; for instance, another and easy route to the same goal is by way of the various forms of masochism. (53, p. 146).

Among the other authors we have considered, those who touch on this question adopt the same cautious scientific attitude, ready to concede pure altruism if evidence is forthcoming, but pointing out that as yet there is no such evidence:

> In this case of altruism after transgression, then, it would seem that the primary motive for helping is a selfish one. Of course, no general statement about the nature of altruism can be made solely on the basis of the present data; it may be that in some other situations helping behavior does involve unselfish concern for the welfare of another. As yet, however, there seems to be no empirical evidence for such selflessness. (28, p. 515).

At the end of Krebs' review of recent literature on altruism he summarizes the findings regarding the most likely beneficiaries of altruism:

> When it came to social roles of recipients, an examination of the effects of friendship status, ingroup affiliation, and social class suggested that people give to those who are similar to them, to those who are prestigious, and to those from whom they stand to gain. (109, p. 298).

The first characteristic, personal similarity to

benefactor, suggests identification at work. The other two characteristics indicate more directly self-oriented motives. Krebs concludes:

> Many have welcomed the new research on the positive aspects of man, but it should be realized that the study of beneficial behaviors does not establish the existence of altruism. Elucidation of the phenomenon of altruism, is, in fact, as capable of shaking the foundation of man's self-conception as elucidation of such things as aggression and anxiety. Unfortunately, the fact that man acts altruistically does not mean that he is altruistic. The hopeful thing about research, however, is that at the same time as it sorts out antecedants, it identifies mechanisms that can lead to a change. (ibid.).

An unsigned article in Human Behavior magazine concludes:

> Thus empathy is still another basis for altruism—in addition to guilt, competence, bribes and favors, dependency and threats. Whatever become of giving for its own sake? (86, p. 54).

Emphasizing a positive note in man's ability to identify and empathize with others, "Guilt-Edged Giving" notes:

> Because a significant part of man's pleasure is derived from the happiness of those with whom he identifies, man is not doomed to eternal selfishness, even though he has hedonistic drives to maximize pleasure and minimize pain. For empathic persons, it is often more rewarding to give than to receive. (110, p. 77).

As a final emphasis, we wish to repeat that not all of this self-orientation in our "altruistic" behavior is to be equated with selfishness. Selfishness means a lack of concern for the welfare of others. In behavior motivated by identification and empathy, indirectly self-oriented though these are, we see strong concern for the welfare of others. Even "altruistic" behavior that is not motivated by identification, but by enlightened self-interest of a more directly self-oriented type, may still be accompanied by a sincere concern for the welfare of others. Therefore it seems quite accurate to say that much helping behavior is definitely unselfish. Indeed, if we bear all these things in mind we can justifiably continue to use the word altruism without "quotes."

CHAPTER IX

The message of this book is that virtually all human behavior springs from two motives: the desire for a good self-image and the desire for sense pleasure.

Each of these motives has also a negative aspect. The negative aspect of the desire for a good self-image is our concern to avoid humiliation, rejection, sense of inadequacy, etc. The negative expression of sense pleasure is our desire to avoid pain, discomfort, effort.

Human behavior, attitudes, and emotions can be analyzed in terms of these motivations, operating singly or in combination. Although sense pleasure is the more evident motivation, the self-esteem desire is more pervasive and powerful. This desire often motivates us subconsciously. The desire for a good self-image moves us to attribute "nobler" motives to our behavior, suppressing into the subconscious the realization that we are operating on the self-esteem motive.

It would be difficult to offer any "it could not be otherwise" proof for the message of this book. The lines of reasoning we have offered may be persuasive to some readers, not so to others. We have presented the testimony of notable thinkers from a variety of fields who have realized the powerful dominance of the self-esteem motive in human behavior. Some of these thinkers consider self-esteem to be the sole motive underlying human behavior, others see the duality of self-esteem and sense pleasure. Secondly, we have considered some key aspects of human behavior and emotions, verifying that they can be explained in terms of their underlying motivation, the desire for a good self-image. Supporting opinions from informed thinkers have been offered in each of these considerations.

Subject to correction and change by you, the discerning reader, it is suggested that this study lays the foundation for a New Science of Human Behavior, based upon the following Laws of Human Behavior:

First Law of Human Behavior: Each human organism seeks to maintain or increase its sense of its own excellence.

Second Law of Human Behavior: Each human organism seeks to maintain or increase its level of sensual gratification.

Third Law of Human Behavior: Virtually all human thoughts, words, and actions spring from the two above motivations, operating singly or in combination.

Fourth Law of Human Behavior: In cases of conflict between the first and second motivation, the desire for a sense of excellence usually prevails.

Some readers may find the first and second laws to be self-evident, as basic principles often are. The fourth law is fairly evident. To make the crucial third law evident has been the aim of this book.

Of what value is this "self-esteem and sense pleasure" theory? If it be true that these are the basic principles of human behavior, then this theory can occupy a similar position in the science of human behavior that Newton's three laws of motion occupied in the science of the behavior of inanimate bodies, physics. To the layman, Newton's laws seemed so general as to have little practical use, but of course they spawned a myriad of practical applications in man's domination of the physical world. The following paragraphs suggest some broad applications of the self-esteem theory. As one delves into these issues the possible applications multiply and become more immediately practical.

The growing awareness among psychologists that neuroses and emotional problems are at root self-esteem problems indicates that the self-esteem motivation is the key to proper analysis and treatment of these maladies. Journal articles indicate that some psychologists are already operating on this premise.

The predominant ways in which a person seeks self-esteem determines his or her personality. This suggests lines for developing an extensive Personality typology. We have touched on this with regard to the stoic/epicurean dichotomy. Alfred Adler has done some work in this direction, based on his theory that personality derives from the life style that the child has chosen in an effort to overcome his inferiority complex (low self-esteem which Adler sees as endemic to all children).

Inasmuch as personal violence and aggression are manifestations of the drive for self-esteem and sense pleasure, a scientific approach to their amelioration should begin with a detailed and extensive analysis of these motivational roots.

The self-esteem theory provides the basis for a detailed philosophy of history. The main thrust of history is the unceasing effort of the human race to eliminate restrictions on collective self-esteem and on gratification of sense desires. This is the thrust for freedom, for equality, for removal of all authority that is seen as restrictive.

Providing as it does the basic principles of human behavior, this theory thus provides the basic principles for the numerous disciplines concerned with human behavior—psychology, sociology, education, ethics, political science, etc. It also offers the much-sought-after integrating principles for relating these disciplines to one another.

Pulitzer prize winner Ernest Becker states that the discovery that the self-esteem motive underlies all our behavior is an achievement of supreme magnitude for establishing the "New Science of Man." In this we concur with one qualification: the independent but junior role of the sense pleasure motive must also be taken into account.

Our desires for self-esteem and for sense pleasure are the basic irreducible principles of the New Science of Man. Scientific analysis of human problems and issues must take its starting point from these two givens. Effective programs for the amelioration of social problems must be based upon these ultimate principles of human behavior.

BIBLIOGRAPHY

1 Adams, John. <u>Life and Works of John Adams</u>.
     Boston: Charles C. Little, 1851.

2 Adams, Stacey. <u>Inequity in Social Exchange</u>. In
     <u>Advances in Experimental Social Psycho-
     logy,</u> Vol. 2. Edited by Leonard Berko-
     witz. New York: Academic Press, 1965.

3 Addison, Joseph. <u>The Spectator</u>. Oxford: Claren-
     don Press, 1965.

4 Aderman, David. "Elation, Depression, and Helping
     Behavior," <u>Journal of Personality and
     Social Psychology</u> 24 (October 1972): 91-
     101.

5 Adler, Alfred. <u>The Individual Psychology of
     Alfred Adler</u>, edited by Heinz L. Ansbacher
     and Rowena R. Ansbacher. New York: Basic
     Books, Inc., 1956; reprint ed., New York:
     Harper & Row, Publishers, Inc., 1967.

6 _____. "Suicide." <u>Journal of Individual
     Psychology</u> 14 (May 1958): 57-61.

7 Allport, Gordon W. <u>The Individual and His
     Religion</u>. New York: Crowell-Collier and
     Macmillan, Inc., 1950.

8 Alvarez, A. <u>The Savage God</u>. London: Weidenfeld
     and Nicholson, 1971; reprint ed., New
     York: Bantam Books, Inc., 1973.

9 Anderson, Camilla M. "The Self Image: A Theory
     of the Dynamics of Behavior, Updated."
     <u>Mental Hygiene</u> 55 (July, 1971): 365-366.

10 Aquinas, Thomas. <u>III Contra Gentes</u>.

11 _____. <u>Summa Theologica</u>.

12 Aristotle. <u>Nicomachean Ethics</u>.

307

13 Augustine, St. Augustine: Earlier Writings.
            Ed. by John H.S. Burleigh. Philadelphia:
            The Westminster Press, 1955.

14 _____. Confessions of St. Augustine.
            Translated by Rex Warner. New York: The
            New American Library of World Literature,
            Inc., Mentor-Omega Books, 1963.

15 Aurelius, Marcus. Meditations. Chicago: Henry
            Regnery Co., 1956.

16 Bachman, Jerald G., and O'Malley, Patrick M.
            "Self-Esteem in Young Men: A Longitudinal
            Analysis of the Impact of Educational and
            Occupational Attainment." Journal of
            Personality and Social Psychology 35 (June
            1977): 365-379.

17 Becker, Ernest. The Revolution in Psychiatry.
            New York: The Free Press, 1964.

18 _____. The Structure of Evil. New York:
            George Braziller, 1968.

19 _____. The Birth and Death of Meaning.
            Second Edition. New York: Macmillan,
            1971.

20 Berkowitz, Leonard. Roots of Aggression.
            New York: Atherton Press, 1969.

21 Branden, Nathaniel. The Psychology of Self-
            Esteem. New York: Bantam Books, Inc.,
            1969.

22 _____. The Disowned Self. Los Angeles:
            Nash Publishing Co., 1971.

23 Breed, Warren. "Suicide and Loss in Social
            Interaction." In Essays in Self-Destruc-
            tion, pp. 188-202. Edited by Edwin S.
            Schneidman. New York: Science House,
            1967.

24 Briggs, Dorothy Corkille. <u>Your Child's Self-</u>
    <u>Esteem</u>. New York: Doubleday & Company,
    Inc., 1970; reprint ed., New York: Dolphin
    Books, 1975.

25 Brown, Bertram S. "What You Should Know About
    Mental Depression." <u>U.S. News and World</u>
    <u>Report</u>, Sept. 9, 1974.

26 Burtt, E. A. <u>The Teachings of the Compassionate</u>
    <u>Buddha</u>. New York: Mentor Books, 1955.

27 Campbell, Robert, and The Editors of Time-Life
    Books. <u>Human Behavior: The Enigma of the</u>
    <u>Mind</u>. New York: Time-Life Books, 1976.

28 Cialdini, Robert B.; Darby, Betty Lee; and Vincent,
    Joyce E. "Transgression and Altruism: A
    Case for Hedonism." <u>Journal of Experi-</u>
    <u>mental Social Psychology</u> 9 (November
    1973): 502-516.

29 Clark, Ramsey. "Crime and Violence in the United
    States." In <u>Aggression</u>, pp. 319-323.
    Edited by Shervert H. Frazier, M.D. Balti-
    more: Association for Research in Nervous
    and Mental Disease, Research Publications,
    1974.

30 Cleaver, Eldridge. <u>Soul on Ice</u>. New York:
    McGraw-Hill Book Co., 1968.

31 Clemens, Samuel. <u>The Complete Essays of Mark</u>
    <u>Twain</u>. Edited by Charles Neider. <u>What Is</u>
    <u>Man?</u> Garden City, N.Y.: Doubleday & Co.,
    Inc., 1963.

32 Comte, Auguste. <u>Catechism of Positive Religion</u>.
    London: John Chapman, 1858.

33 Cohen, Arthur R. "Some Implications of Self-
    Esteem for Social Influence." Chap. 38 in
    <u>The Self in Social Interaction</u>, ed. by
    Chad Gordon and Kenneth Gergen. New York:
    John Wiley & Sons, Inc., 1968.

34   Cooley, Charles Horton. *Human Nature and the Social Order*. New York: Schocken Books, 1964.

35   Coopersmith, Stanley. *The Antecedents of Self-Esteem*. San Francisco: W. H. Freeman and Co., 1967.

36   _____. "Studies in Self-Esteem." *Scientific American* 218 (Feb. 1968): 96-100.

37   Diggory, James C. *Self-Evaluation: Concepts and Studies*. New York: Wiley, 1966.

38   Dodge, Raymond, and Kahn, Eugen. *The Craving for Superiority*. New Haven: Yale University Press, 1931.

39   Dollard, J. C.; Doob, L.; Miller, N.; Mowrer, O.; and Sears, R. *Frustration and Aggression*. New Haven: Yale University Press, 1939.

40   Douglas, Jack D. "The Absurd in Suicide." In *On the Nature of Suicide*, pp. 111-119. Edited by Edwin S. Schneidman. San Francisco: Jossey-Bass, Inc., Publishers, 1969.

41   Dublin, Louis I. *Suicide, A Sociological and Statistical Study*. New York: The Ronald Press Co., 1963.

42   Durkheim, Emile. *Suicide*. New York: The Free Press, 1966.

43   Eastman, Max. *Enjoyment of Laughter*. New York: Simon and Schuster, 1936.

44   _____. *The Sense of Humor*. New York: Schuster and Schuster, 1922.

45   Epstein, Seymour. "The Self-Concept Revisited." *The American Psychologist* 28 (May 1973): 404-416.

46 Evans, Richard I. _Dialogue With Erich Fromm._
New York: Harper & Row, Publishers, 1966.

47 Evans, Richard I. "Conversations with Konrad
Lorenz." _Psychology Today_, November 1974,
pp. 83-93.

48 Fedden, Henry R. _Suicide, A Social and Historical
Study._ New York: Benjamin Bloom, Inc.,
1972.

49 Fenichel, Otto. _The Psychoanalytic Theory of
Neurosis._ New York: W. W. Norton & Com-
pany, Inc., 1945.

50 _____. _The Collected Papers of Otto Fenichel._
New York: W. W. Norton & Company, Inc.,
Second Series.

51 Franks, David D., and Marolla, Joseph. "Effica-
cious Action and Social Approval as Inter-
acting Dimensions of Self-Esteem: A Ten-
tative Formulation Through Construct Vali-
dation." _Sociometry_ 39 (No. 4, 1976):
324-341.

52 Fingarette, Herbert. _Self-Deception._ London:
Routledge and Kegan Paul, 1969.

53 Freud, Anna. _The Ego and the Mechanisms of
Defense._ New York: International Uni-
versities Press, 1946.

54 Freud, Sigmund. "Humour." _The International
Journal of Psychoanalysis_ 9 (January 1928):
1-6.

55 _____. _Jokes and Their Relation to the
Unconscious._ New York: W. W. Norton &
Co., 1960.

56 _____. _A General Selection from the Works
of Sigmund Freud._ Edited by John Rickman.
Beyond the Pleasure Principle. _The Ego
and the Id._ _Instincts and Their Vicissi-_

tudes. On Narcissism: An Introduction. Garden City, N.Y.: Doubleday & Co., Inc., 1957.

57 _____. The Future of an Illusion. Garden City, N.Y.: Doubleday & Co., Inc., Anchor Books, 1961.

58 _____. Sexuality and the Psychology of Love. New York: Collier Books, 1963.

59 _____. New Introductory Lectures on Psychoanalysis. New York: W.W. Norton & Co., 1965.

60 _____. Moses and Monotheism. New York: Vintage Books, 1967.

61 _____. The Standard Edition of the Complete Psychological Works of Sigmund Freud. Edited by James Strachey. Vol. II: Psychotherapy of Hysteria. London: Hogarth Press, 1955.

62 _____. Civilization and Its Discontents. New York: W.W. Norton & Co., Inc., 1961.

63 _____. The Complete Psychological Works of Sigmund Freud. Edited by James Strachey. Vol. XXII: Why War? London: Hogarth Press, 1964.

64 _____. Collected Papers. Edited by James Strachey. Vol. 5: Analysis, Terminable and Interminable; and Why War? New York: Basic Books, Inc., 1959.

65 _____. "Mourning and Melancholia." Sigmund Freud: Collected Papers. New York: Basic Books, Inc., 1959.

66 _____. The Ego and the Id. Edited by James Strachey. New York: W.W. Norton & Company, Inc., 1960.

67 _____. The Interpretation of Dreams. Trans-
       lated by James Strachey. New York: Avon
       Books, 1965.

68 Fromm, Erich. Man for Himself. New York:
       Fawcett Publications, 1947.

69 _____. The Anatomy of Human Destructiveness.
       Greenwich, Conn.: Fawcett Publications,
       1973.

70 Gazzaniga, Michael S. "Violent Man." Psychology
       Today, June 1969, pp. 52-63.

71 Geen, Russell G. Aggression. Morristown, N.J.:
       General Learning Press, 1972.

72 Gergen, Kenneth J. The Concept of Self. New
       York: Holt, Rinehart and Winston, Inc.,
       1971.

73 Gergen, Kenneth J., Gergen, Mary M., and Meter,
       Kenneth. "Individual Orientations to
       Prosocial Behavior." Journal of Social
       Issues 28 (No. 3, 1972): 105-130.

74 Gibbon, Edward. The Decline and Fall of the
       Roman Empire.

75 Gillette, Paul J., and Hornbeck, Marie. Depres-
       sion: A Layman's Guide. New York: Outer-
       bridge and Lazard, Inc., 1973.

76 Goble, Frank. The Third Force. New York: Pocket
       Books, 1970.

77 Goldstein, Kurt. The Organism. New York:
       American Book Company, 1939.

78 _____. Human Nature, In the Light of Psycho-
       pathology. New York: Schocken Books,
       1940.

79   Greenwald, Anthony G., and Ronis, David L. "Twenty
         Years of Cognitive Dissonance: Case Study
         of the Evolution of a Theory." Psycholog-
         ical Review 85 (No. 1, 1978): 53-57.

80   Gregory, J. C. The Nature of Laughter. New
         York: Harcourt, Brace & Co., 1924.

81   Greig, J.Y.T. The Psychology of Laughter and
         Comedy. New York: Dodd, Mead and Co.,
         1923.

82   Grier, William H., and Cobbs, Price M. Black
         Rage. New York: Basic Books, Inc., 1968.

83   Hall, Calvin S. A Primer of Freudian Psychology.
         New York: The New American Library, Mentor
         Books, 1954.

84   Hall, Calvin S., and Lindzey, Gardner. Theories
         of Personality. 2nd ed. New York: John
         Wiley & Sons, Inc., 1970.

85   Havighurst, Robert J. "Suicide and Education."
         In On the Nature of Suicide, pp. 53-67.
         Edited by Edwin S. Schneidman. San Fran-
         cisco: Jossey-Bass, Inc., 1969.

86   "Helping Out." Human Behavior, July 1973, p. 53.

87   Hendin, Herbert. "Suicide: Psychoanalytic Point
         of View." In The Cry for Help, pp. 181-
         192. Edited by Norman L. Farberow and
         Edwin S. Schneidman. New York: McGraw-
         Hill Book Co., Inc., 1961.

88   _____. Suicide and Scandanavia. New York:
         Grune and Stratton, Inc., 1964.

89   Hilgard, Ernest. "Human Motives and the Concept
         of the Self." The American Psychologist 4
         (September 1949): 374-382.

90   Hobbes, Thomas. The Elements of Law. Cambridge:
         Cambridge University Press, 1928.

91 _____. Hobbes Selections. Edited by Frederick
     J.E. Woodbridge. Leviathan. New York:
     Charles Scribner's Sons, 1930.

92 _____. The English Works of Thomas Hobbes.
     Vol. IV. N.p.: Scientia Aalen, 1962.

93 Horney, Karen. Self-Analysis. New York: W.W.
     Norton & Company, Inc., 1942.

94 _____. New Ways in Psychoanalysis. New York:
     W.W. Norton & Co., 1966.

95 Hutcheson, Frances. Reflections on Laughter
     and Remarks upon the Fable of the Bees.
     New York: Garland Publishing Co., 1971.

96 Ibn Hazm, Ala. "A Philosophy of Character and
     Conduct." Anthology of Islamic Litera-
     ture. Ed. by James Kritzeck. New York:
     Holt, Rinehart and Winston, 1964.

97 Isen, Alice M. "Success, Failure, Attention,
     and Reaction to Others: The Warm Glow of
     Success." Journal of Personality and
     Social Psychology 15 (August 1970): 294-
     301.

98 Jacobson, Edith. The Self and the Object World.
     New York: International Universities
     Press, Inc., 1964.

99 James, William. The Principles of Psychology.
     London: Macmillan and Company, Ltd.,
     1910.

100 Johnson, Samuel. The Rambler. London: Jones
     & Co., 1825.

101 Jones, Stephen C. "Self- and Interpersonal Eval-
     uations: Esteem Theories Versus Consis-
     tency Theories." Psychological Bulletin
     79 (No. 3, 1973): 185-199.

315

102   Kaplan, Howard B., and Pokorny, Alex D.   "Self-
           Derogation and Psychosocial Adjustment."
           Journal of Nervous and Mental Disease 149
           (1969): 421-434.

103   Kaplan, Howard B.   Self-Attitudes and Deviant
           Behavior.   Pacific Palisades: Goodyear
           Publishing Company, Inc., 1975.

104   Kaplan, Howard B., and Pokorny, Alex D.   "Self-
           Derogation and Suicide——I: Self-Derogation
           as an Antecedent of Suicidal Responses."
           Social Science and Medicine 10 (1976):
           113-118.

105   Kernberg, Otto.   "Why Some People Can't Love."
           Psychology Today, June, 1978, pp. 55-59.

106   Kohut, Heinz.   "Thoughts on Narcissism and Nar-
           cissistic Rage."   The Psychoanalytic Study
           of the Child 27 (1972): 360-400.

107   _____.   The Restoration of the Self.   New
           York: International Universities Press,
           Inc., 1977.

108   Krauss, Herbert H., and Critchfield, Leslee L.
           "Contrasting Self-Esteem Theory and Con-
           sistency Theory in Predicting Interper-
           sonal Attraction."   Sociometry 38 (No. 2,
           1975): 247-260.

109   Krebs, Dennia L.   "Altruism——An Examination of
           the Concept and a Review of the Litera-
           ture."   Psychological Bulletin 73 (April
           1970): 258-302.

110   Krebs, Dennis, and Whitten, Phillip.   "Guilt-
           Edged Giving: The Shame of It All."   Psy-
           chology Today, January 1972, pp. 50-77.

111   La Rochefoucauld.   Maxims.   Baltimore: Penguin
           Books, 1959.

316

112 Levine, Jacob, ed. Motivation in Humor. New
         York: Atherton Press, 1969.

113 Litman, Robert E. "Sigmund Freud on Suicide."
         In Essays in Self-Destruction, pp. 324-
         344. Edited by Edwin S. Schneidman. New
         York: Science House, Inc., 1967.

114 Leung, Jup-chung. Self-Esteem and Emotional
         Maturity. Unpublished dissertation, San
         Diego State University, 1972.

115 Levy, David M. "The Hostile Act." In Under-
         standing Human Motivation, Revised Edi-
         tion, pp. 351-355. Edited by Chalmers L.
         Stacey and Manfred F. DeMartino. Cleve-
         land: The World Publishing Co., 1965.

116 Lorenz, Konrad. On Aggression. New York: Har-
         court, Brace and World, Inc., 1966; re-
         print ed., New York: Bantam Books, 1966.

117 Lovejoy, Arthur O. Reflections on Human Nature.
         Baltimore: Johns Hopkins Press, 1961.

118 McCall, George J., and Simmons, J.L. Identities
         and Interactions. New York: The Free
         Press, 1966.

119 McDougall, William. The Energies of Men. New
         York: Charles Scribner's Sons, 1933.

120 McMillen, David L. "Transgression, Self-Image,
         and Compliant Behavior." Journal of Per-
         sonality and Social Psychology 20 (No. 2,
         1971): 176-179.

121 Madow, Leo. Anger. New York: Charles Scribner's
         Sons, 1972.

122 Malcolm X. Malcolm X Speaks. New York: Merit
         Publishers, 1965.

123 Maslow, Abraham. Motivation and Personality.
         New York: Harper and Row, 1954.

124   . Toward a Psychology of Being. 2nd ed.
         New York: Van Nostrand Reinhold Co., 1968.

125   . "Toward a Humanistic Biology." The
         American Psychologist 24 (August 1969):
         724-735.

126   , ed. New Knowledge in Human Values.
         Chicago: Henry Regnery & Co., 1970.

127 Marx, Melvin H., and Hillix, William A. Systems
         and Theories in Psychology. New York:
         McGraw-Hill Book Co., 1963.

128 May, Rollo. The Meaning of Anxiety. New York:
         The Ronald Press Company, 1950.

129   . Power and Innocence. New York: W.W.
         Norton & Company, Inc., 1976.

130 Megargee, Edwin I. The Psychology of Violence
         and Aggression. Morristown, N.J.: General
         Learning Press, 1972.

131 Melniker, Robert C. "Self-Acceptance and the
         Mechanism of Identification." Unpublished
         doctoral dissertation, New York Univer-
         sity, 1957.

132 Mendelson, Myer. "Intrapersonal Psychodynamics
         of Depression." The Nature and Treatment
         of Depression. Ed. by Frederic F. Flach
         and Suzanne C. Draghi. New York: Wiley
         Medical, 1975.

133 Miller, Neal E.; Sears, R.; Mowrer, O.; Doob, L.;
         and Dollard, J. "Frustration and Aggres-
         sion Hypothesis." In Understanding Human
         Motivation, pp. 347-351. Edited by Chalm-
         ers E. Stacey and Manfred F. DeMartino.
         Cleveland: The World Publishing Co., 1965.

134 Mindess, Harvey. Laughter and Liberation. Los
         Angeles: Nash Publ. Co., 1971.

135   Monro, D.H. Argument of Laughter. New York: Cambridge University Press, 1951.

136   Moynier, Miles R. "Helping Behavior: Self-Sacrificing or Self-Serving." M.A. dissertation, San Diego State University, 1975.

137   Murphy, Gardner. Outgrowing Self-Deception. New York: Basic Books, Inc., 1975.

138   Neuringer, Charles. "Attitudes Toward Self in Suicidal Individuals." Life Threatening Behavior 4 (Spring 1974): 96-106.

139   Nietzke, Ann. "Hostility on the Laugh Track." Human Behavior, May 1974, pp. 64-70.

140   Oates, Whitney J. The Stoic and Epicurean Philosophers. New York: Random House, 1940.

141   O'Brien, Edward J., and Epstein, Seymour. "Naturally Occurring Changes in Self-Esteem." Proceedings of American Psychological Association, Division of Personality and Social Psychology, 1974.

142   Pascal, Blaise. Pensees. London: Penguin Books, 1966.

143   Pepitone, Albert. "An Experimental Analysis of Self-Dynamics." Chap. 34 in The Self in Social Interaction, ed. by Chad Gordon and Kenneth Gergen. New York: John Wiley and Sons, Inc., 1968.

144   Piddington, Ralph. The Psychology of Laughter. London: Figurehead, 1933.

145   Plato. The Portable Plato. Ed. by Scott Buchanan. New York: The Viking Press, 1948.

146   Plutarch. Plutarch's Lives. Vol. 12. New York: P.F. Collier and Son, 1909.

147 Rado, Sandor. "The Problem of Melancholia."
         International Journal of Psychoanalysis 9
         (1928): 420-437.

148 Rapaport, David. "On the Psychoanalytic Theory
         of Motivation." _Nebraska Symposium on
         Motivation_, 1960, pp. 173-247.

149 Reif, Adelbert. "Erich Fromm on Human Aggres-
         sion." _Human Behavior_, April 1975, pp.
         17-23.

150 Rieff, Phillip. _Freud: The Mind of the Moralist_.
         Garden City, NY: Doubleday & Co., Inc.,
         1961.

151 Robert, Marthe. _The Psychoanalytic Revolution_.
         New York: Avon Books, 1966.

152 Robinson, John P., and Shave, Philip R. _Measures
         of Social Psychological Attitudes_. Ann
         Arbor: University of Michigan Survey Re-
         search Center, 1973.

153 Rochlin, Gregory. _Man's Aggression: The Defense
         of the Self_. Boston: Gambit, Inc., 1973:
         reprint ed., New York: Dell Publishing
         Co., Inc., 1974.

154 Rogers, Carl R. _Client-Centered Therapy_. New
         York: Houghton Mifflin Company, 1951.

155 Rosenberg, Morris. "Psychological Selectivity in
         Self-Esteem Formation." Chap. 33 in _The
         Self in Social Interaction_, ed. by Chad
         Gordon and Kenneth Gergen. New York: John
         Wiley & Sons, Inc., 1968.

156 Rosenhan, D.L.; Underwood, Bill; and Moore, Bert.
         "Affect Moderates Self-Gratifications and
         Altruism." _Journal of Personality and
         Social Psychology_ 30 (October 1974): 546-
         552.

157 Rounds, J. "Social Desirability and Machiavel-
     lianism Artifact in the California Self-
     Esteem Measure." Journal of Research in
     Crime and Delinquency, Jan. 1977: 84-87.

158 Rousseau, Jean-Jacques. Julie. In French Thought
     in the Eighteenth Century, ed. by Romain
     Rolland, Andre Maurois and Edouard Her-
     riot. New York: David McKay Company,
     Inc., 1953.

159 Runyon, Richard, and Haber, Audrey. Fundamentals
     of Behavioral Statistics. 2nd ed. Read-
     ing, Mass.: Addison-Wesley Publ. Co.,
     1971.

160 Schopenhauer, Arthur. The Essential Schopen-
     hauer. New York: Barnes & Noble, Inc.,
     1962.

161 Schuller, Robert H. Self-Love: The Dynamic Force
     of Success. New York: Hawthorne Books,
     Inc., 1969.

162 Schur, Max. Freud: Living and Dying. New York:
     International University Press, Inc.,
     1972.

163 Shulman, Bernard H. and Mosak, Harold H. "Various
     Purposes of Symptoms." Journal of Indivi-
     dual Psychology 23 (May, 1967): 79-87.

164 Silverberg, William V. "The Factor of Omnipo-
     tence in Neurosis." Psychiatry 12 (Nov.
     1949): 387-398.

165 _____. Childhood Experience and Personal
     Destiny. New York: Springer Publishing
     Company, Inc., 1952.

166 _____. "Toward a Theory of Personality and
     Neurosis." In An Outline of Psychoanaly-
     sis, pp. 48-76. Edited by Clara Thompson,
     Milton Mazer, and Earl Wittenberg. New
     York: The Modern Library, 1955.

167 Sjoback, Hans. The Psychoanalytic Theory of Defensive Processes. New York: John Wiley & Sons, 1973.

168 Skinner, B.F. Walden Two. Toronto: The Macmillan Co., 1962.

169 _____. Beyond Freedom and Dignity. New York: Knopf, 1971.

170 Snygg, Donald, and Combs, Arthur. Individual Behavior. New York: Harper & Bros. Publishers, 1949.

171 Spielberger, Charles D. "Theory and Research on Anxiety." Anxiety and Behavior. New York: Academic Press, 1966.

172 _____. "Current Trends in Theory and Research on Anxiety." Anxiety: Current Trends in Theory and Research. New York: Academic Press, 1972.

173 Spencer, Herbert. The Data of Ethics. New York: American Home Library, 1902.

174 Storr, Anthony. Human Aggression. New York: Antheneum Press, 1968.

175 Strodach, George K. The Philosophy of Epicurus. Chicago: Northwestern University Press, 1963.

176 Swabey, Marie Collins. Comic Laughter. New Haven: Yale University Press, 1961.

177 Symonds, Percival M. The Ego and the Self. New York: Appleton-Century-Crofts, Inc., 1951.

178 Veblen, Thorstein. The Theory of the Leisure Class. New York: The Macmillan Co., 1912.

179 Verkko, Veli. Homicides and Suicides in Finland. Copenhagen: G.E.C. Gads Forlag, 1951.

180 Vernon, M.D. Human Motivation. London: Cambridge Univ. Press, 1969.

181 Voltaire. The Portable Voltaire. Edited by Ben
        Ray Redman. New York: The Viking Press,
        1963.

182 Wagenknecht, Edward. Mark Twain: The Man and his
        Work. Norman, Okla.: University of Okla-
        homa Press, 1961.

183 Walster, Elaine; Berscheid, Ellen; and Walster,
        William G. "The Exploited: Justice or
        Justification." In Altruism and Helping
        Behavior, pp. 179-204. Edited by J. Mac-
        auley and L. Berkowitz. New York: Aca-
        demic Press, 1970.

184 Warner, Rex. The Greek Philosophers. New York:
        The New American Library of World Litera-
        ture, Inc., Mentor Books, 1958.

185 Wells, Edward L., and Marwell, Gerald. Self-
        Esteem. Beverly Hills: Sage Publications,
        1976.

186 White, Ralph K., and Lippitt, Ronald. Autocracy
        and Democracy. New York: Harper & Bro-
        thers, Publishers, 1960.

187 Woodman, Loring. Perspectives in Self-Awareness.
        Columbus, Ohio: Charles E. Merrill Publ.
        Co., 1973.

188 Wylie, Ruth C. The Self-Concept. Revised edi-
        tion. Lincoln, Neb.: University of Nebra-
        ska Press, 1974.

189 Maltz, Maxwell. The Search for Self-Respect.
        New York: Bantam Books, 1973.

190 Sullivan, Harry Stack. The Interpersonal Theory
        of Psychiatry. Ed. by Helen Swick Perry
        and Mary Ladd Gawel. New York: W.W. Nor-
        ton & Company, Inc., 1953.

191 _____. Clinical Studies in Psychiatry. Ed.
by Helen Swick Perry, Mary Ladd Gawel, and
Martha Gibbon. New York: W.W. Norton &
Company, Inc., 1956.

192 Mullahy, Patrick. "The Theories of H.S. Sulli-
van," in The Contributions of Harry Stack
Sullivan. Ed. by Patrick Mullahy. New
York: Hermitage house, 1952.

193 Goffman, Erving. "On Face-Work: An Analysis of
Ritual Elements in Social Interaction,"
Psychiatry 18 (August 1955): 230.

194 Felker, Donald W. Building Positive Self-Con-
cepts. Minneapolis: Burgess Publishing
Company, 1974.

195 Wilson, John P. and Wilson, Stephen B. "Sources
of Self-Esteem and the Person X Situation
Controversy," Psychological Reports 38
(1976): 355-358.

196 Worchel, Philip, and Hillson, Joseph S. "The
Self-Concept in the Criminal: An Explora-
tion of Adlerian Theory." Journal of
Individual Psychology 14 (Nov. 1958): 173-
181.

197 Foulds, G.A. "Attitudes Toward Self and Others
of Psychopaths," Journal of Individual
Psychology 16 (May, 1960): 81-83.

198 Meerloo, Joost A.M. Suicide and Mass Suicide.
New York: E.P. Dutton & Co., Inc., 1968.

199 Locke, John. Essays Concerning Human Under-
standing. London, Dent, 1961.

200 Jung, C.G. "Jung on Freud." Atlantic Monthly,
Nov., 1962, p. 50.

201 Freud, Sigmund. An Outline of Psychoanalysis.
New York: W.W. Norton and Company, Inc.,
1949.

202   . Group Psychology and the Analysis of
the Ego. New York: Bantam Books, 1960.

203   . The Standard Edition of the Complete
Psychological Works of Sigmund Freud. Ed.
by James Strachey. Vol. XVII: A Diffi-
culty in the Path of Psychoanalysis. Lon-
don: Hogarth Press.

204 Rothgeb, Carrie Lee, ed. Abstracts of the Stand-
ard Edition of the Complete Psychological
Works of Sigmund Freud. Rockville, Md.:
U.S. Department of Health, Education and
Welfare, n.d.

205 Aquinas, Thomas. Commentary on John.

206 Wispe, Lauren G. Journal of Social Issues 28
(no. 3, 1972), preface.

207 Aristotle. Rhetoric.

208 Bogard, Howard M. "Collected Thoughts of a Sui-
cidologist," in Identifying Suicide Po-
tential. Eds. Dorothy B. Anderson and
Lenora J. McClean. New York: Behavioral
Publications, 1971.

209 Darwin, Charles. The Expression of the Emotions
in Men and Animals. London, 1904.

210 Kohut, Heinz. The Analysis of the Self. New
York: International University Press,
Inc., 1971.

211 Hunt, Morton M. The Natural history of Love.
New York: Grove Press, 1959.

212 Schmalhausen, Samuel D. Why We Misbehave. New
York: The Macauley Company, 1928.

213 Reik, Theodor. Of Love and Lust. New York:
Farrar, Straus, and Cudahy, 1957.

214 Smith, Adam. The Theory of Moral Sentiments.
          New York: Augustus M. Kelley, Publishers,
          1966.

215 Dobson, James. Hide or Seek. Old Tappan, NJ:
          Fleming H. Revell Co., 1974.

216 Kant, Immanuel. Lectures on Ethics. Gloucester,
          Mass.: Peter Smith, 1978.

217 _____. The Moral Law. (or, Groundwork of the
          Metaphysics of Morals.) New York: Barnes
          & Noble, 1950.

218 _____. The Crituque of Pure Reason. Great
          Books Series. Chicago: Encyclopedia Brit-
          tanica, 1952.

219 _____. The Critique of Practical reason.
          Great Books. Chicago: Encyclopedia Brit-
          tanica, 1952.

220 _____. On the Old Saw: That May Be Right in
          Theory But It Won't Work in Practice.
          Philadelphia: University of Pennsylvania
          Press, 1974.

221 _____. Religion Within the Limits of Reason
          Alone. LaSalle, Ill.: The Open Court
          Publishing Co., 1960.

222 _____. Lectures on Philosophical Theology.
          Ithaca: Cornell University Press, 1978.

223 _____. The Critique of Aesthetic Judgement.
          Great Books. Chicago: Encyclopedia Brit-
          tanica, 1952.

224 Beck, Lewis White. A Commentary on Kant's Cri-
          tique of Practical Reason. Chicago: Uni-
          versity of Chicago Press, 1960.

225 Paton, H.J. The Categorical Imperative. Phila-
          delphia: University of Pennsylvania Press,
          1948.

226 Luther, Martin. <u>Luther's Works</u>. St. Louis: Con-
cordia Publishing House, 1967.

227 Edwards, Jonathan. <u>Jonathan Edwards: Basic Writ-
ings</u>. New York: The New American Library,
1966.

228 Clemes, Harris, and Bean, Reynold. <u>Self-Esteem:
The Key to Your Child's Well-Being</u>. New
York: G.P. Putnam's Sons, 1981.

229 Ellison, Craig W., ed. <u>Self-Esteem</u>. Oklahoma
City: Southwestern Press, Inc., 1976.

230 Rubin, Theodore Isaac. <u>Compassion and Self-
Hate</u>. New York: Ballantine Books, 1975.

231 Maltz, Maxwell. <u>The Magic Power of Self-Image
Psychology</u>. New York: Pocket Books, 1970.

232 Narramore, S. Bruce. <u>You're Someone Special</u>.
Grand Rapids, Mich.: The Zondervan Corp.,
1978.

233 Harris, Thomas A. <u>I'm OK—You're OK</u>. New York:
Avon Books, 1967.

234 May, Rollo. <u>Love and Will</u>. New York: Dell Pub-
lishing Co., Inc., 1969.

235 Nietzsche, Friedrich. <u>The Complete Works of
Friedrich Nietzsche</u>. Edited by Dr. Oscar
Levy. Vol. Fourteen, <u>The Will to Power</u>.
Translated by Anthony M. Ludovici. New
York: Russell & Russell, Inc., 1964.

236 _____. <u>The Will to Power</u>. Translated and
edited by Walter Kaufman. New York: Vin-
tage Books, 1969.

237 _____. <u>The Complete Works of Friedrich Nietz-
sche</u>. Edited by Dr. Oscar Levy. <u>The
Twilight of the Idols</u>. Vol. 16; <u>Ecce
Homo</u>. Vol. 17: <u>The Dawn of Day</u>, <u>Vol. 9</u>;
<u>The Joyful Wisdom</u>, Vol. 19; <u>The Geneology
of Morals</u>, Vol. 13. Translated by Anthony

M. Ludovici. New York: Russell & Russell,
Inc., 1964.

238 _____. Thus Spake Zarathustra. Edited by
Manuel Komroff. New York: Tudor Publish-
ing Company, 1928.

239 _____. The Basic Writings of Nietzsche. Ed-
ited and translated by Walter Kaufman.
New York: The Modern Library.

240 _____. Selected Letters of Friedrich Nietz-
sche. Edited and translated by Christo-
pher Middleton. Chicago: The University
of Chicago Press, 1969.

Note: For "SE" read "self-esteem."